# WHERE THE ANGELS COME TOWARD US

# Where the Angels Come Toward Us

SELECTED ESSAYS, REVIEWS & INTERVIEWS

## DAVID ST. JOHN

WHITE PINE PRESS • FREDONIA, NEW YORK

Acknowledgements:
*The American Poetry Review*: A Generous Salvation: The Poetry of Norman Dubie; An Interview by Karen Fish.

*The Antioch Review*: Raised Voices in the Choir (1981, 1982, & 1983); Scripts and Water, Rules and Riches; Memory As Melody; Where the Angels Come Toward Us: The Poetry of Philip Levine

*The Denver Quarterly*: The Poetics of Light

*Field*: Eugenio Montale's "Two In Twilight"; "Seele Im Raum" (On Randall Jarrell); "Walking Around" (On Pablo Neruda).

*Hayden's Ferry Review*: Reaching To Touch Mystery

*Acknowledgements continue on page 256.*

Publication of this book was made possible, in part, by grants from
the National Endowment for the Arts and the New York State Council on the Arts.

Book design: Elaine LaMattina

Cover painting: *Music* by Gustav Klimt, 1895.
Used by permission of Neue Pinakothek Müchen

ISBN 1-877727-46-6

Manufactured in the United States of America

First Printing 1995

9  8  7  6  5  4  3  2  1

Published by
White Pine Press
10 Village Square • Fredonia, New York 14063

# WHERE THE ANGELS COME TOWARD US

# CONTENTS

III. Interviews

*For Vivienne*

# WHERE THE ANGELS COME TOWARD US

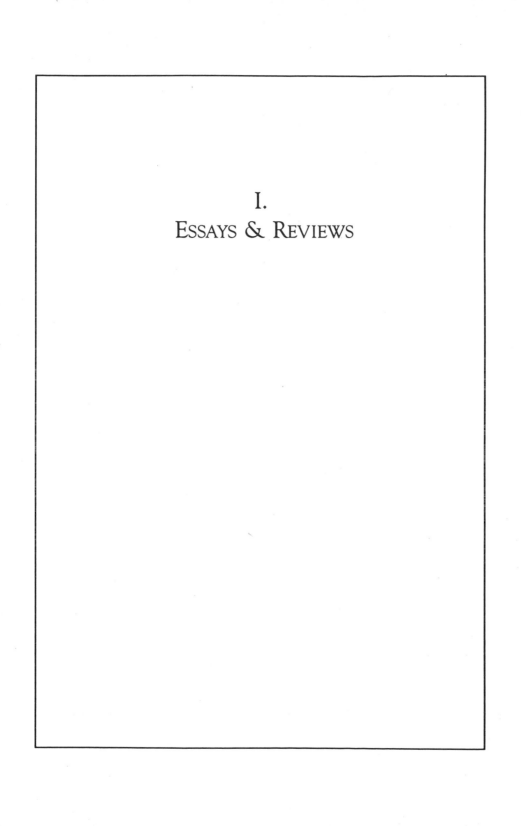

# I.
## ESSAYS & REVIEWS

# A GENEROUS SALVATION:
# THE POETRY OF NORMAN DUBIE

For the past ten years one of the most intriguing presences in American poetry has been that of Norman Dubie. Since 1969 he has published five collections and six limited edition books of poetry, and his work has grown in power and depth with each new collection. From this prodigious body of work, Norman Dubie has made a startlingly severe selection from his early work and has added thirty pages of new poems for this volume of *Selected and New Poems*. It is a collection which will establish Dubie beyond dispute as one of the major voices in contemporary literature and it will confirm the claims of many critics that Dubie is one of the most radical poetic imaginations to have appeared in Post-War American poetry.

It will surprise some that in this *Selected and New Poems* Dubie has chosen to include no poems from his first book, *The Alehouse Sonnets*, and that he has also omitted some of his longer, more operatic poems. Some readers will miss these latter poems, all uncompromisingly ambitious works ("Indian Summer," "The Aster," "Popham of the New Song," "The Piano," "The Ambassador Diaries," and "Principia Mathematica: Einstein's Exile in an Old Dutch Winter"). Yet my own feeling is that Dubie has been quite shrewd in choosing to be represented here by a more densely lyrical body of work, as this allows his readers a more immediate access to what are the complexities and delights of his poetry. (Dubie is planning a *Selected Longer Poems* with a small press.) Dubie's selections from his other collections—*In the Dead of the Night, The Illustrations, The City of the Olesha Fruit,* and *The Everlastings* (three of which are now no longer available)—has been rigorous and unsentimental; one feels there is not a poem here which hasn't in some way won its place. Especially satisfying is the group of new poems Dubie has included, many of them exhibiting an exceptionally quiet and highly personal side of the poet.

Most often, Norman Dubie's poems exist at the place of juncture of several "realities," sometimes historical and sometimes personal. For Dubie, "reality" is a condition of perception; that is, it is a complex of perceptions in constant flux. In each poem, a "sensibility" works to define the nature of the poem's "reality" as details of history (or of "objective" reality) begin to intrude upon and intersect with the speaker's own meditation and perceptions, his own sequence of realities. In this way, multiple correspondences arise out of Dubie's poetry even as their constant narrative impulses drive them on. With the very first poem in *Selected and New Poems*, "For Randall Jarrell, 1914-1965," we are introduced to the condition common to many of Dubie's poems—we are caught at the juncture of two worlds. Here, in a realm touched by both the world of the living and the world of the dead, is the poem:

FOR RANDALL JARRELL, 1914-1965

*What the wish wants to see, it sees.*

All the dead are eating little yellow peas
Off knives under the wing of an owl
While the living run around, not aimlessly, but
Like two women in white dresses gathering
Hymnbooks out on a lawn with the first
Drops of rain already falling on them.

Once, I wrote a sudden and enormous sentence
At the bottom of a page in a notebook
Next to a sketch of a frog. The sentence
Described the gills of a sunfish
As being the color of cut rhubarb, or
Of basil if it is dried in a bundle
In a red kitchen with the last winter light
Showing it off, almost purple.

Anything approaching us we try to understand, say,
Like a lamp being carried up a lane at midnight.

Jeremy Taylor knew it watching an orange leaf
Go down a stream.
Self-taught, it came to us, I believe,
As old age to a panther who's about to
Spring from one branch to another but suddenly
Thinks better of it.
She says to us from her tree:
"Please, one world at a time!" and leaps—

Making it, which could mean,
Into this world or some other. And between.

In the leap which ends this poem, all possibilities are true; we are given the suspended emblem of the panther, invoking the twinned quality of the living world with that of the dead, and of the interpenetration of those worlds. The transgression of one world by another remains a constant preoccupation in Dubie's work; often, the transgression of reality by illusion or imagination—the objective by the subjective—is a poem's true occasion. For Dubie it is this multiplicity of worlds which creates whatever universal harmonies exist.

Norman Dubie's poems look out into our world and find the replication and repetition of image and emblem, of the figure and the figurative, of the shifting perspective and the broken tableau—he finds these all in movement, in the world's shifting mutations of context. His poems consider the nature of experience as influenced by the multiplicity of our perceptions and by the multiplicity of correspondences available in those perceptions. Often, in a Dubie poem, we find the natural, the violent, and the intimate all conjoined in a single poetic whole. There is a melancholy of detail, often painterly in ambition and scope, and through the disruption of those details—sometimes a syntactic disruption; Dubie is one of the most complex and yet absolute lyricists of the moment) the reader finds the vision both in and of the poem being dramatically transformed. The fine, delicate confusions of mind and eye are transfigured for us into the speech and voices of poetry. Dubie's narratives work on the principle of *release*—detail, nuance, gesture—and this allows an accretion of understandings to coalesce as his landscapes quietly reveal themselves. Every story turns visual in Dubie's meditations, just as all of his landscapes imply latent narratives. Dubie is always positing the congruent possibilities of an experience and, in spite of their overwhelmingly elegiac tenor, his is a poetry of celebratory illustration and illumination. Here is one such illustration detailing Dubie's concern with repetition and replication, coupled with his persistent visual richness:

## FEBRUARY: THE BOY BREUGHEL

The birches stand in their beggar's row:
Each poor tree
Has had its wrists nearly
Torn from the clear sleeves of bone,
These icy trees
Are hanging by their thumbs
Under a sun
That will begin to heal them soon,
Each will climb out
Of its own blue, oval mouth;
The river groans,
Two birds call out from the woods
And a fox crosses through snow
Down a hill then, he runs,
He has overcome something white
Beside a white bush, he shakes
It twice, and as he turns
For the woods, the blood in the snow

Looks like the red fox,
At a distance, running down the hill:
A white rabbit in his mouth killed
By the fox in snow
Is killed over and over as just
Two colors, now, on a winter hill:

Two colors! Red and white. A barber's bowl!
Two colors like the peppers
In the windows

Of the town below the hill. Smoke comes
From the chimneys. Everything is still.

Ice in the river begins to move,
And a boy in a red shirt who woke
A moment ago
Watches from his window
The street where an ox
Who's broken out of his hut
Stands in the fresh snow
Staring cross-eyed at the boy
Who smiles and looks out
Across the roof to the hill;
And the sun is reaching down
Into the woods

Where the smoky
red fox still
Eats his kill. Two colors.
Just two colors!
A sunrise. The snow.

It is not often enough said that Dubie's poems are quite commonly con-
cerned with situations of dailiness. Even in those poems, often monologues,
in which conspicuously "famous" artists, writers, scientists, or musicians
appear, these figures are always dealt with in basic and human terms. The
poems that employ these presences are never contingent upon the speaker's
or subject's renown for their power as much as upon the richness and sur-
prise of their perceptions. For Dubie, the intuitive and intimate response is
consistently the most primary concern, not the literary, well-read response.
There has always been, it seems to me, a basic misunderstanding of Dubie's
use of renowned personages as speakers and subjects. For Dubie, they hold
no special attraction simply because of that renown; instead, he sees them as
crucial historical exemplars of new and radical ways of thinking and perceiv-
ing from throughout our past. These speakers are the very voices of those
historical junctures in the arts and the sciences, in music and philosophy,
that have changed the ways in which we think about ourselves as human
beings. Dubie's poems about or spoken by artists and scientists are not sim-

ply considerations of art and science, they are more basically meditations on thought itself and the nature of perception, on the process of *seeing* and *think-ing* that is common to us all but which, in some, seems raised to a higher power.

Dubie's regard for the past is one which finds itself manifested repeatedly in elegiac homages to those sensibilities (those "perceivers") he admires and finds most instructive, most honorable. It is the dignity of the radical pursuits and perceptions of these figures that Dubie wishes to champion and preserve. Invariably, Dubie's great "perceivers" are minds at work against the odds of convention. Yet he allows us to see them in their most ordinary and human moments; sometimes, in fact, we see them exposed in some element of ugliness or cruelty. Dubie finds it crucial to allow his speakers to find as their backdrops the ordinary, *lived* world.

Dubie's poems exemplify a world view which posits the congruence and simultaneity of all acts and temporalities, all artistic and daily endeavors. Necessarily, this interaction and interdependence of memory and experience, of one's perceptions and hopes, includes the interweaving of the worlds of the living and the dead. In his *APR* interview, Dubie said in regard to his own work, "in any tradition of talents, the new artist is completed by the dead artist." Dubie's monologues can sometimes suggest a collaborative effort between the poet and the past "perceiver"; yet, even when the poems convey a serious and weighty historicity their speakers continue to wear their destinies calmly, usually with great grace and even humor. The list of renowned figures in Dubie's work is long, including Chekhov, Klee, Jacob Boehme, Ovid, Gide, Virginia Woolf, Mayakofsky, Ibsen, Beethoven, Rodin, Melville, and Coleridge. Yet one of the most powerful and moving of all of Dubie's speakers is a failure on many counts and not a terribly illuminating thinker at all—he is the prideful, captive, and soon to be executed Czar Nicholas of Russia:

## THE CZAR'S LAST CHRISTMAS LETTER: A BARN IN THE URALS

You were never told, Mother, how old Illya was drunk
That last holiday, for five days and nights

He stumbled through Petersburg forming
A choir of mutes, he dressed them in pink ascension gowns

And, then, sold Father's Tirietz stallion so to rent
A hall for his Christmas recital: the audience

Was rowdy but Illya in his black robes turned on them
And gave them that look of his; the hall fell silent

And violently he threw his hair to the side and up
Went the baton, the recital ended exactly one hour

Later when Illya suddenly turned and bowed
And his mutes bowed, and what applause and hollering

Followed.
All of his cronies were there!

Illya told us later that he thought the voices
Of mutes combine in a sound

Like wind passing through big, winter pines.
Mother, if for no other reason I regret the war

With Japan for, you must now be told,
It took the servant, Illya, from us. It was confirmed.

He would sit on the rocks by the water and with his stiletto
Open clams and pop the raw meats into his mouth

And drool and laugh at us children.
We hear guns often, now, down near the village.

Don't think me a coward Mother, but it is comfortable
Now that I am no longer Czar. I can take pleasure

From just a cup of clear water. I hear Illya's choir often.
I teach the children about decreasing fractions, that is

A lesson best taught by the father.

Alexandra conducts the French and singing lessons.

Mother, we are again a physical couple.
I brush out her hair for her at night.

She thinks that we'll be rowing outside Geneva
By the spring. I hope she won't be disappointed.

Yesterday morning while bread was frying
In one corner, she in another washed all of her legs

Right in front of the children. I think
We became sad at her beauty. She has a purple bruise

On an ankle.
Like Illya I made her chew on mint.

Our Christmas will be in this excellent barn.
The guards flirt with your granddaughters and I see...

I see nothing wrong with it. Your little one, who is
Now a woman, made one soldier pose for her, she did

Him in charcoal, but as a bold nude. He was
Such an obvious virgin about it, he was wonderful!

Today, that same young man found us an enormous azure
And pearl samovar. Once, he called me Great Father

And got confused
He refused to let me touch him.

I know they keep your letters from us. But, Mother,
The day they finally put them in my hands

I'll know that possessing them I am condemned
And possibly even my wife, and my children.

We will drink mint tea this evening
Will each of us be increased by death?

With fractions as the bottom integer gets bigger, Mother, it
Represents less. That's the feeling I have about

This letter. I am at your request, The Czar.
And I am Nicholas.

This is a poem of tremendous tenderness, generosity, and beauty. In the extremity of these historical circumstances, we find a voice which transfigures our understanding of a person and a period. Dubie is a master of the impassioned, elliptical story. In his monologues (Dubie once called the dramatic monologue "a chosen profession"), Dubie asks: What is it that grants this speaker a unique place along the continuum of history? What, in each figure, is *like us*; what, in fact, is universal and human? Dubie doesn't so much recall history as recast histories; we constantly find his speakers redefining their relationships to their world, to their own observations and experiences. History is what time has left us in its wake; history is the story, the compilation of stories, we tell about time. Time has only one story it wishes to tell us: we are heading toward our deaths. Dubie, in his rescue of the dead and their visions, is able to forestall that sense of passage. Like Scheherazade, each poem, each story keeps him alive against time. It is in part this that makes Dubie so unafraid to champion ennobling acts, just as he is equally unafraid to champion the idiosyncratic, the momentary, and the domestic.

The object of Dubie's poetry is twin: natural sympathy and psychic renewal, or if you prefer, psychic sympathy and natural renewal. It is perhaps because of his capacity for sympathy with his speakers that Dubie has written the finest monologues in the voices of women (that is, of those written by a man) of anyone since Randall Jarrell; in my view, Dubie's monologues in the voices of women surpass Jarrell's (because they avoid the pathos so many of Jarrell's poems enjoy). What a pleasure it is to reread these poems: "The Pennacesse Leper Colony For Women, Cape Cod: 1922," "Monologue of Two Moons, NudesWith Crests: 1938," "Nineteen Forty" (spoken by Virginia Woolf), the stunning "Aubade of the Singer and Saboteur, Marie Triste," and a new poem, "Penelope." In "The Pennacesse Leper Colony For Women, Cape Cod: 1922," a young woman writes to her father about her life as a leper on the island. What she describes is the living and physical replication of the body's disintegration after death; what we as readers discover is that the poem's true subject is the transcendence and issuance of the spirit. As she says in her letter, "We are not kept/In; even by our skin."

Many of Dubie's poems want to ask of history: What is primitive? What is civilized? How does *this* world supersede *that* world, if not by a more open and humane understanding of itself? The poems ask: What is the place of the will in the natural world? Is this the source of our constant struggles? Yet Dubie's poems are often also tinged with a light that is almost mystical; they invite into themselves a spirituality that itself transcends any conventional sense of spirituality because it is contingent upon the mind's simultaneous intersection with and recognition of many worlds beyond the natural world. In one of his new poems, "Revelations," we find this visionary side of Dubie, just as it exists perhaps in its most finely orchestrated state in the superb poem, "Elegies for the Ochre Deer on the Walls at Lascaux," a masterfully conceived meditation on will and being, on death and regeneration. Another poem concerned with a figure caught at a juncture of two worlds, a juncture infused with an impending transformation, is another of the new poems, "To a Young Woman Dying at Weir":

TO A YOUNG WOMAN DYING AT WEIR

She hears a hermit laughing
Like a great scapegrace of waxwings and crows.
He is laughing about the burdock seed

That is in the horse manure
That is in the Sheriff's compost.
Last night, unable to sleep,
She recalled the catbird
Wheezing out in the chinaberry tree.
Soon frost would splatter
Iodine all over the hydrangeas
And the deer would no longer graze
Under the blood maples along the hill.

Sometimes her spirit grows and she remembers
A mountain dulcimer being played

While a woman sews. When the fear is largest
She remembers the old hermit poling his boat
Back along the cooling pond, he's taken burlap bags
Of the whitest sand from the cove
For plastering the walls of his autumn shack:
This comforts her,

              errand and prospect,
A freshened sense of snow
Feathering over the frozen pond. She says
          in a hush
That she loves something she has not found.

In reviewing the book *The City of the Olesha Fruit*, Peter Stitt noted that Dubie's poems "are not, no matter how obliquely, written in honor of the personality. They are written to celebrate the power of the imagination. The stance of the poet is objective, curious, interested in the known wonders of the world and in its possibilities." Indeed, the power, resiliency, and scope of the imagination often figure as subjects in many of Dubie's best poems, including the title poem of the volume above. In "The City of the Olesha Fruit" we find one of Dubie's most marvelous figures, Rumen, "an old man without legs," who, unable to go out into the real city, "has/invented the city outside the window." Rumen (whose "favorite writer is the great Russian/Yuri Olesha") not only gives his city its people and its stories, he provides and changes the weather as well. Rumen is the author of his own city, filling it with his memories and his imagination. Rumen shares his stories, the stories of his city, with Yuri Olesha—that is, with the Olesha of his imagination, the "companion" Olesha he addresses in his mind. In the second section of the poem, the narrator of the story of Rumen and his city *himself* addresses Olesha with stories of his own life and experiences. Quietly, the poem has turned towards a meditation on the indelibility of memory (and on the perpetual constructions of the imagination as well). As readers, we're presented with three fictive levels—Rumen's, the narrator's, and the poet's; and all of these are drawn against the background of Yuri Olesha's own fictions. Yet it is not the sophisticated leveling of narrative which so moves us in "The City of the Olesha Fruit"; it is the sympathy we feel with both Rumen and the narrator, and the desire we feel to join them in their imaginative constructions and creations of cities, people, and grand stories. We can understand the great nourishing power of memory and the imagination, the healing it holds available to us. Rumen's novelistic inventions help us to understand that, for the self to survive, in Dubie's work as well as in all others, the imagination must make a profound investment in the real.

To say that Dubie's poems are not autobiographical and not, as Stitt puts it, written "in honor of the personality" is not to say they are not personal. To the contrary, there is always the freedom of great intimacy and the privilege of the highly personal at work—and always vulnerable—in Dubie's poems. Even when his poems clothe autobiographical urges and urgencies in the voices of history and in the concept of the "other," Dubie still treats every voice and every speaker as if it were himself; he speaks with the urgency of that self and so makes each narrative monologue in some part autobiographical. And of course there are the deeply personal poems such as "Comes Winter, the Sea Hunting," a poem about his daughter's birth, and love poems like the marvelous new poem, "At Midsummer." Because so many readers are first struck by the persistent verbal imagination in Dubie's work, the deeply natural and simple voices in his poetry are rarely given their due. Let me suggest, as an antidote to this, the poem "A Grandfather's Last Letter," with its wisdom and understated tenderness. It is a moving and memorable poem.

Though what I consider to be the more operatic of the long poems are absent from this selection, Dubie has included many of his better-known longer poems, including the aforementioned "Elegies for the Ochre Deer on the Walls at Lascaux" and "The City of the Olesha Fruit," as well as "The Composer's Winter Dream," "The Parallax Monograph for Rodin," "The Scrivener's Roses," and a powerful new poem (about artistic responsibility and personal urgency), "Pictures at an Exhibition." In these longer poems, Dubie's architectures are simultaneously delicate and complex. He loves to employ disguised technical apparatuses and his phrasings seem as proper to a cinematic grammar as to a linguistic grammar. The impulse in Dubie's narratives is almost always compositional, in painterly and musical terms, and it is also theatrical in that he often invokes a dramatic staging for his poems. And over and over, in delivery and syntax, we find the cinematic textures of the poems coloring and disturbing the expected order of perception. There is, as Lorrie Goldensohn saw in her comprehensive review of Dubie's work, "that cross-cut, frame-cancelling gesture which is very nearly a Dubie signature."

Goldensohn also noted "a slow, prosaic specificity of utterance peculiarly Dubie's own." Dubie manages to write a poetry that exhibits those virtues seen by, for example, poet and critic Robert Pinsky in a highly discursive poetry while losing none of the activated surface, none of the muscular and energetic rhythms, none of the complexities of syntax sometimes absent in a more discursive poetry. There is also a great quiet and stately integrity to these poems. Here, for example, is the poem "Parish":

PARISH

i

God only knows what he'd been doing. Painting or sewing?
All I can say is that from my window
In the old yellow-and-black parsonage
I had been looking across falling snow
To the brick mortuary on the other side of the road.
It had one lamp burning, the mortician
Had thrown off his white gown, washed
His hands above the forearms, was exhausted,
And sat down. The water still running.

ii

I had a little friend once
Who fixed her own dolls: the walleyed, the lame,
And the gutted. She lived in a small town like this one.
She grew up to be odd.
All day I'd waited for a visitor
Who wasn't coming, all highways
Now closed by bad weather.

iii

He'd left the water running cold over porcelain.
He'd thrown down his gown. Looked out at the road.
Hypnotized by the snow and running water,
He gazed off to the body of hills.

iv

The wind grew for some hours, then it was dawn.
The storm over. I could see footprints
That had shallowed with the drifting snow, that had
Come to our door in the dark—

Perhaps some transient
Looking for an early breakfast after a night
Of journeying and enchantment. I smelled
Dahlias—thoughts of Saint Jerome's lion
  Carrying a burden of wood in for the stove.
  I glanced
  To the footprints,
  Which had circled, waited, circled some more,
  And left our door, leaping the fence

  Or passing through it, all signs
  Of them vanishing into the hills.

Dubie's poems show a quality of poetic thought capable of absorbing a rhetoric of discourse without suffering its constraints. Perhaps, in part, this is due to the fact that Dubie sees the function of language as providing a fluent body of possibility; that is, he constantly wants to ask: What is the sustaining character of poetry? What is its capacity for generosity, hope, and tolerance? With Dubie's speakers we are faced with a testimony of history, yet the conjunctions of moral questions appear without any judgmental impositions. As such, the poems force us to consider the potentiality of each voice, and the lines build as a sequence of permissions. Dubie's poems are important because structures of language and structures of thought are our only models for self-consideration aside from visionary or hallucinatory models. In this regard, Dubie has sought a style which both subtly instructs us about and consequently frees us from the ordinary structures of poetic investigation. And we ourselves must ask, reading Dubie, what constitutes "hope" at any time in history except the possibility of alternative structures of thought and language and consciousness, structures that will allow us to understand ourselves in new ways and free us from our repetitive and constraining despairs. It seems to me the responsibility of poetry, and of all of the arts, is to rehearse eternally these possible alternatives for us.

For Dubie, and for other poets as well, a sense of unity can be found through the acceptance and inclusion of the world's great variance, its multiplicity of realities. Like Kepler attempting to show the "harmony" of the cosmos, Dubie's response to the fragmentary nature of experience is to gather and balance it, showing its echoes and refractive or reflective qualities. Still, however philosophical, artistic, or spiritual the concerns of Dubie's poems, the stories and tableaus illustrating those concerns remain resolutely human. More than ever, Dubie's new poems show the powerful intimacy active in all of his work. It therefore seems to me proper that this *Selected and New Poems* ends with an elegy for two of American poetry's most personal and intimate poets, James Wright and Richard Hugo. The poem, a parable about Saint Jerome, is another of Dubie's gifts to his readers. In calling his poem simply "Elegy For Wright & Hugo" Dubie allows his story of Jerome's wisdom and saintliness to reflect upon our own understanding of the compassion and sympathy of the two poets. Obliquely, yet inevitably, we feel in the poem the way in which poetry is the repeated story of human understanding and misunderstanding—of each other, of ourselves, of all other sentient creatures, and of nature itself. For a man or woman who lives, at whatever expense, the life of those stories (Dubie seems to be saying), that realm of what we call "poetry" allows us the most generous salvation we have any right to expect. In Norman Dubie's *Selected and New Poems* that sympathy and generosity can be found on every page, and the great power and inventiveness of these poems make this volume one of the richest and most challenging of many years. It is a book the reader must live with; it is a book to return to over and over again.

# OXYGEN AND SMALL FRICTIONS

*Stars Which See, Stars Which Do Not See,* Marvin Bell's fourth volume, is a disarming book, deceptive in its simplicity and altogether seductive in its beauty. If others have made much of the verbal intelligence and knotty wit in Bell's work, and rightly so, what has most often been ignored is the extreme delicacy of the voice in his most lyric poems. Though Bell's playful, metaphysical intelligence is always pleasing, it is when this intelligence grows most fluid and intimate that the poems most completely succeed. It is this same delicacy, for example, which informs the much anthologized poem "Treetops" from Bell's first book, *A Probable Volume of Dreams.* It is the immediacy of this voice and the implicit pleas which draw us to a poem such as "We Have Known" from *The Escape Into You,* his second book:

> We have known such joy as a child knows.
> My sons, in whom everything rests,
> know that there were those who were deeply
> in love, and who asked you in,
> and who did not claim a tree of thoughts
> like family branches would sustain you.
>
> My sons, in whom I am well pleased,
> you will learn that a man is not a child,
> and there is that which a woman cannot bear,

but as deep wounds for which you may hate
me, who must live in you a long time,
coursing abrasively in the murky passages.

These poems, also, are such and such passages
as I have had to leave you. If very little
can pass through them, know that I did,
and made them, and finally did not need them.
We have known such joys as a child knows,
and will not survive, though you have them.

That same sense of being, as readers, invited into the landscape of a *privacy overheard* continues throughout Bell's third book, *Residue of Song*. The fluid self-dialogue of the title poem ("There was a certain inconsolable *person.*/You felt you had to discover who./You would be shocked to discover it was/not yourself.") as well as the intimate address of the sequence "You Would Know" (for his dead father) both serve to join us with the experiences Bell seizes. Again, notice the music of this final stanza of a poem from that sequence:

Now I want you as you were before they hurt you,
irreparably as you were as in another country.
The harvest moon, sunset's clockwork, can show us
what to pick, but not whom to pick on.
Step here with me, and stay, and blame the birds
whose unschooled bedlam in the sweltering cherries
is all the blame and harm a tree can bear.

("Father and Russia")

For some time now, it has seemed as if Bell has wanted to abandon the complications of syntax which have sometimes marked other of his poems, even though they were nearly always genial complications. He has sought a plainer speech, as American and colloquial as Williams'. Since Gary Snyder's haybucker in "Hay For The Horses" many poets have tried to appropriate into their poems a gritty, tough-talking American character, and to thereby earn for themselves some similar authority or "authenticity." But in *Stars Which See, Stars Which Do Not See*, Bell has found within his *own* voice that

American voice, and with it the ability to write convincingly about the smallest details of a personal history. He has found the maturity to meet with an enviable generosity those otherwise ordinary domestic events and routines of a daily life. When reading the titles of the poems, one thinks of a natural history book or an American tour guide ("The Wild Cherry Tree Out Back," "Two Pictures of a Leaf," "The Great South Bay," "A Catch of Weakfish from Peconic Bay," "John Clare's Badger," "Three Parts Mud," "The Great American Search for the Perfect Home Town"), but Bell has taken his admiration for Stafford to a higher plane; there is never the temptation to mutter "Aw, shucks" at these poems. And what in some poets has always seemed a Puritan underpinning to our ideas of American speech ("straight talk, no nonsense") instead reads in Bell simply as a belief that words might possibly mean what they say. Yet this never leads him to contend, as it apparently has others, that beauty in language is the snake-oil of poetry. Nor does Bell ever feel called upon to abandon his intelligence to retain his identity as an American.

Throughout *Stars Which See, Stars Which Do Not See*, the overwhelming concern is for *wholeness*. The poems seek to establish the self in relation to the natural, as in poems such as "The Self and the Mulberry" ("I wanted to see the self, so I looked to the mulberry") and "Bits and Pieces of Our Land" ("The land thinks/by watching you look around;/in its stopped-down time/ it will become what you want it to be, and then become/all that it wanted you to"). The poems consider the self's relation to the fragments of the past and the vague promises we name the future, yet they rely on nothing so grand as these summations imply. The poems are invariably located in the moment, the idea arising from the fact. Each seems as earthbound as a prayer, for what but a life on earth prompts us to prayer?

*Stars Which See, Stars Which Do Not See* begins with a poem bearing all the earmarks of an *Ars Poetica*. Aptly titled, "The Poem" indeed speaks, telling us repeatedly of its rather ordinary nature. There is nothing heavenly or angelic about it, for it says, "I had no wings, just shoulders." And later, "I cured no one./When I died, my bones turned to dust, not diamonds." Then "The Poem" accuses us and its author, "Had you survived/the silliness of the self,/you would have treated me better." Finally, "The Poem" confronts us:

> I said only that life continues.
> I did not mean a life like yours.
> Not life so proud to be life.

Not life so conscious of life.
Not life reduced to this life or that life.
Not life as something—to see or own.
Not life as a form of life
which wants wings it doesn't have
and a skeleton of jewels,
not this one of bones and becoming.
How perfect are my words now,
in your absence!
Ungainly yet mild perhaps,
taking the place of no field,
offering neither to stand in the place of a tree
nor where the water was,
neither under your heel nor floating,
just gradually appearing,
gainless and insubstantial,
near you as always,
asking you to dance.

("The Poem")

"The Poem" continually forces us back upon ourselves. The insistence of
the rhythm, the small "not life" litany propelling us to the poem's conclu-
sion, the aggressive diction and weary-yet-resilient tone all demand we recog-
nize that "The Poem" has refused to bear our burdens in our stead. "The
Poem" will not serve us, only its world. And it is in this world of detail
throughout Bell's poems—a catfish battered to death on a pier, the poet as a
boy killing sick young ducks by breaking their necks against a tree—that we
find those lessons learned by the child. In other poems, we find lessons we
knew and had forgotten, about failures, returns, and of course, love. Each les-
son has found its embodiment: in a passing goldfinch, a woman brushing
her hair, in the fish-like spine of a leaf. Bell tells us, "Listen! I speak to you in
one tongue,/but every moment that ever mattered to me/occurred in anoth-
er language."

Slowly, through a reading of the book, we assume a trust in the voice of
these poems, a trust enhanced by the instances of sheer lyric beauty. The
title poem, for example, seems a model of composure. Yet in the course of
the poem we find our sense of the verbal surface violated by our own recog-
nition of a subtle, if inevitable, moment of dislocation. In "Stars Which See,

Stars Which Do Not See," the illusory surface is literally broken within the poem:

> They sat by the water. The fine women
> had large breasts, tightly checked.
> At each point, at every moment,
> they seemed happy by the water.
> The women wore hats like umbrellas
> or carried umbrellas shaped like hats.
> The men wore no hats and the water,
> which wore no hats, had that well-known
> mirror finish which tempts sailors.
> Although the men and woman seemed at rest
> they were looking toward the river
> and some way out into it but not beyond.
> The scene was one of hearts and flowers
> though this may be unfair: Nevertheless,
> it was probable that the Seine had hurt them,
> that they were "taken back" by its beauty
> to where a slight breeze broke the mirror
> and then its promise, but never the water.

The poem takes, of course, Seurat's *La Grande Jatte* as a point of departure. The figures of the poem remain, like the rest of us, in that zone of being which is neither the world of pure beauty and seductive illusion nor that of the cold, final depths of the water. We stand between those stars above, which see us enacting our perpetual couplings and uncouplings, and those below reflected on the river's mirror, those stars being broken by the breeze. It is that sadness of the failed promise, that moment of the past frozen and clarifed by our present, which holds us to the ending of the poem. Like Carlos Drummond de Andrade's poem, "Souvenir of the Ancient World," Bell's poem infects us with a nostalgic clarity, only to carry us through to a point of suspension in which we feel those imminent but unspoken terrors of (our present) the future. As in Andrade's poem, it is the precise composure of the diction which prepares us to be most surprised by the reality of fear.

In "The Mystery of Emily Dickinson" Bell weaves an homage to Dickinson ("You were divine./While others wrote more and longer,/you wrote much more and much shorter.") into a dream-like encounter between the poet at a weekly chore ("only/a sleepy householder at his routine/bending to trash") and a young girl, Dickinson's physical echo, out walking in the rain-soaked, early morning. Addressing Dickinson throughout, the poem concludes, "I should have called to her, but a neighbor/wore that look you see against happiness./I won't say anything would have happened/unless there was time, and eternity's plenty."

As in "The Mystery of Emily Dickinson," it is the daily incident transformed, the minute detail serving as fulcrum to the poem, which informs nearly all of *Stars Which See, Stars Which Do Not See.* Bell has sought out the most physical mirrors for his considerations of the self. He refuses to dazzle us with mysterious possibilities; instead, he is happy now to talk with us plainly, until we feel we understand.

It is in the poem "Trinket," which I take to be the real and secret Ars *Poetica* of the book, that Bell most clearly outlines his methods and concerns. The pacing is deliberate and exact, like the movement of the poem's water through a crack in a fern pot. The poem's humor is measured and human. It is not in grandeur that the self is to be found, but in this minute trickle of water though the cracked, baked earthen pot. It is this trinket, this gift, which is to be found and shared. The poem enacts the same balance of self Bell has sought in all of the book, and the pervasive presence in the poem steadies as we, like the water, move slowly out of what contains us. It is this delicate balancing act, between ambition and peace, between those two networks of stars, between our self-consciousness and the natural, which "Trinket" allows us to perform:

> I love watching the water
> ooze through the crack in the fern pot,
> it's a small thing
>
> that slows time
> and steadies
> and gives me ideas of becoming
>
> having nothing to do
> with ambition or even reaching,
> it isn't necessary at such times
> to describe this,

it's no image for mean keeping,
it's no thing that small

but presence.
Other men look at the ocean,
and I do too,

though it is too many
presences for any
to absorb.

It's this other,
a little water, used, appearing
slowly around the sounds


of oxygen and small frictions,
that gives the self
the notion of the self

one is always losing
until these tiny embodiments
small enough to contain it.

("Trinket")

# CHARLES WRIGHT'S COUNTRY MUSIC

It has been ten years since the first edition of Charles Wright's Country Music: Selected Early Poems, which gathers work from his first four collections of poetry: The Grave of the Right Hand, Hard Freight, Bloodlines, and China Trace. In that time, Wright has dazzled his readers with four more quite extraordinary new volumes: The Southern Cross, The Other Side of the River, Zone Journals, and Xionia, which have now been collected into one volume entitled The World of the Ten Thousand Things. For the many readers who have been longtime admirers of his poetry, it has been gratifying to note that the critical reception to Charles Wright's work has also kept pace with the widening of his audience, an audience which has been increasingly drawn to his poetry by its great power and beauty, its incisive spirituality and meditative elegance.

Certainly, the fact that Helen Vendler, David Kalstone, Peter Stitt, Calvin Bedient and others have championed his poetry in their thoughtful and perceptive reviews has helped this audience at large to recognize that Charles Wright is without question one of our preeminent American poets. His many prizes, including the 1983 National Book Award for Country Music, The Academy of American Poets' Edgar Allan Poe Award, and the Brandeis Creative Arts Citation for Poetry, have also shown the high regard in which he's held by his peers. Yet it strikes me that Charles Wright's poetry is highly unusual in that it stands not only in the context of its own time (and such temporal accolades), but that its lucid illuminations are also intended to reflect far into—while casting light upon—those dark recesses of our futures.

For his readers, Charles Wright's poetry often serves as a kind of prayer book, a kind of poetic hymnal or speculative field guide we might carry with us on our own metaphysical journeys.

Over the past twenty years Charles Wright has written an impressive and demanding body of work that can stand in its accomplishments as the equal of *any* poet's in the latter part of the twentieth century. This has been not only an artistic achievement of notable dimension but a spiritual one as well. Quite simply, Charles Wright has emerged as the most visionary American poet since Hart Crane; he is that most rare of poets—one who is stylistically (and tirelessly) inventive, yet who speaks to and from a tradition that harkens back to Dante. With the mirror of his collection *The World of the Ten Thousand Things* so recently before us, it seems to me a proper occasion to look back at the rich and complex harmonies of Charles Wright's selected early poetry, *Country Music.*

\* \* \*

Throughout his career, Charles Wright has been a highly adept literary architect; he is not only a formal master, he is also an endlessly imaginative sculptor of larger unifying structures for his work. *China Trace*, Wright's fourth full collection, completed the triptych of books begun with *Hard Freight* (his second volume) and which he'd continued through his much praised third book, *Bloodlines*. In *County Music*, Wright has selected only five brief prose poems from his first book, *The Grave of the Right Hand*, as a kind of prologue to this triptych of his subsequent books.

It has always seemed natural to me (after the finely crafted, visually acute and precise poems of his debut volume) that Wright should feel the need to gather his past, in some sense to write—and rewrite—not only that past, but also the self (the poetic self and voice) which he was bringing to maturity in his newer and more ambitious poems. Clearly, in terms of both style and subject matter, this new direction was signaled by the poem "Dog Creek Mainline" from the book *Hard Freight*. Knotty, rhythmically muscular, alliterative, yet still highly imagistic and visual, Wright's poetry took on a beautiful rasping quality; his work began more deliberately to reflect the abstract concerns embodied in his retrieval of the past, all the while exhibiting the enjambed music that seemed to arise so magically from his lines. Wright also began revealing in these new poems from *Hard Freight* and *Bloodlines* his self-conscious choice to use both overt and covert autobiographical subject matter. These now familiar impulses in Wright's poetry began to grow, it seems, along with his conviction that the "unknown," or the spiritual and metaphysical, could best be encountered or mediated through the "known." For Wright this meant a reclamation of his past, an attempt at the recuperation of his childhood, was necessary before he could begin to look toward the yearnings and desirings of the *"beyond"* we find so delicately considered in the volume *China Trace,* the final panel of Wright's triptych.

In *Hard Freight* (and to some extent in the poems of *Bloodlines)* familial memories and episodes of Wright's youth in Tennessee and North Carolina mix quite easily—"naturally" we might say—with the rich landscapes of their settings. Yet, in *Bloodlines,* Wright begins the rigorous process of not only attempting to orient himself to his past, now as a mature speaker, but of orienting himself in relation to his own *present* and *presence* as well. *Bloodlines* is a fiercely elegiac book, detailing the losses of people, places, and times that have passed out of the poet's life. In addition to the powerful elegies for his parents, Wright provides a double axis of personal reckoning to *Bloodlines;* the intimate losses of the book revolve around two masterful poetic sequences, "Tattoos" and "Skins" (each consists of twenty numbered sections and each sequence serves to echo the concerns of the other).

"Tattoos" illustrates a list of psychologically potent events which have, each in some distinct way, "marked" Wright. "Skins" is a highly abstract inquiry into the materials of existence, from the most elemental to the most ethereal. The philosophical and metaphysical issues of "Skins" combine in a complex verbal music. And even though he questions his own ordering of the present, Wright nevertheless attempts to lay to rest his reclamation of the past while looking toward the certain—if ill-defined—terrain of his future, a terrain which takes as its horizon Wright's own death. Although, in *China Trace,* Wright will ask what may exist beyond that horizon (albeit in his own yearnings and imaginings), it is in *Bloodlines,* at the end of the final section of "Skins," that the meditations found in *China Trace* really begin:

> And what does it come to, Pilgrim,
> This walking to and fro on the earth, knowing
> That nothing changes, or everything;
> And only, to tell it, these sad marks,
> Phrases half-parsed, ellipses and scratches across the dirt?
> It comes to a point. It comes and it goes.

So, it is with these "sad marks" that Wright begins his attempt to tell not only what it comes to, but where—and why—his pilgrimage must continue.

\* \* \*

*China Trace* remains one of the most remarkable books of American poetry of recent years. Though made up of individual pieces, *China Trace* functions also as a single book-length poem, beginning with the speaker's childhood and concluding with his assumption into the sky, into what Wright has called "a man-made heaven." *China Trace* is a personal history pushed toward its future; its speaker reaches toward his own death and the desired salvation it may or may not bring. In the course of these poems, Wright often clearly does *not* believe, yet he feels called upon to continue the search that his spiritual yearnings have prompted. The book is filled with portents of what's to come, as in the poems "Next" ("I want to lie down, I am so tired, and let/The crab grass seep through my heart,/Side by side with the inchworm and the fallen psalm..." and "January" ("In some other life/I'll stand where I'm standing now, and will look down, and will see/My own face, and not know what I'm looking at"). Much as in the poem "Skins," it is the elemental regeneration of a life—its death into decay, the body passing through its cycle of water, earth, fire, and air—which seems as much as one might ask of salvation. Here in "Self-Portrait in 2035" is Charles Wright imagining himself at 100 years old:


>The root becomes him, the road ruts
>That are sift and grain in the powderlight
>Recast him, sink bone in him,
>Blanket and creep up, fine, fine:
>
>Worm-waste and pillow tick; hair
>Prickly and dust-dangled his arms and black shoes
>Unlinked and laceless, his face false
>In the wood-rot, and past pause...
>
>Darkness, erase these lines, forget these words.
>Spider recite his one sin.


The poems in *China Trace* are often offered as small cosmologies, many posited by Wright as approximations of both what is and what's to come. Even if, as he says in the poem "Morandi" (for the great Italian painter), it is "the void/These objects sentry for, and rise from," it is clear that the poems of *China Trace* are firmly rooted in the objects of everyday life, in the earth itself (as well as in natural landscape), and in the domestic experience reflected in the journal-like quality of many of the poems. It is no accident these poems are often fixed not only by place names, but by specific times of day or night, phases of the moon, dates, and personal references as well. In his diary of passage, the quotidian and the natural must balance what otherwise could simply seem the illusions all dreamers must perform. Thus, it remains vital to Wright that he must continuously mark and notate his search with the facts of his existence. Otherwise, without these resolutely concrete notes in the log, what future resonance could such a spiritual search have?

*China Trace* is a pilgrim's book, the same "Pilgrim" who is addressed at the conclusion of "Skins." It carries a strong and dramatic narrative—the soul's search for salvation, a man's yearning for the other. *China Trace* also shows Charles Wright to be one of the most formally inventive poets writing. The weblike structures of his poems reverberate with his characteristic verbal music, and their individual images seem to radiate through *Country Music* as a whole. *China Trace* grows slowly into a guidebook of spiritual passage, with nods to fellow travelers along the way. Sometimes, we feel that the speaker of these poems has suffered his own silence, in seclusion, for a long while. Sometimes, we listen as the poems take on the tone of a wanderer who has walked off from the tribe, the city, in order to turn and speak for it, at last. In "Depression Before the Solstice," Wright sees:

> The watchers and holy ones set out, divining
> The seals, eclipses
> Taped to their sleeves with black felt,
> Their footprints filling with sparks
> In the bitter loam behind them, ahead of them stobbed
>     with sand.
> And walk hard, and regret nothing.

Many have remarked upon the hermetic tone of *China Trace*, attributing it in part to the influence of Eugenio Montale, the superb Italian poet whom Wright has translated so well. Yet the impulse to touch mystery has always been present in Wright's work. In the illuminating instants of *China Trace*, we are in the presence—as in all of the finest religious works—of the mystery of the *one*, the individual, confronted by the expanse of the greater and more fluent *other*. Here is the poem "Stone Canyon Nocturne":

> Ancient of Days, old friend, no one believes you'll come back.
> No one believes in his own life anymore.
>
> The moon, like a dead heart, cold and unstartable, hangs
>        by a thread
> At the Earth's edge,
> Unfaithful at last, splotching the ferns and the pink shrubs.
>
> In the other world, children undo the knots in their tally strings.
> They sing songs, and their fingers blear.
>
> And here, where the swan hums in his socket, where bloodroot
> And belladonna insist on our comforting,
> Where the fox in the canyon wall empties our hands, ecstatic
>        for more,
>
> Like a bead of clear oil the healer revolves through the night
>        wind,
> Part eye, part tear, unwilling to recognize us.

Once again, Wright tries to explore the nature of our proper relationship to what "lies beyond," since fear and acquiescence are both regarded as inadequate. For Wright, this simple search always leads back to language; for that reason his poetry has, over the years, developed a more heightened and exremely graphic sense of what characterizes verbal enactment. As a result, Wright has often been called "painterly" in his use of wordplay and in his execution of dazzling verbal chromatics. It is as if many of Wright's poems keep seeking some ideogrammatic form, and as such exist almost as some other language—something between the language we know and the glyphs of an obscure, yet resilient poetic cult. There is, in Charles Wright's poetry, much of the tone of Yeats' occult clarity and Rilke's sonorous passion. It's no accident that the natural elements often appear in the act of "writing" themselves across the face of the earth or the sky. It is this singularly physical signature of passage, both man's and the world's, which so intrigues Wright, perhaps because so much of his poetry reflects his struggle against the impossibility of inscription.

Certainly one can trace Pound behind some of Wright's ambitions, just as one can find echoes of Hart Crane's revisionist-symbolist impulses, or the devotional grandeur of Gerard Manley Hopkins. Yet I'm convinced that, in the forging of this new line and new language for himself, Charles Wright has responded to a tremendously personal, internal pressure—a pressure to discover the proper word construct, the right syllable mobile, the most pleasing sound ladder—in his search for an appropriate aesthetic to reflect and convey his anxious, metaphysical explorations. There is some risk, certainly, when so demanding a notion of language is coupled with so abstract a subject matter. But Charles Wright is an impeccable stylist, and his poems remain rooted in real experience even while seeking some greater, perhaps more universal, equation.

*Country Music* as a whole traces Charles Wright's grand passions: his desire to reclaim and redeem a personal past, to make a reckoning with his present, and to conjure the terms by which we might face the future. If we wonder where the road of these poems can possibly end, it is the end we knew would be reached from the very beginning. If we wonder what will become of the "pilgrim" who has disguised himself so often as "I," "You," and "He," then we are answered in the final poem of *China Trace*, with its devotional pun on hymn, "Him":

> His sorrow hangs like a heart in the star-flowered boundary tree.
> It mirrors the endless wind.
>
> He feeds on the lunar differences and flies up at the dawn.
>
> When he lies down, the waters will lie down with him,
> And all that walks and all that stands still, and sleep through
>     the thunder.
>
> It's for him that the willow bleeds.
>
> Look for him him in the flat black of the northern Pacific sky,
> Released in his suit of lights, lifted and laid clear.

In *Country Music* we see the same explosive imagery, the same dismantled and concentric (or parallel) narratives, the same resolutely spiritual concerns that have become so familiar to us in Wright's more recent poetry. The idea of using a fluid "journal" construct, which becomes the central formal aspect of *The World of the Ten Thousand Things*, can be discovered in the poems of *China Trace*. The charged verbal rhythms and the crystalline music that have become hallmarks of Wright's poetry both have their poetic workbooks contained in *Country Music*. And it is here, especially in those poems of overt autobiographical reckoning, that we come to recognize the importance of Charles Wright as an American poet, most specifically as a Southern poet. The "country" in *Country Music* is meant to signal a fierce regionalism in Wright, as well as to honor the "lyric, the human theme" of country music itself; an art whose story line, Wright says, seldom varies: "change your life or else heaven won't be your home." Yet the title also announces the importance of understanding how elements of landscape in Charles Wright's poems have been first remembered and recovered, then precisely reinvented and constructed as poetic entities (and melodies). In his prose book, *Halflife*, Wright says of his poems from *Zone Journals* something that is applicable to all of his work, that his poems "are about language and landscape, and how they coexist in each other, and speak for, and to, each other." In his poetry, Wright looks to the landscapes that have nourished him, contained him, and inspired him, and tries to give them worthy poetic voices.

We need also to keep in mind the interwoven quality of Wright's spiritual aspirations with the poetic materials of his poems. In Charles Wright's poetry, reticence is a kind of faith and style is an articulation of virtue. As Wright says elsewhere in *Halflife*, "True vision is great style." Wright's poems are not only truly devotional, they are each secular prayers begging to break into a realm far beyond their own seclusion or privacy. It is perhaps Charles Wright's greatest accomplishment that, while his poems remain very much of the world, they are nevertheless resolutely spiritual in character. It is this, even more than his technical virtuosity, formal prowess, and astounding imaginative range which makes him unique among his contemporaries. Charles Wright's poetic maps are drawn with humor and tenderness, great clarity and imagistic precision; yet it is his reverberating metaphors and complex verbal overlays that continue to dazzle his readers. Like his master, Cézanne, Wright insists that the very nature of perception itself changes within us, that we might see more clearly the world which is without. This remarkable volume, *Country Music*, is an essential key to understanding the delicate poetic cosmology that resonates in Charles Wright's poetry. Lastly, let me remind the reader that one of the many rewards of these poems is that they seem so often to arise, in their consummate grace and power, in voices we slowly come to recognize as the simple echoes and lost harmonies of our own.

# OR YOURS TO KEEP:
## THE POETRY OF PAMELA STEWART

In Pamela Stewart's poems, the lyrical articles of *attention* catalogue the simultaneities of a layered, shifting world. We watch ourselves upon a stage of suspended perceptual delay, as each experience finds its reflective and multiple intersections with other finely detailed—and ever spiraling sequences of—narrative episodes. These poems describe the elemental congruities of fact and imagination, the distentions of anxiety through repose, in what seems a richly gestural, cinematic grammar of progression. The poems celebrate the *textual* and *textural* relief of language in our increasingly disjunctive world, in the most intimate terms and tone. They are the poems one writes *to continue*.

*The St. Vlas Elegies*, which includes several poems from the earlier chapbooks *The Hawley Road Marsh Marigolds* and *The Figure Eight At Midnight*, is Pamela Stewart's first book-length collection. The narrative impulses in these poems often filter through a series of problematic asides, seeking their courses, as water seeks its circuit along the face of a smooth sheet of rock. What remains essential to each poem is the way in which its particular imaginative transformation is enacted; in many of the poems, we find that a piece of visual inscription serves, in turn, as the metaphorical tracing of the poem's voice, much as the skater's figure eight is first etched in ice, to be erased by wind and snow. Even the most abstract, rhetorical conjectures find themselves delivered into resolutory equations. Often, it is the literal and physical terrain of the poem which functions as the "ground" against which the poem's verbal figures are activated. An example of this kind of perceptual unraveling is the poem, "The Columbine Fields At Easter," where the transfigurative use of colors is especially clear:

It burns, this idea of red and white, a finger
Pricked in snow behind a shed: a ceremony
That wishes to marry an absence:
A sister, itself, or the small season
That flickers in April when the tiny


Points of a wildflower we shouldn't touch
Are irresistable as those old, bonewhite
Fingers stitching up
The ragged breast of an ornamental dove.

It fell too many times
From the Easter branch by the door
Surviving, after all, its first self
As sawdust and crushed glass. The pale columbine

By the edge of the woods dips its beak
Like a needle in the mouth of a dead bird
That drills
Through the diamond wreckage of someone
Whose hollow bones spilled out all the words
Of a visit, or flight across a dappled field
With water and ice that's torn from us.
The audience

Of the dead is our most demanding, a soft
Flower bell that can't endure us, or
This fire from nowhere:
A flock of returning birds
That drops down on our meadow to be fed

By God: by men weaving through the gate
From the woods as though a thin

Seam bound our worlds of light
And dark, that are

These bundles of flaming columbine, gentle
In our arms like the bodies of the dead.

*The St. Vlas Elegies* is filled with women and their voices, both personal and historical, issuing notice on the prevailing conditions of their lives and times. The poems occasionally take up the congruent voices of literary personages (Edith Wharton, Emily Dickinson, Edna St. Vincent Millay) as well as more anonymous voices of isolation and fatigue. Yet, it is in the poem, "Elegy For Agatha Christie," that we find the finest example of the interaction of self, life, and literature. It is Stewart's seriously imaginative playfulness at its best:

In the pantry a decanter reflects topaz pools
On pastries and the tins
As the late sun flows in through an open window.
Outside, a tall woman bends and clips off
Red roses for a perfect setting, the guests'
First meeting. That picturesque,
Elegant dinner will be disturbed by which

Person's memory of an incident in Egypt?
The butler yawns behind the door, pauses
Before crossing the hall and hears
The guests rising from their chairs.
The sticky mark above an ear
Locks every door that night. Upstairs,
A girl in a flowered dress holds a photograph
And weeps; the man in the corridor

Makes a fist at his own image in the glass
And all over the world
People sit up, not wanting to finish, and still
Not able to sleep. They think they know,
Knowing themselves!

Now one woman is missed as our lost hours
Are not. For us she killed the individual,
Evil people, and the hours. Characters
For results. They are not
Ourselves or even like
The crystals of our hatred and distrust.

The airs of a murder clearing up,
And the lost hours
That saved us for the accomplishment of sleep—
We are grateful for the murders, and we know
That all she killed for us has, now, killed her:
Time and boredom, preparing us for the rest
That's dark and formal,
Like the butler sleeping in a chair, his large
Hands innocently folded between his knees.

Some of the greatest pleasures of Pamela Stewart's poems are the intima-
cies and desired joinings—of the self with others, of the self with its frag-
ments. We find in the voices quiet adoptions of tenderness, or a sudden
admission of another's presence within the faintly startled speaker. In "The
Pages," a love poem for her husband, she invites our presence as readers in
the delicate duality of passage; in "Haploscore," we find a self-portrait (com-
plete with disclaimer) in which the stereoscopic image, the dual, becomes the
one—the focused "I" which continues throughout the book to define itself in
absence, or as "other." In the title poem, "The St. Vlas Elegies," which takes
Tolstoy's *War and Peace* as a remembered context, we are confronted by a
series of shifting monologues which detail the elegiac longings of their fictive
characters, so that we as readers become enveloped in the poem's twelve part
memory play, not as audience but as equals, prompters from the wings. It is
this capacity to embrace a reader into the fabric of the poem which remains,
for me, one of the major strengths in Pamela Stewart's work. Still, it is a
poem of, quite clearly, personal reckoning, a poem of tremendous quiet and
restraint, which continues to move me most. Here is "The Hawley Road
Marsh Marigolds":

April returns this constellation of flowers
In a ditch, butter-shadows with green orbs

In water. Sometimes we eat them, our details
Of morning. Little lights strung
In a black mirror inside us. The mirror is
Inside us, not, as we thought, in the faces
Of our children looking back, and up, even into

Our eyes. The ditch widens in winter.
I once painted a small boy skating on it
Out of these glazed windows in a blue coat.
He had yellow gloves and was visible just
For a moment this side of the trees. I've lost
The idea of him. His bright hand in black water is
The curve of my own arm which is wet.
There is a little girl who lives with me, not

Inside me, but here with us. Everything
Scares me. Once she was just yours,
Your idea of someone skating a distance
When there were no details. Now,
Everything is ours and these incidents of love
Scare me. They are specific like that unexpected swarm
Of yellow stars. Day and night.

In her most recent chapbook, *Half-Tones*, Pamela Stewart has gathered her strongest work to date. In the marvelous sequence, "Cascades," she manages a unique performance, mixing autobiographical narrative incident with meditative interlude with metaphysical conjuring. Her lyrical innocence, her delicate ironies, and her inventive couplings combine in these poems to show that never have Pamela Stewart's abstract considerations found more beautiful or more physical embodiments. Here, embracing and amplifying many of her earlier concerns, is the poem, "Camera Lucida":

Just before dawn, outside the window,
When we're restless
Pulling back from dreams, a pale
Glimmer arrives from nowhere, a slow
Aerial spinning above the lawns.
This is shade and foreplay, the strobe lights

Of the purposeful ghost moths. The males
With their sheen and carroty scent
Are waking the females
Who've been closed over thin
Stalks of grass all night. These females

Are dusky and ochre, hidden
In the dim morning. Suddenly,
They fly up
Toward that mysterious light that comes
And goes as the alternate
Dark and white sides of their partner's wings.
For us,

Drawn out of sleep or from our houses, the best
Show in town is a stranger
Dancing: a large hat slung
Across her buttocks, a white feather
Caught in the labia while a live
Canary follows down an invisible wire.
Like us, the crowd is tipped on their chairs
Somewhere between themselves
And what they see. We all see

What the body sees, in daylight
On the street or in the long grasses
Of adolescence flattened
Under cold stars; the white daisies staring
Back up beneath us. Or this:

The sound of someone dreaming
Beside you whose hand is suddenly on you;
You accept it in sleep.
And even as the familiar
Has motion, scent and color, you have woken

As someone being discovered
In a world between worlds. Strange

Duration that tilts you back to sleep:
What the body saw
When it was no longer rising
In a field of wild carrots

Or yours to keep.

Pamela Stewart's poems invoke a system of gestural causalities and suspensions. Instead of definitions we find tracings; the outlines of experience are drawn over the emotional grids of her concerns. From the resulting intersections, we find how the poems often issue probabilities of circumstance, a collated spectrum of conditions in which the declarative resolve of the speaker either triumphs or, on occasion, fails. As with the best of poets, Pamela Stewart's poems continue to speak for their faith in the obscured correspondences within the world.

# THE HAPPY MAN

In *String Too Short to Be Saved*, his marvelous book of recollections of his childhood summers at Eagle Pond Farm, Donald Hall recounts memories and narratives of a time and place he thought was forever lost to him. Yet because the world is a mysterious and sometimes generous place, Hall found himself living at Eagle Pond Farm (where his great-grandfather had begun farming in 1865) in the fall of 1975, and he has lived there ever since. Hall's remarkable collection of poems, *Kicking the Leaves* (1978) was the announcement and celebration of that homecoming, that return to New Hampshire.

*String Too Short to Be Saved* is a loving album of family portraits, landscape sketches, and quiet paeans to the rural values Hall recalled. *Kicking the Leaves* became Hall's farewell to his life in Ann Arbor ("a life of parties and schools, lectures and plays, English departments and picnics, tennis, tenure and Volvos"), as he stepped simultaneously back into his past and forward into his future, into the hope that any new life carries with it.

*Kicking the Leaves* is a compelling and powerful volume of poems. Deceptively straightforward in its style, the book is haunting in its human resonances. It is a book in which a man makes peace with the natural world—with the land, in this case the rugged and beautiful landscape of southern New Hampshire, and with its animals, seen by Hall with a sense of loving kinship.

In his return, Hall found his own place in a lineage of values, his own rightful inheritance in a world of *trust*, and work; he found *his* place in a real place, a physical landscape—not in a place of the imagination, of the mind.

And not, I should add, in an unlived landscape, but a landscape with a history that was both personal and familial.

In the poems of *Kicking the Leaves,* we see how Eagle Pond Farm becomes both a source and a resource for Hall. Even the harshness and elemental quality of rural farm life give, with the dailiness of physical work, a kind of clarifying urgency. The poems all become hymns of praise for the men and women and animals that populate, or once populated, the farm and its surrounding villages. For Hall, the farm quietly came to represent the timelessness of place, a timelessness he could see reflected in the mountains around him. In the face of the shifting horrors of contemporary life and politics, this created, for the speaker of these poems, a place of solace, a vantage point of strong witness. And at the end of the book *Kicking the Leaves,* in the poem "Stone Walls," Donald Hall is exactly where he wishes to be:

> Pole beans raise their green flags in the summer garden.
> I grow old, in the house I wanted to grow old in.
> When I am sleepy at night, I daydream only
> of waking the next morning—to walk on the earth of the present
> past noons of birch and sugarbush, past cellarholes,
> many miles to the village of nightfall.

Yet in his new collection, *The Happy Man,* Hall can see in the distance that "the village of nightfall" is all too quickly approaching.

\* \* \*

In *The Happy Man,* Donald Hall may indeed still be as happy as ever, yet the sunlit vistas of the past are now shown complete with their complicated shadows. One has only to note the book's marvelous and scary epigraph from Tolstoy for the title to acquire its proper irony:

> Behold me then, a man happy and in good health, hiding the rope in order not to hang myself to the rafters of the room where every night I went to sleep alone; behold me no longer shooting, lest I should yield to the too easy temptation...

Hall introduces his new volume with a section of ghosts, both animal and human; he is a conjurer who summons, in "Great Day in the Cows' House," the spirit of his grandfather and those of his grandfather's cows! The effect is startling and poignant; we feel ourselves drawn slowly into the living pulse of the natural world, yet of the natural world that belonged to Hall's dead grandfather. Of these spirits, we presume, of those that follow in this opening section, Hall says, "They are long dead; they survive...." The presence of this past, its men and women and landscapes, invades every poem in *The Happy Man*, but it's nowhere more explicitly apparitional than in this opening section. In "Whip-poor-will" the poet is summoned to the day by a "ghost bird" calling him by a ghostly name—the name of his dead grandfather, whose place he has taken. "Scenic View" provides its ghost mountains, a landscape certain to take its vengeance upon the tourists who've drained it of color with their endless photography. "The Rocker" supports a grandmother and her story, a ghost story of a suicide. The poem concludes "Her kettle screams;/her fat old tomcat/turns his head/when a mouse skitters/over linoleum." The unrelentingly predatory quality of nature and natural processes, of which time's ravagement is one, is present everywhere in *The Happy Man*. Here is one of the stanzas of the poem "Twelve Seasons":

> A doe walks in the railroad's trench on corrupt snow.
> Her small hooves poke holes in the crust,
> melted and frozen again, that scrapes her ankles
> as her starved head swivels for bark. So the dogpack,
> loosened one by one from stove-warm houses, gathers
> seven leaping bodies that larrup, sliding
> along the crust, like twelve year-old boys at recess
> chasing a sissy. They rip her throat out.
> Walking on a mild day, as snow melts from the tracks,
> we find the body hollowed by birds and coyotes
> and drag it aside, into a grove of yellow birch
> that beavers forested, leaving spiky stumps behind.

In "Twelve Seasons" (a poem of twelve stanzas of twelve lines each), Hall recounts a passage through real seasons and seasons of memory. The poem is a meditation on aging and survival, strength and fortitude, the brother-and-sisterhood of the old and the young.

Hall says, "Ghosts rise, ghosts whirl in the aftenoon leaves,/as the dead visit the declining year. We take them in...." Indeed, there is a place for the dead in this cycle of seasons. Hall treasures these passages and the human resilience they reveal. The poem concludes in this lovely and ambigous way; it is winter, December:

> Now we gather in the black evening, in Advent,
> as our nervous and reasonable fingers continually reach
> for the intangible. Now we wait together;
> we add wood to the cast iron stove, and midnight's
> candlelight trembles on the ceiling
> as we drowse waiting. Someone is at the door.

The second section of *The Happy Man* is the single long poem "Shrubs Burnt Away" (which is one part of a projected book-length poem to be entitled *Build A House*), a startling and riveting meditation on mortality and aspects of self-destruction. The poem takes its title from this passage from Hsu Hsia-K'o: "Mi-t'o Temple after thirty li. A most desolate spot... For fear of hiding tigers, all trees and shrubs have been burnt." As "Shrubs Burnt Away" progresses, we increasingly recognize the irony of this passage (an epigraph to the poem), as we see that the most serious predators of the lives recounted—madness and alcoholism and adultery—arise from within those lives. And, sadly, we see the elements of self-destruction as that paradoxical burning away of the shrubs.

The project of this ambitious poem is to build a house of the spirit, and to build it from within the house of the body, by definition already a corrupted house, a house which will fall—a house of death. "Shrubs Burnt Away" opens with a mother's tale to a sleepy child, a tale of a brother and sister who build a secret house in the woods. This ideal of refuge then gives way immediately to the poem's next scene in which the poet, middle-aged, "starting/the night's bottle," says, "I daydream to build the house of dying...."

Flights—both flights from difficulty and real flights in the early history of air navigation—weave their metaphorical escapes throughout the poem, as the corruptions of place (Hollywood and Sunset Strip) begin to mirror the self-inflicted corruptions of the body, alcoholism and destructive cigarette smoking (from which the poet's father, we learn, has died). And the real flights, we should note, are all flights of unfortunate consequences, from Wrong-Way Corrigan to Amelia Earhart.

The only proper adjective for this poem is *searing*. There is such an extraordinarily complex investigation of the psyche at work here; using filmic shifts of time and locale, Hall is able to trace the threads of disintegration through the lives of his speakers (there are two speakers here, a man and a woman) and his incidental characters as well. Hall, in this poem, wants to confront the violence one finds not only in the external world, but also within himself—or herself, as the case may be—as well. Again, the insistence of mortality drives every line.

"Shrubs Burnt Away" reveals all of the tigers still lurking in our lives. The house of marriage collapses; the poet says, "I told my wife: Consider me a wind/that lifts square houses up and spins them/into each other...." The male speaker in the poem is often adrift, numbed; he is a false Sinbad, an adventurer who can't make it off the motel-room bed. The house of sexuality seems to tremble everywhere around him, but the true home of the sensual, nowhere. The poem concludes with the male speaker, "waking dozing twisted in the damp clothes/of lethargy, loathing, and the desire to die." The female speaker, in her last address, recounts a vision in which "the children," who one presumes are her own, are sentenced to death; a "visitor" then enters her kitchen to give her a lesson, using a rag-doll and scissors, in how to then dismember them—"as I must do," the speaker says, "as it seems that I want to do."

The horrors of "Shrubs Burnt Away" are all the more stunning as the reader comes to understand how much they are all horrors of consciousness and self-consciousness. Can art, can poetry do anything to mitigate the force of these horrors? The stringent conscience that arises from the objectified diction of "Shrubs Burnt Away" has two functions: the first, to imply yes, art can; and the second, to keep the poem from crumbling under the force of its emotions. The poem has a second epigraph, central to this question, which forces us to recognize that much of the project of this poem has been to make poetry out of what cannot become poetry. It also leads us to question the premise from which the poem sets out. From Matthew Arnold: "What then are the situations, from the representation of which, though accurate, no poetical enjoyment can be derived? They are those in which the suffering finds no vent in action; in which a continuous state of mental distress is prolonged, unrelieved by incident, hope, or resistance; in which there is everything to be endured, nothing to be done." It is from precisely this state that this spectacular poem emerges.

Hall conjures, in the third section of *The Happy Man*, voices and characters both local and historical, from his acquaintances, literature, and even baseball. The baseball poems are always, of course, more about the passing of time than the crack of the bat (though perhaps those two are the same).

Here, in every poem, we find lives emptied out by circumstance, by time. These are in some ways the voices of living ghosts, women and men who've suffered great losses, whose voices rest at the edge of violence, each in danger of imploding. These are characters latent with anger and frustration, figures doing their best to simply keep on. For me, the most frightening aspect of several of these poems is their composure in the face of great internal pressure, in the face of the fragmentation of a life. The characters are, one feels, each, in his or her own choice of life over death, spectacularly courageous. The "affliction" of the soul each faces becomes the occasion for Hall's meditations, several in the form of monologues. Again, our undeniable transience on earth and the "concealment" of life's terrors beneath its glossy surface are the facts that trouble each of these poems. Yet these are all speakers who tell themselves the truth; they confront, despair, and prevail. Even their own self-loathing engenders in us, because of the lack of self-pity, only the most generous response. In this section, entitled "Men Driving Cars," the men of these poems all believed they were going *somewhere*, only to find they had no destination at all.

What, then, does the soul look toward in this fragmented world? Hall provides a partial answer in his epigraph to the concluding section of the book, a passage from Meister Eckhart (a presiding spirit in *The Happy Man*): "If I were asked to tell the truth about God's purposes, when he created us, I would say 'Repose.' If I were asked what all creatures wanted, in all their natural efforts and motions, I would answer 'Repose.' " This section, entitled "Sisters," once again makes peace with the world, the natural world. The women in these poems become "sisters" in spirit to the men driving cars. The poems urge us towards a sense of kinship, of brother-and-sisterhood with the natural world, its people and animals, its grasses, its stones. We are, after all, the most transitory aspect of this planet of grass and earth; yet it is essential, Hall repeatedly shows, that we not forget that we are *of* this world. In the poem "Granite and Grass" Hall notes that we worship granite as an "emblem of permanence," yet it is only the grass which "generates again" each spring. Nature's cycles of recomposition and regeneration mirror the mortal, yet the changing is, therefore, everlasting. The last stanza of this poem reads:

> Ragged Mountain was granite before Adam divided.
> Grass lives because it dies. If weary of discord
> we gaze heavenward through the same eye that looks at us,

vision makes light of contradiction:
Granite is grass in the holy meadow of the soul's repose.

Like many of Hall's poems, the poems of *The Happy Man* have genera-
tional and regenerational impulses; one must live both through and beyond
those generational echoes and reverberations. The spirits and souls and char-
acters here have chosen to stand, as steadfastly as they are able, against the
wastes of time. These poems want to insist upon a transcendence (though
Hall would prefer, of course, Eckhart's "repose" as the term to embody that
transcendence) over the body's destruction and the world's griefs. There is a
determined, at times willed, quality to this insistence—I don't mean forced, I
mean chosen—that makes me feel that though Hall sees the spirit's victory as
natural, perhaps as natural as the body's betrayal and the occasional vacuum
of human values, he still sees and wishes to honor the fierce courage of his
characters, the courage necessary to find belief or, rather, repose. In this way,
confronting the seeming "defeat" of mortality, the spirit joins itself to the
timelessness of landscape and natural process. To be *of* nature is, in a basic
way, to be no longer the *object* of its seemingly destructive (though regenera-
tive) processes. Merging times and generations, Hall concludes *The Happy
Man* with a gesture of affirmation and generosity and triumph; it is a simple
offering, as simple as the milk his grandfather carries, or the words he holds
forth:

From the Studebaker's backseat, on our Sunday drives.
I watched her earrings sway. Then I walked uphill
beside an old man carrying buckets
under birches on an August day. Striding at noontime,
I looked at wheat and at river cities. In the crib
my daughter sighed opening her eyes. I kissed the cheek
of my father dying. By the pond an acorn fell.
You listening here, you reading these words as I write them,
I offer this cup to you: Though we drink
from this cup every day, we will never drink it dry.

# ANCIENT EYES

In October of 1951, at the end of an audience with T. S. Eliot, budding young poet Donald Hall receives this memorable wisdom: "Let me see," Eliot tells him, "forty years ago I went from Harvard to Oxford. Now you are going from Harvard to Oxford. What advice may I give you?" After what Hall calls "the comedian's exact milliseconds of pause," Eliot asks, "Have you any long underwear?" Hall confesses, "I suppose it was six months before I started laughing." We've always loved to read about the lives of our writers. Long before our taste for celebrity profiles of movie and rock 'n' roll person-alities foamed into its present lather, we feasted on the details of poets' lives, given what seemed their special bent for suicide or early death, drunkenness and rancid literary pettiness. Yet even the most clichéd cautionary tale of a literary life is never so simple as it first seems.

It takes a book as shrewd and balanced as Donald Hall's *Their Ancient Glittering Eyes* to begin to set us straight. This expanded and mildly revised version of *Remembering Poets*, Hall's well-known but long-out-of-print memoir of Robert Frost, Dylan Thomas, T. S. Eliot, and Ezra Pound, now adds to its gallery of portraits the faces of Marianne Moore and two of Hall's former teachers, Archibald MacLeish and Yvor Winters. Donald Hall is a deft chron-icler of his acquaintance with the already famous elders he encounters as a young poet. In several cases—Eliot, Pound and Moore—the visits arise from Hall's role as interviewer for *The Paris Review* (these original interviews are reprinted in the book's appendix). He is, at first meeting, somewhat in awe of these figures; it is an awe that is inevitably tempered by experience.

In Hall's reflections on Frost, we find troubling if sometimes amusing accounts of the warping effects of a poet's desire for fame. When MacLeish decides to enlist Frost's aid in trying to get Pound released from St. Elizabeth's Hospital (where Pound was being held, charged with treason for his World War II radio broadcasts from Italy), Hall asks MacLeish "how he planned to persuade Frost to intervene. Oh, he said, he would just tell Robert that Ezra was getting *too much attention,* locked up down there; if we get him out, people won't notice him so much."

Hall tries to provide a balanced account of Frost, measuring the *Life* magazine version of the "rustic, witty, avuncular, *benign*" Frost against the man later biographies depict, in the words of one critic, as a "monster of egoism." For Hall, neither extreme will do. Instead, he posits a complicated double vision that reveals not only the public Frost pandering to audiences by playing the role of the simple New Englander, but also the private Frost, wracked by guilt over the wreckage of his family. It is a Frost, Hall says, who "lived in terror of madness and suicide."

Though Frost reveled in his late celebrity, his ambition, Hall says, "was never merely to be a celebrated poet; it was larger and more serious than that, for he knew that to write great poems he had to make perfect works of art which embodied wisdom and knowledge beyond the perfections of art." Still, in Hall's remarkable framing of Frost's self portraiture, a Grant Wood mask hangs over a face by Francis Bacon.

Hall shows the outrageous Dylan Thomas in all his riotous glory, a genius of excess. At one point, during a full day of pub-crawling all over London, Thomas, a glass in *each* hand, invents for his audience an American gangster movie, playing all the parts and doing "a sampler of American accents, each of them exaggerated, accurate enough, and hilarious." The young Hall returns to his hotel room that evening flush with his new friendship, not to mention endless pints of bitter. He dashes off a celebratory letter to his parents, noting with classic filial understatement, "Dylan is fine, though he drinks a bit heavily."

This "public suicide," as Hall calls Thomas' drinking, leads him to an exceptionally powerful discussion of the relationship of artistic endeavor and personal self-destruction. Hall concludes that the poet "who survives is the poet to celebrate; the human being who confronts darkness and defeats it is the one to admire."

Yet throughout this book, Hall is unapologetic about the often life-altering demands of art, especially great art. Paraphrasing Rilke's advice to the young poet, Hall says, "You will never be any good as a poet unless you arrange your life by the desire to write great poems, always knowing (and if you do not know it, you are foolish) that you are likely to mess up your life for nothing." Hall is devoted to the power of poetry. He says, "the great poets as they turn older look...to pursue vision, to discover motions of spirit and of human consciousness, which it is art's task to enlarge."

Hall's recollections of T.S. Eliot commend that enlarged sense of self in the man himself toward the end of his life. No longer the "cadaverous" figure of their first meeting, the newly remarried Eliot (at 70) appears "debonair, sophisticated, lean, and handsome" and very much, Hall reports, "like George Sanders." Hall adds that a friend of the Eliots "later told me that he had seen Eliot at a dinner party eating his soup left-handed, with some difficulty, because he was seated on his wife's left and his right hand was engaged with her left, under the table." Hall tells us, in this shrewd and succinct reckoning, "Eliot's deadpan hidden (Old Possum) humor smiled at the center of his behavior."

Sometimes reconciling the life and the art can be more difficult. The aptly titled chapter "Fragments of Ezra Pound" reveals the shattered Pound of 1960, living again in Italy after his release from St. Elizabeth's, awash in fatigue, often disconsolate, and physically fragile. These fragments, Hall tells us, "assembled themselves in half a second, turned strong, sharp, and insistent; then dissipated quickly, sank into flaccidity, depression, and silence."

We all know about Pound's paranoia (in the mid-1930s in Rapallo, he believed that, because of his economic ideas, Wall Street spies watched him with binoculars from the hills above the tennis courts where he played), his megalomania and his anti-Semitism. We also know of his quite extraordinary and lifelong generosity to other writers, including Eliot, Yeats, and William Carlos Williams. Pound's personal courage here late in his life, in the face of these devastating fluctuations in his capacities, gives this chapter a genuine poignancy. Never have the greatness of the work and the contradictions of the man seemed more compelling.

Of the new materials, Hall's memoir of Marianne Moore shows her to be, of course, charming and eccentric (lunch items are served in pleated paper cupcake cups), and above all else, *precise*. Hall says, "Precision was her passion, definition at the forefront of duty. She constructed her poetry of terms made exact." Hall is terrifically useful in situating Moore in the context of her times and peers, but it's in his two interviews with Moore (collected here) that her peculiar and often comic turns of mind become most evident and intriguing.

In his sketches of Archibald MacLeish and Yvor Winters, Hall seems to carry still the same ambivalence toward MacLeish and his work that he describes himself having as a student at Harvard. About Winters, however, with whom Hall disagreed about almost everything concerning poetry, Hall is both wry and generous. An early Winters story, "The Brink of Darkness," leads Hall to a startling conjecture—that the critic's aesthetic ferocity and rigidity came, in part, from the fact that "Winters feared madness all his life. The right ideas, combined with willpower, could keep madness off."

The title of Hall's book is drawn from the famous Yeats poem "Lapis Lazuli," which concludes, "Their eyes mid many wrinkles, their eyes,/Their ancient, glittering eyes, were gay." The irony here is that this passage ends a page of epigraphs Hall begins with Wordsworth's well-known couplet, "We Poets in our youth begin in gladness/But thereof come in the end despondency and madness." Yet, Hall also says, "Whatever old poets feel as they come toward the end of their lives, they have spent their lives trying to make antidotes to death; we honor this making when we attend to their lives and characters."

It is rare to find such an expert witness in the defense and celebration of poetry, such a champion of artistic courage, as we find in Donald Hall.

# RAISED VOICES IN THE CHOIR:
## A REVIEW OF 1981, 1982 & 1983
### POETRY SELECTIONS

## 1981

It is easy to love Gerald Stern's poetry. Like the wonderful poems in his earlier book, *Lucky Life*, the poems in his new collection, *The Red Coal*, are generous, energetic, and immediate. The intimate and conversational manner of the poems sometimes draws us so close to them that, at last, they seem to close around us in a great, grinning bear-hug. Stern's subjects are passion and compassion, earned friendship, and individual love. In his open, expansive voice, Stern gestures as broadly as Whitman in drawing us a portrait of the world he loves and of the smaller, more private worlds within that larger one. Indeed, it's hard to find a piece of the world that hasn't at one time or another fallen into Stern's tumbling, kaleidoscopic vision of experience. With their tolerant and wry humor, their anecdotal jauntiness, and their infectious enthusiasm, each poem of Gerald Stern's exhibits the wisdom of its excesses, and each poem convinces us that beauty and consolation—as well as the sensation of *hope* Stern's poems convey—remain poetry's most lasting and most difficult of gifts. Here is one of my favorites from *The Red Coal*, the poem

"Waving Good-bye":

> I wanted to know what it was like before we
> had voices and before we had bare fingers and before we
> had minds to move us through our actions
> and tears to help us over our feelings,
> so I drove my daughter through the snow to meet her friend
> and filled her car with suitcases and hugged her
> as an animal would, pressing my forehead against her,
> walking in circles, moaning, touching her cheek,
> and turned my head after them as an animal would,
> watching helplessly as they drove over the ruts,
> her smiling face and her small hand just visible
> over the giant pillows and coat hangers
> as they made their turn into the empty highway.

One of the most startling and individual books of the year is Michael Burkard's *Ruby For Grief*. Although Burkard is widely known among younger poets for his two small-press collections, *In A White Light* and *None, River*, he has yet to win the readership he deserves. Even to readers well acquainted with the disjunctions of modern and contemporary poetry, Burkard's poems may at first seem difficult, elliptical, and disturbing. Yet Burkard's demanding and beautiful poems exist in a lineage that honors not only Wallace Stevens but the Objectivists, primarily Louis Zukofsky, as well. Still, to point to his precursors is to provide only the most rudimentary literary context for these poems, and the work itself remains truly inimitable. Full of syntactic and grammatical derailments, the poems are tragic and passionate, tender and playful, seductive and obstinate. They portray psychological states and emotional complexities with an often holographic effect. These dense textures and honed verbal mazes provide us, under Burkard's sure touch, with a collection that is deeply satisfying and compelling. From this remarkable and powerful book, here is a very brief passage from its title poem:

> I'm fond of the bridges the sea makes in my mind, although far
>     away.
> Even with a shallow life before this one, or a life
> after, I know my life is short, each is. The sea
> bridges such familiar territory the life makes. The sea

measures such mending I make, and gives it colors:

ruby for grief, yellow for choice, flint green for staying awake.

What strikes one immediately about Marvin Bell's wonderful new book, *These Green-Going-to-Yellow*, is the pervading sense of *quiet* and the deceptive understatement of nearly every poem. Even more than Bell's previous book, *Stars Which See, Stars Which Do Not See*, his new collection offers poems that express their fluent and steady peace with the world. Although many of the poems in *These Green-Going-to-Yellow* are set in distant locales—Hawaii, Tangier, Alaska, Cuba, Italy, Spain, France—they seek not to appropriate the exotica of their surroundings but to recognize the dailiness and immediacy, yet intrinsic *otherness*, of their settings. The traveler, the speaker in these poems, acknowledges again and again the statement that begins the poem, "Letters from Africa," a fact continually impressed upon him by his travels: "The self is small, and getting smaller."

Throughout this volume, Bell has chosen a more straightforward and unadorned diction, a diction capable of becoming alternately reflective and immediate. Yet there is still the verbal play and sly wit, the marvelous turns and reversals familiar to readers of Bell's earlier books. Because the poems in *These Green-Going-to-Yellow* are more consistently, more unashamedly narrative than in the past, Marvin Bell's aphoristic gifts have never seemed more successful; interwoven in the narrative fabric of the poems, these moments seem so inevitable and yet so surprising. Bell is constantly able to bring the reader up short with a sudden shift in tone; he has become masterful at quite invisibly shifting the grounds of argument upon the reader, and he often makes his exit in these poems with a disarming and winning directness. At the close of "Letters from Africa." Bell says, "What good is it to be away/ and not want to go home?" Yet each of the poems in *These Green-Going-to-Yellow* holds within it that resolute core of self that Bell recognizes as the one "home" he will carry within himself always and to any distance. This careful, subtle book needs to be read more than once, as with each reading it accrues with power and vision.

There is a spare, lovely reticence to many of the poems in *Bazaar*, Susan Wood's first collection. The poems are discreet and precise, almost stark at times, yet there is always a rich music echoing within and a deft melding of images that propels each poem to its conclusion. Though the content of many of these poems is clearly private and potent, the poems' true subject seems often to be the painful detachment felt by their speakers. This conflict demands, in the action and the meditative course of each poem, a sequence of difficult personal resolutions. This fine first book is sometimes witty and charming, sometimes oblique and reserved. Here is a lovely poem titled after a painting by Helen Frankenthaler, "What We Really Are We Really Ought To Be":

> Imagine a woman
> with a gift for centers:
> how she moves to master
> space by flooding it
> with light that holds
> the dark. That shape
> says taking risk
> is taking heart, that color
> is a way of bending
> time until it breaks
> on a field of white where
> what we are is what
> we ought to be. The suicides
> of her friends rise
> on the air, and she dances—
> she dances among them
> like a woman who knows
> what it means
> to continue: to begin,
> to begin again.

Larry Levis's third book of poems, *The Dollmaker's Ghost*, will come as something of a surprise to readers who continue to associate him with the more highly imagistic, mildly surreal poems of his earlier books. Levis's work has become far more narrative and reflective; almost all of the poems in *The Dollmaker's Ghost* exploit a more extended meditative progression. The poems resonate with the idea of history, of its passage in both a personal and public sense; the narrative episodes in this book examine and exhibit the way events and individuals find themselves placed in, then erased by, time. Dates abound in the poems (and in their titles) with a documentary urgency. Yet though these are poems of a world always cognizant of its own passing, in their insistence to place us (and their stories) in particular times and locales, these poems project a gripping, authoritative immediacy. Still, it is Levis's constant and passionate imaginative sympathy with the figures and human dilemmas in his poems that allows the reader the necessary entry into their disparate worlds and situations; we find ourselves held and absorbed by their conversational intimacy. What we learn, as we read the stories in *The Dollmaker's Ghost*, is that they are ours, and everyone's. Here is a very short but electrifying passage from a poem for the friend and fellow poet named in its title, "For Zbigniew Herbert, Summer, 1971, Los Angeles":

> And though I don't know much about madness,
> I know it lives in the thin body like a harp
> Behind the rib cage. It makes it painful to move.
> And when you kneel in madness your knees are glass,
> And so you must stand up again with great care.

In *Globe*, Elizabeth Spires' first collection, there is a lucid ease that informs every poem. Roughly, the poems are of three kinds: poems recollective of childhood; historical portraits in the voices of other women; and love poems, some of which take as their physical context, their settings, the backdrop of an earth eclipsed by snow or by the sea's constant, uncertain shiftings. Many of the poems recall the grace and invisible architectures of Elizabeth Bishop. Spires is capable of high drama, as in the poem, "Exhumation," spoken from the grave by Elizabeth Siddall, Rossetti's wife, as well as finely detailed and delicate lyrics, as in the poems "Blame" and "Dark Night on Cape Cod." To give some sense of the imagination and power consistently at work throughout *Globe*, here is the poem "Blame":

> I do not believe the ancients—
> the constellations look like nothing at all.
>
> See how their light scatters itself
> across the sky, not bright
>
> enough to guide us anywhere?
> And the avenues of trees, leaking
>
> their dark inks, are shapes I can't identify.

The night is too inconstant, a constant

injury, alchemical moonlight
changing my body from lead to silver,

silver to lead. I lie
uncovered on the bed, unmoved

by the love you left, bad dreams,
bad night ahead. All summer

you held me to your chest:
*It's the heat,* you said, accounting

for our sleeplessness, so that
touch became metaphor for what kept us

separate. Our lives construct
themselves out of the lie of pain.

I lied when I sent you away.
To call your name would be another lie.

Charles Wright's stunning new book, *The Southern Cross,* is full of the familiar verbal iconographies and textural chromatics that have made his earlier books so distinctive and powerful. Wright's palpably physical sense of language—of language as sensual, supple *material*—invites us to see him in terms one usually reserves for the visual arts. Yet Wright's poems are clearly aware of and delighted by their own painterly and sculptural qualities; their architectures are simultaneously intellectual and spiritual, an achievement executed, as Wright once wrote, by "setting the Imagist technique loose in the Symbolist current." Though Wright has always spoken of the profound influence Pound and Montale (the latter of whom he has translated) have had upon his work, *The Southern Cross*—even by its title—shows the enormously rich resource the poetry of Hart Crane has become for him. It could just as easily be Wright quoting, from Crane's "General Aims and Theories," these lines by Blake: "We are led to believe in a lie/When we see *with* not *through* the eye."

In many of the poems in *The Southern Cross*, Wright's concerns revolve around the idea of self-portraiture—not autobiography, with its implication of self-absorption and completeness, but self-portraiture. The distinction is important to Wright, as a quality of self-objectification details all of his poems. Just as each of the emblematic and imagistic strokes (of each poem's lines) in each self-portrait serves to approximate the figure, so the sequence of self-portraits in *The Southern Cross* serves to give us perhaps a less literal but more vivid and multidimensional reading of the poet.

For Wright, it is always language, its textures and music, that reclaims and collates all of the images of the self, all of the moments lost to the freeze frame of the blinked eye. Self, in Wright's poems, is the necessarily constant but web-cracked lens through which the world and the body are seen in their decomposition and regeneration. Self is that zero, that perfect circle of consciousness, through which all elemental shiftings—the blown dust, the drowned flame—and all spiritual aspirations are, for better or worse, to be regarded. Perhaps some of the special force of Wright's poetry can be illustrated by this poem, "Dead Color," one of the many astonishing pieces in *The Southern Cross*:

> I lie for a long time on my left side and my right side
> And eat nothing,
>                 but no voice comes on the wind
> And no voice drops from the cloud.
> Between the grey spiders and the orange spiders,
>                 no voice comes on the wind...
>
> Later, I sit for a long time by the waters of Har,
> And no face appears on the face of the deep.
>
> Meanwhile, the heavens assemble their dark map.
> The traffic begins to thin.
> Aphids munch on the sweet meat of the lemon trees.
> The lawn sprinklers rise and fall...
>
> And here's a line of brown ants cleaning a possum's skull.
> And here's another, come from the opposite side.

Over my head, star-pieces dip their yellow scarves toward their
black desire.

Windows, rapturous windows!

By now the virtues of Philip Levine's poetry are well known: his poems
are deeply humane; they are eloquently persuasive in their convictions, both
personal and political; and they are fiercely concerned with their accessibility
to unacademic readers. Although Levine, in his early work, exercised a vari-
ety of voices in his poems in his attempt to give voice to a whole realm of
everyday working experience for which there was no voice, it has been his
most recent books, *The Names of the Lost*, *Ashes*, and *7 Years From Somewhere*,
that have fixed him in the minds of most readers. For that reason, when
most readers think of one of Levine's poems, they think of a very personal
first-person poem, generally serious and impassioned, sometimes gently lyri-
cal, sometimes politically charged and rhetorically urgent.

In Philip Levine's most recent book, *One For The Rose*, those recognizably
*Levine* poems are present. Yet, for me, some of the most exciting poems of
the book are those that issue out of an exuberant sideshow of voices; they are
full of such sassiness and wit, such buoyancy and good humor. A partial sam-
pling of the speakers of these poems includes: the world's first pilot (quite
possibly for the Wright brothers); "The Conductor of Nothing," a man who
dresses in the shabby parody of a conductor's uniform in order to ride trains
endlessly back and forth across the country; a man who believes he once
lived as a fox (that deliciously unsocial creature), and who continues to
behave accordingly; and a foundling who, left on a woman's doorstep at
seven years old, seems to have grown up to be embodiment of the Second
Coming! These are wonderful rich, and funny poems. In fact, *One For The
Rose* is filled with Levine's marvelous humor, at times burlesquing his sub-
jects or speakers and at times creating a remarkable poignancy.

Yet I don't mean to slight the work in a vein more expected of Levine. Two
of the poems in *One For The Rose*, "Having Been Asked 'What Is A Man' I
Answer," and "To Cipriano, In The Wind," stand among the best poems—
the most beautiful and powerful poems—Levine has ever written. And there
is of course no need to feel one must choose between the poems of the per-
sonas here and the poems of the more recognizable serious-minded poet. All
of these voices speak for the same man, just as he is speaking in them all.
I've come to feel that *One For The Rose* is one of Philip Levine's finest, richest

books.

Pablo Neruda's *Isla Negra: A Notebook*, translated by Alastair Reid, is both an autobiography in poetry and a daily diary infected by the past. *Isla Negra* consists of five books, published separately when first published in Spanish in 1964, which follow Neruda's biographical chronology from his birth up to the writing of *Isla Negra*. The book was to be, Alastair Reid says, not "a systematic autobiography in poem form but a set of assembled meditations on the presence of the past in the present, an essential notebook." Another distinction between this book and the autobiographical life presented in *Memorias*, Neruda's prose memoirs, is that the memoirs, as Enrico Mario Santi says in his excellent afterword, "come from retrospection, the 'notes' from introspection." What remains constant is the vantage point from which the past and the present are seen to intersect—Isla Negra, the village on the Chilean Pacific Coast where Neruda bought an old sea captain's house in 1939 and where he lived while writing these poems.

I should say now that when I read Neruda I most often become hopelessly unobjective. I allow the most prosaic and sentimental passages to move me terribly. This problem, for me, is compounded when the Neruda I am reading has been translated by Alastair Reid, who is so skillful and so naturally graceful that I sometimes could be convinced the poems were first written in English. With the exception of some of the early work that W. S. Merwin has translated, I have found only in Reid's translations that true sense of, to quote Reid, "that spoken intimacy that pervades [Neruda's] poetry." For Neruda's poetry not to collapse too often into that prosaic sentimentality, a reader must be able to feel the conviction of his intimacy. And this is exactly Reid's great achievement here: we feel it, and we believe it. With *Extravagaria* and *Fully Empowered*, *Isla Negra: A Notebook* makes the third complete volume of Neruda that Alastair Reid has translated. I've long believed that Mr. Reid is Neruda's most talented and imaginative English translator; *Isla Negra* exceeds my own high expectations.

Finally, let me recommend a fine book of criticism, *Whatever Is Moving*, by Howard Moss. In this superb collection of essays and critical appreciations, Moss' direct and incisive style deftly steers the reader along a perpetually intelligent, unerring course. Having read and admired many of these pieces when they first appeared in periodicals, I find it a double pleasure now to have them all in one volume. The tender reminiscence of Jean Stafford and the fascinating essay, "Interior Children," on Elizabeth Bowen are especially wonderful. This is an important, long-overdue collection.

# 1982

In his superb new book, *The Passages of Joy*, Thom Gunn is writing with truly exceptional power and authority. As is Gunn's habit, the collection includes poems in both traditional (rhymed and metered) and "free" forms; yet in spite of their deceptive appearance of casualness and colloquial off-handedness, the "free" poems are as taut and sinewy as any of Gunn's poems in traditional forms. In all of his work, the polished surfaces are counterbalanced by an immediacy of subject matter and a directness of tone; the poems win us with their intimacy. *The Passages of Joy* takes its title from Samuel Johnson's poem, "The Vanity of Human Wishes" "Time hovers o'er, impatient to destroy/And shuts up all the Passages of Joy." There is a sexual punning in Gunn's use of this title, though of course it refers more generally to his concern with our passages through experience.

*The Passages of Joy* is made up primarily of Gunn's quiet portraits of individuals in the throes of those passages through experience, which are most often less than joyful. The lost, the mad, the alcoholic, a few friendly *poseurs*, old lovers, and a jaunty cab driver are all drawn with Gunn's careful hand; yet it is not only these figures but the backdrop sketches of their lives, the details of each landscape or cityscape, that make these poems so compelling. The portraits are rendered with a sympathy and compassion that is always restrained and understated, objective, and even seemingly cool. The effect is almost photographic, though better, of course, as the results are three-dimensional and human. Often, the poems consider the raw sexual hunger of their subjects, and all the consequent sadnesses and joys.

One of the book's central poems, "Talbot Road" (given the epigraph, "where I lived in London 1964-5"), is both the portrait of a friend and a double self-portrait. Gunn considers himself as a young man, when he first lived in Talbot Road, and then as his later self, the man who returns first twelve, then fifteen years later to the London he had left. The parallel portrait Gunn draws as the counterpoint to his own double image is that of his friend Tony White, who also figures prominently in the autobiographical sketches included in Gunn's recent prose volume (which also includes shrewd critical pieces), *The Occasions of Poetry*. And, though it doesn't represent some of the harder-edged poems of *The Passages of Joy*, the poems of contemporary life and anguish (and joy), here is a sonnet that conveys some of the tonal charm and lyric ease that seem always at work in Thom Gunn's poetry, "Keats at Highgate":

> A cheerful youth joined Coleridge on his walk
> ('Loose,' noted Coleridge. 'slack, and not well-dressed')
> Listening respectfully to the talk talk talk
> Of First and Second Consciousness, then pressed
> The famous hand with warmth and sauntered back
> Homeward in his own state of less dispersed
> More passive consciousness—passive, not slack,
> Whether of Secondary type or First.
>
> He made his way toward Hampstead so alert
> He hardly passed the small grey ponds below
> Or watched a sparrow pecking in the dirt
> Without some insight swelling the mind's flow
> That banks made swift. Everything put to use.
> Perhaps not well-dressed but oh no not loose.

*Yellow Light*, Garrett Kaoru Hongo's first collection of poems, is a beautifully written and extremely moving book. A Japanese American, Hongo asks his readers to consider the historical dilemma of the postwar Japanese living in Hawaii and California (those living in California had, of course, been living as American citizens for many years before being interned in camps at the war's outbreak). Yet the politics of these poems are intimate and personal, as in those poems about family, friends, and cultural double lives, and when Hongo's anger and indignation break loose in his work, as in the wonderful poem "Stepchild," the effect is exhilarating and liberating. All memory is an act of recovery, and in these poems the acts of reclamation concern that emotional and psychic territory scarred by the conflict of two cultures. Though Hongo, in the tone of many of the poems, is often jazzy and sassy, full of pleasing verbal syncopations, he can also be, as at the conclusion of the poem " Yellow Light," equally powerful in passages that are more descriptive, quiet, and reflective:

> But this is October, and Los Angeles
> seethes like a billboard under twilight.
> From used-car lots and the movie houses uptown,
> long silver sticks of light probe the sky.

From the Miracle Mile, whole freeways away,
a brilliant fluorescence breaks out
and makes war with the dim squares
of yellow kitchen light winking on
in all the side streets of the Barrio.

She climbs up the two flights of flagstone
stairs to 201-B, the spikes of her high heels
clicking like kitchen knives on a cutting board,
props the groceries against the door,
fishes through memo pads, a compact,
empty packs of chewing gum, and finds her keys.

The moon then, cruising from behind
a screen of eucalyptus across the street,
covers everything, everything in sight,
in a heavy light like yellow onions.

Margaret Gibson's second book of poems, *Long Walks in the Afternoon*, the 1982 Lamont Poetry Selection, is broken into three groups of poems, all of which concern themselves with self-reckoning. Gibson's poems have a pared gracefulness, a care and composure to their craft. In the book's first group, the speaker confronts the daily disaffectedness of a sensibility, including, in the fine poem "Inheritance," the complex legacies of a personal history. In the second grouping, Gibson considers the self in the context of a more public history and against the impinging backdrop of violence—war and oppression and sexual aggression. The most winning poem of this batch is "Fugitive," based on Ronald Fraser's marvelous book, *In Hiding*, the story of Manuel Cortes, the one-time mayor of the Spanish city of Mijas, who, with Franco's victory in 1939, went into hiding for thirty years (the first two of those years were spent hiding in a wall). Here, as in other of her poems, Gibson celebrates the faith and human courage of men and women oppressed by historical circumstances, that is, by other, more powerful men and women. *Long Walks in the Afternoon* concludes with a meditative sequence of ten elegies occasioned by a cosmology of loss—of innocence, of life, of the unborn's hope for life; but most crucially the poems consider a *desire* for loss, a desire to lose oneself to what seems a greater force—a force of primacy, life-and-death giving. This attendant *other* that shadows this

sequence is called by Gibson "*No one*, you beautiful one just beyond grasp. "
These elegies invoke a consistent elemental imagery—air, earth (dust), water,
and fire abound—and in the concluding poem of the book, "Fire Elegy," the
speaker is both consumed and reconciled: "the sticks of my body, arms and
feet, all/the bones kindle, and I burn with last light/unafraid, and part of it."
Still, it is the poem "Glass Elegy" that stays with me, and it is where a self, by
the loss of its sanity, most completely finds its reflective wholeness in "no
one." A woman who has gone mad believes she is "transparent,/a single
bloom in a glass bowl of water." And the poem concludes:

> I can't account for her words that morning, what she later
> saw, or the calm finally out of which she spoke
> with such authority.
>
> She described a random, long walk in the afternoon
> when the woods breathed with her
> and she lived through the power
> of death and the earth's rotation
>
> as ordinarily
> you do, she said, if you're ready to notice.
>
> In the mirror that evening, dark branches tangled
> weaving my face with their fire, and almost
> I could reach through and touch the ripening
>
> long sweep of wind toward morning.

Daniel Halpern's fifth book, and his finest, *Seasonal Right*, is a wonderfully
unassuming and genial collection. The poems are full of a quiet wit and
pleasing elegance as they survey landscapes and passions in America and
abroad. Halpern has always written with grace and clarity, but there's a fuller
sense of strength and command to these poems, a confidence that gives this
new work a deeper resonance. There is the tenderness of his meditation,
"The Last Days of the Year," and the restrained power of the poem,
"Portoncini die Morti," as well as many delicately achieved modulations of
tone, as in this lovely poem, "Nude":

In one of Watteau's pencil sketches
there's a woman sleeping on her side,
partly covered, the space behind her
darkly penciled in, her right arm
reaching out, probably around someone
who has left.
What makes me think her arm
is not merely cast out
is the way Watteau sketched dampness into her hair,
the way he remembered to pencil in
the good-time cloth-bracelet on that wrist,
and the space next to her,
which he left without a mark.

Yet the poem I return to repeatedly, the one that for me best represents the warm humor and narrative ease of *Seasonal Rights*, is "The Storm." After being stopped for speeding by the Italian police, the speaker, who'd been trying to beat home an oncoming storm, argues his case and, naturally, loses both the argument and a small fine. Undaunted:

We drove on into the storm and beat it home
as I knew we would, past the guinea fowl
and geese in our village of Polgeto,

and soon the rain began to fall, large drops
at first raising the dust, then gluing it down,
then filling the water tanks of Umbria.

The peasants sitting outside Polgeto's shops
stopped talking awhile, and the tree insects
too stopped their chirrs, as if to acknowledge

the storm. And then they started up again.
I awaited this beginning—nothing
is plain when heard again after silence.

I wanted to say more, how a storm registers
on the stony faces of the men outside

the *alimentari*, the insects' shutdown.

What will survive, remembering all this,
is something else—not the police or the rain
or the skies building up over the north,

but how out of the daily incidents
we find the distance not too long to go,
that we can go that distance, and continue on.

*Monolithos: Poems, 1962 and 1982* is Jack Gilbert's first collection of poems since, in 1962, his book *Views of Jeopardy* was chosen as the Yale Younger Poets Selection. *Monolithos* contains a section that includes work from *Views of Jeopardy* and it is fascinating to see how, both stylistically and in terms of content, Gilbert's poetry is—over a period of more than twenty years—very much of a piece. Jack Gilbert effects the stoniest and most ascetic Romanticism in American poetry. There is a stark, Oriental quality to many of the poems, just as many employ a purposely halting, telegraphic phrasing. Gilbert uses sentence fragments like building blocks, or perhaps more aptly, like pieces of glass or shards of ceramic hung upon the arms of a mobile—in Gilbert's poems, all depends upon balance. The sense of constant abbreviation and looping redirection in the poems is not, for me at least, as displeasing as I may be making it sound. Gilbert's fragments illuminate and accrue, and if some of his insights seem merely glancing, others are unquestionably penetrating and exact. It would be easy to suspect the poems of being too self-conscious, too self-enclosed—but I can't help but feel, taking *Monolithos* as a whole, that there is a tremendous (and sympathetic) personal vulnerability expressed; and what to some might seem a quality of arrogance in the poems strikes me as simply the visible edge of a particular, extremely personal brand of courage.

For Gilbert, a life and the poetry of a life must be one; the values of the poetry must embody and express the values, decisions, and failures of a life. The sensibility in Gilbert's work can be described as "self-chiseled," honed like a skater's blade, and rubbed—like the porcelain rim of an espresso cup—with the rind of bitter lemon. In Italy, Greece (primarily), and Japan, against a cyclorama of what Gilbert feels are the enduring legacies of those cultures and the accomplishments of their heightened civilizations, the poet enacts an existentially contemporary morality play. Most centrally, whenever the subjects of marriage—its hopes and disappointments—or love are at issue, the poems are activated by a current of sexual lawlessness; for Gilbert, the equations of love are dependent upon, and perhaps best solved by, the axioms of lust. The poems in *Monolithos* are troubling, exciting, maddening, and even, at times, latently aggressive—which is to say I find them to be quite wonderful. Here is a representative poem, "A Description of Happiness in København":

All this windless day snow fell
into the King's Garden
where I walked, perfecting and growing old,
abandoning one by one everybody:
randomly in love with the paradise
furnace of my mind. Now I sit in the dark,
dreaming of a marble sun
and its strictness. This
is to tell you I am not coming back.
To tell you instead of my private life
among people who must wrestle their hearts
in order to feel anything, as though it were
unnatural. What I master by day
still lapses in the night. But I go on
with the cargo cult, blindly feeling the snow
come down, learning to flower by tightening.

There is once again a taste for traditional forms manifesting itself in American poetry. This is good news in that it allows the reevaluation and a new appreciation, by a whole generation of younger poets, of those traditional forms and of some of our formal masters, poets like Anthony Hecht, Richard Wilbur, Donald Justice, Howard Moss, James Merrill, and W. D. Snodgrass. It is bad news because, perhaps predictably, it is helping to usher in a whole new era of decorative parlor poetry and exceedingly vapid verse. In our hunger for the least trace of formal consciousness (as teachers, poets, and reviewers), we've been too eager to leap upon the slightest trace of formal competence as the evidence of genius. As a result, we're finding too many young poets beginning to write, in my view, the same accomplished and inconsequential verse (not poetry) that finally convinced us it was time to leave the 1950s (of poetry) in the first place. While it may be true that style and content are inseparable, it is not true that technique—formal or otherwise—makes up for lack of content, or that technique itself is style. If American poetry is going to backpedal, I wish it would do it with some grace, and perhaps some substance too, though I realize I may be pushing my expectations in this regard. It should also be said that it was the popularity and fine poetry of three non-American poets, Joseph Brodsky, Seamus Heaney, and Derek Walcott, that helped initiate the present return to a concern for traditional meters and forms.

Therefore it is a special pleasure and relief to find a young poet writing in traditional forms who also has in her grasp both powerful subject matter and the intelligence to command her technique. Gjertrud Schnackenberg's *Portraits and Elegies* is an exceptional first book of poems. *Portraits and Elegies* is a book of three poems, two of which are long sequences: "Laughing with One Eye," an elegy for the poet's father, and "19 Hadley Street," a wonderful narrative poem about a house and the lives it sheltered. The book's centerpiece is an affectionate portrait of "Darwin in 1881" (a year before his death). This charming poem follows Darwin as, sleepless, he rises for a night walk; reflectively, he and the poem look back over the events of his life, of both the recent and distant past. Coming back to bed, where his wife is sleeping:

> He lies down on the quilt
> He lies down like a fabulous-headed
> Fossil in a vanished riverbed.
> In ocean-drifts, in canyon floors, in silt,
> In lime, in deepening blue ice,
> In cliffs obscured as clouds gather and float;
> He lies down in his boots and overcoat,
> And shuts his eyes.

The book's concluding sequence, "19 Hadley Street," creates a portrait across time of a pre-revolutionary house in which the poet once lived. In drawing its cameos of the past residents (real or imagined, it is unclear) of 19 Hadley Street, the sequence very shrewdly moves backwards in time from its present owner, an unnamed contemporary speaker, to its original owner, one Ebenezer Marsh, in 1725. Punctuating this movement back in time are sections set in the present tense and spoken by the contemporary speaker, sections that juxtapose her life and her reflections with the lives and stories of

19 Hadley Street's past (but clearly, in spirit, still resident) occupants—those "voices rising like smoke from time's wreckage."

What the reader of *Portraits and Elegies* soon realizes is that Schnackenberg is absorbed, in the best sense, with the idea of history and its role in our lives. Whether offering the history of a house or of Charles Darwin (history's own great revisionist), she makes us aware of the *idea* of the past, and of the way a past, a history, resounds within and intrudes upon the present. Nowhere is this more clear than in her book's first sequence, "Laughing with One Eye." An elegy for Schnackenberg's father, himself a professor of history, it is a remarkable and powerful poem. The sequence not only envelops the poet's relationship with her father, and her changing views of him as she recognizes his mortality, it also collates into its structure the importance of the father's love for history and his devotion to it: "your filing cabinet/Heavy with years of writing working toward/A metaphysics of impersonal praise." "Laughing with One Eye" often resonates with the destructive forces and brutality—the wars, the madness—found in our world history, and it is a world, as she says, thinking about her father after his death, "Where men trying to think about themselves/Must come to grips with grief that won't resolve." And, as she finds in this elegy, private grief is equally difficult to resolve.

A book equally resonant with an historical imperative, and one as formally adept, is Jordan Smith's *An Apology for Loving the Old Hymns*, another exceptional first book of poems. Jordan Smith has broken his book into two titled sections: the first, "A Lesson from the Hudson River School," and the second, "A Mirror for Loyalists." The former section includes dramatic monologues, often in syllabics, spoken by Marina Tsvetayeva, Chaim Soutine, and August Strindberg; and though other artists and writers are invoked (Edvard Munch and Weldon Kees), these monologues are set off against other poems whose settings, either named or implicit, are the Hudson River Valley of upstate New York. Though all of Smith's monologues are quite amazing ("For the Orthodox," Marina Tsvetayeva's dramatic monologue, is an especially subtle and stunning elegy for an entire era of Russian history and for the poets it consumed), it is these poems set in upstate New York, along the Hudson River Valley, in which we sense the recurring primary concern of Smith's work—the forging of the American spirit. In poems like "Vine Valley," a superb, elegiac poem about two brothers after the death of their father, and "A Lesson from the Hudson River School," which takes as its subject a painterly discourse, only to quietly subvert the meaning of

"American light" from a visual to a spiritual and ethical emphasis, we feel as if we're being shown the stripped roots—both historical and psychological—of a uniquely American code, touching the moral, artistic, and spiritual attachments to the land and the landscape.

This examination of the American spirit is most dramatically enacted in "A Mirror for Loyalists," an extraordinary triptych of poems. Subtitled "Being/a Portrait by Several Hands of the Late Sir William Johnson/ Baronet Royal Superintendent of Indian Affairs/& Proprietor of Johnson Hall/Tryon County, New York/1715-1774/Deo Regique Debito," the sequence consists of letters, all in syllabics, from Walter Butler (in 1778), British commander of His Majesty's Rangers and leader of the savage attack on Cherry Valley; from Guy Johnson (in 1788, in London), Sir William's nephew and his former cartographer; and from Joseph Brant (in 1804, in Niagara), the Mohawk leader who, with his tribe, fought with the British in the Revolutionary War (and also the brother-in-law of Sir William Johnson). In these quite amazing epistolary poems, what emerges is not only a portrait of Sir William (as both a greedy and a visionary man), but of the basic moral questions that accompany the birth of a nation—what is savage (of nature) and what is civilized (of man and God). In establishing these questions from a Loyalist perspective, Jordan Smith forces us to once again select—as if it were 1776 all over again—what will be our American values.

These are not fashionable, philosophically glib poems; Smith's work must be read slowly and carefully in order to absorb their depths and complexities. The moral and philosophical questions at the heart of these poems are always understated, always inextricably bound up with each speaking voice, just as they are the same questions always relevant to our lives.

One of the most appealing and exciting books of this year or any other is Denis Johnson's *The Incognito Lounge*. Johnson's personae are so playful and so expert at verbal sleight-of-hand that a reader, this reader at least, could wish he or she might stay forever happily ensconced on a bar stool listening to the most recent (and ever more curious) details of their hapless lives. The sad and defiant characters who drift through *The Incognito Lounge* are fortunate to have been given voice by a poet as masterful as Denis Johnson. Though he has had a following among poets for his books *The Man Among the Seals* and *Inner Weather*, it is only with *The Incognito Lounge* that Johnson has begun to reach the much larger readership he deserves. The scalding wit of the poems, with their savagely funny and heartbreaking unravelings of American culture and its many—for Johnson, endless—lies and pretensions, makes *The Incognito Lounge* a welcome antidote to any number of literary and spiritual malaises. It is that very rare thing, an *essential* volume of poetry. Here is one of the many marvelous poems in the collection, "Ten Months after Turning Thirty":

> We've been to see a movie, a rotten one
> that cost four dollars, and now we slip
> in a cheap car along expensive streets
> through a night broken open like a stalk
> and offering up a sticky, essential darkness,
> just as the terrible thing inside of me,
> the thick green vein of desire or whatever it was,
> is broken and I can rest.
> Maybe in another place and time, people
> drive slowly past the taverns
> with black revolvers reaching from their windows,
> but here in the part of night where every
> breath is a gift tremendous as the sea,
> thousands of oleanders wave
> blossoms like virgins after a war.
> I can hear my own scared laughter coming back
> from desolate rooms where the light-bulbs
> lunge above the radios all night,
> and I apologize now to those
> rooms for having lived in them. Things
> staggered sideways a while. Suddenly
> I'm stretched enough to call certain of my days
> the old days, remembering how we burned
> to hear of the destruction of the world,
> how we hoped for it until many of us were dead,
> the most were lost, and a couple lucky
> enough to stand terrified outside the walls
> of Jerusalem knowing things we never learned.

*Of the Great House: A Book of Poems* is Allen Grossman's fifth collection of poetry. His previous book, *The Woman on the Bridge over the Chicago River*, generated enormous enthusiasm and wide praise. Grossman is without question one of the most powerful American poets of the middle generation, and for those just becoming acquainted with his work, let me recommend *Against Our Vanishing: Winter Conversations with Allen Grossman*, conducted and edited by Mark Halliday. This sequence of interviews provides a brilliant introduction and gloss to Grossman's poetry and poetics. As an index to a poet's intellectual life, it is a unique and fascinating record. Of all the recent volumes on "poetry and poetics" by contemporary poets (often, like this, a collection of interviews), I find *Against Our Vanishing* to be by far the most engaging and instructive.

Allen Grossman's poetry is a poetry of great pain and great passions mediated by, as Grossman sees it, the intelligence of art. Often the poems bear a prophetic, even oracular quality, and classical echoes resonate regularly in his lines. The music of the poems is broadly expansive while at the same time being internally measured, often unobtrusively rhymed, and seemingly inevitable in its congruence to the poet's thought. For Grossman, "poems are the pictures in a man's life—first the present, later pictures, and then behind them the early ones." To that end, in *Of the Great House*, Grossman has included a section of early poems from his first collection, *A Harlot's Hire* (1961). Yet it is the more muscular and fiercely elegiac poems, which typify Grossman's most recent work, that make a more lasting claim upon the reader. In many of these poems there is the ever-present attendance of death ("Death," to Grossman), and the pages of *Of the Great House* often seem lit by the violet of black light. But it is precisely *against* that vanishing, our vanishing, that Grossman's poems issue and are addressed. Though this short passage can't reflect, offered out of its context, all of the rich religious and familial overtones it holds, this concluding movement of the final section of the poem "Of the Great House" helps convey what Grossman feels is a deliverance from—and *of*–the "Great House" (which, Grossman says, "the poem makes clear is mind, but as mind it is also world"):

> Let me tell you how the thunder grew,
> And seemed mingled with familiar women's voices;
> Sirens entered, then,
>
>        and in rain were lost,
> Or overtaken by the unmistakable word—
> Streak of birthcry;
> And the white, white lightning—wounds as they are
> Known to God—

Inscribed one stroke on the black stone above.

Now, there is nothing in the place of what
I know,

the only thing that is—

the world

With winds and rivers.
The house is first a torch, and then a ruin,
And then a sweetening field, quiet after storm.
Songs flower in the night by whose light we dance
And go up.

Finally, let me note the appearance of James Merrill's *From the First Nine: Poems 1946-1976*, which is a well-edited and suitably sumptuous collection of Merrill's lyric work, and also *The Changing Light at Sandover*, which includes Merrill's triptych, *The Book of Ephraim*, *Mirabell's Books of Number*, and *Scripts for the Pageant*, as well as a "new coda" entitled *The Higher Keys*. I would caution the new reader of *The Changing Light at Sandover* not to be put off by the somewhat intimidating critical claims that have often been made for the book (certainly not Mr. Merrill's fault), and I'd advise the uninitiated to read *The Changing Light at Sandover* as the superbly written, divine poetic comedy it is—that is to say, for *pleasure*, as well as for instruction. Its rewards are endless.

# 1983

What a pleasure it is to read W. S. Merwin's new collection, *Opening the Hand*. It is perhaps his strongest collection since *The Carrier of Ladders*, and the supple, muscular lines of these new poems exhibit the quiet authority we've come to associate with Merwin's finest work. The first section of *Opening the Hand* is concerned with family portraits, most specifically of the poet's father. This section is in some ways a poetic correlative to Merwin's superb prose recollections of his family, *Unframed Originals*, and it is equally powerful. One of Merwin's finest poems ever, "Apparitions," seems to me to be the gravitational center of his poems of the family. A dazzling meditation upon his parents' hands, "Apparitions" is as fine an interweaving of mystery, personal myth, and family intimacy as appears anywhere in Merwin's work. In the book's other two sections, Merwin writes often of his two homes—Hawaii and New York City. The poems of Hawaii are delicate and lovely, full of Merwin's great sympathy for the natural world. But it is his new poems about New York City—"Coming Back in Spring," "Sheridan," and "The Fields"—that show that Merwin is also one of our most powerful poets of urban experience (as earlier witnessed by his poems "St. Vincent's" and "Numbered Apartment" from *The Compass Flower).* Here is the close of one of those exceptional poems, "Coming Back in Spring":

> the trains rattle under the hooves
> of the mounted police riding
> down the Avenue at eleven in blue helmets
> and past the iron skeleton
> girders and stairs and sky
> of the new tower risen
> out of the gutted core
> of St. Vincent's Hospital
> most beautiful
> of cities and most empty
> pure Avenue behind the words of friends
> and the known music
>
> the stars are flaking in the apartment ceiling
> and the lights of lives
> are reflected crossing the floating night
> the rain beats on the panes
> above the Avenue
> where I have watched it run
> for twelve years in the spring
> ambulances shriek among the trucks
>
> this is an emergency the walkers
> in the street in ones and twos
> walk faster
> those in groups walk more slowly

the white tower beyond Union Square
is lit up blue and white
during the first few
hours of darkness

we all sleep high off the ground

There is often the sense in *Opening the Hand*, as in all of Merwin's best work, that the experience of the poem has occasioned the invention and generation of a language that feels *new* and original. Merwin continues to explore and to surprise—which is what we always wish to ask of our strongest poets—and so he has remained one of America's most imaginative and satisfying writers. Turning once again to Merwin's powers of portraiture, let me call attention to another of this book's finest moments, the conclusion of the wry and revealing homage/elegy entitled "Berryman." The poem ends,

I had hardly begun to read
I asked how can you ever be sure
that what you write is really
any good at all and he said you can't

you can't you can never be sure
you die without knowing
whether anything you wrote was any good
if you have to be sure don't write

Guilt is the vortex out of which all of Frank Bidart's speakers attempt to call to us in his disturbing and compelling new book, *The Sacrifice*. And it is the way in which guilt both articulates and manifests itself *through* and *out of* the body, seeking its own expiation and explication, that fascinates Bidart and directs his poetic vision. Bidart necessarily considers the nature and capacity (or rather the incapacity) of (and for) forgiveness in human affairs. If guilt is the motivating force driving Bidart's speakers, forgiveness and the possibility of forgiveness (of self or of others) are the ephemeral twin horizons toward which his speakers are aimed. Along the way, the human way, the body (which is also to say the flesh) enacts and wrestles with the corruption of the spirit. It is the choreography of spiritual struggle that Bidart's characters follow, and his proper metaphor is dance.

So perhaps it should be no surprise that the triumph of *The Sacrifice* is without question the poem "The War of Vaslav Nijinsky." In this poem, Nijinsky's interior guilt and madness are joined with the world's (the historical, objectified guilt and madness of World War I) by the dancer's will and art; Nijinsky creates and dances a piece he believes will let war and the guilt of war pass through (and *out of*, to an audience) his body. Bidart is constantly at perfect pitch in this poem, as both Nijinsky's voice and the voice of his wife, Romola, provide the counterpoint of the poem's narrative. Subtly, the conflict of the physical and metaphysical plays itself out in Nijinsky's monologues. The poem is itself a kind of superb poetic ballet, and it remains one of the most beautiful and disquieting poems of recent years.

In the poems "The Sacrifice" and "Confessional," Bidart again examines the mirroring, reflective qualities of guilt. The latter poem is in part autobiographical, and its concerns revolve around the complex relationship of the poet and his mother, using a story (from *The Confessions*) of St. Augustine and his mother as a counter-narrative. Yet the poem that best exemplifies what are for me Bidart's most important virtues as a poet, psychological depth and human compassion, is a much briefer poem, an elegy for a friend, that remains one of his most haunting works. Here is "For Mary Ann Youngren ( 1932-1980)":

> Mary Ann, as they handed you the cup
> near the black waters of Lethe,
>
> (the cup of *Forgetfulness*,
> the waters of *Obliteration*.
>
> did you reach for it greedily—
>
> just as, alive, you abruptly needed
>
> not to answer the phone for days: ballet tickets
> unused: awake all night: pacing
>
> the apartment: untouchable: chainsmoking?
>
> Dip a finger into the River of Time,—

it comes back
    STAINED

No, that's *not* enough,—
*not* true, wrong—

dying of cancer, eager to have the whole thing
over, you nonetheless waited

for your sister to arrive from California
before you died,—

you needed to bring up your cruelest, worst
adolescent brutality, asking:

DO YOU FORGIVE ME?

Then: WILL YOU MISS ME?

At the Resurrection of the Dead,
the world will hear us say

*The phone is plugged in, please call,*
*I will answer it.*

For many years I've been excited and charmed by the poems of Brenda Hillman. In her first collection, *Coffee, 3 A.M.*, she is writing with truly exceptional grace and skill. There is a quiet elegance to these poems and their clarity is at times almost crystalline. Yet Hillman's poems are never decorous, never satisfied by beautiful surfaces, however pleasing. Her poems are subtle and understated, and they most often revolve around unstated yet emotionally and psychologically complex impulses. The deceptive simplicity of the poems' surfaces makes all the more startling their powerful resolutions. Hillman is a poet of great restraint; she is an exacting craftsman and an impeccable lyricist. She is never a showy or flashy poet, and perhaps because of that her work shows a composure and maturity that is rare in young poets. Of the many superb pieces in this book here is a typically lovely and moving poem, "Anonymous Courtesan in a Jade Shroud":

In an unknown century of your country's life
They staked your body out,
Bound it with rocks the color of grass
And sewed the rocks with golden filaments.
They flattened your breasts, and in your bald
Head, made a hollow valley for the eyes.

I walk around you, wanting to see
Inside—how the chandelier of sun
Makes its way through, and what
Became of your fingernails, your hair;
Are they rock too?

Perhaps you were not beautiful, but had
A sickly look, nothing to recommend you
But a famous mother or a gift for talk.

I wonder how you made it
To the afterlife; did your soul
Seep out those narrow cracks?
Or was it better than anything you knew

Just to lie flat on your back
Like a garden, well cared-for, unchanging,
And so valuable—each frozen cell—
Nothing could tempt you to let the rich man in.

In his fine new book of poems (his third), *Keeping Company*, Gibbons
Ruark exhibits a formal mastery that should claim the attention of all his
peers. Ruark's conversance with traditional meters and rhyme is enviable, and
the subtlety with which he employs traditional forms is exemplary. Behind
Ruark's great accomplishment stand his acknowledged masters: Yeats and
Keats, as well as the vital presences of Rilke and of Ruark's close friend, the
late James Wright. In *Keeping Company*, Ruark allows the landscapes of both
Ireland and Italy to stand as both occasion and backdrop to his meditations.
These are a traveler's poems, *not* a tourist's—and the distinction is great. The
traveler seeks in his journeying, and Ruark's poems seek constantly for the

spiritual and fraternal life as it appears in human affairs. The landscapes and place names he invokes are made impassioned by his search for what is artful and poetic in the natural, just as he searches for what is most natural in a culture's art and poetry. Ruark's continual project is the consideration of human fellowship (see, for example, his extraordinary elegy, "Lost Letter to James Wright, With Thanks for a Map of Fano"), and the kinship he feels with both the figures and landscapes of his travels resonates throughout his poems. There is both exuberance and melancholy in Ruark's poetry, as he is a poet of both extremes. Yet neither extreme ever mars his amazing craftsmanship; indeed, Ruark's range of great humor to great sadness is impressively and carefully presented in these poems. Also, it should be said that Ruark is a poet of quite memorable love poems, and though he risks great sentiment in these poems, he refuses to indulge in the sentimental. As an all too brief taste of Ruark's enormous talents, let me offer the last stanza of his marvelous poem, "Written in the Guest Book at Thor Ballylee":

> If you want to believe our life is possible, come
> Look out the window where the wind blows a brief shower
> Of leaves on the stream, swift with earlier rainfall,
> And try to imagine that they love their vanishing
> Merely to leave the surface untroubled and clear.
> Then listen for breath in this room without music.
> While you can hear it the stream makes a personal sound.

One of the most refreshing books of the year is Arthur Vogelsang's *A Planet*. The poems are full of a conversational jauntiness and a maniacal rhythmic energy that even Frank O'Hara would envy. Vogelsang's lines are powered by a breathless *drive* to explain to us, to talk with us, about the nature of all the marvelous American madness in which we live. They are sardonic and comic poems, but they are filled with Vogelsang's sense of the rich pleasures of that comedy as well. And just as we begin to feel cozy with the wry poignancy of Vogelsang's poems, he startles and shocks us out of our new complacency with his searing wit and syntactical gear-shifting. It's marvelous.

In some ways, Vogelsang reminds me a bit of John Ashbery, and much that I admire in Ashbery I find in Vogelsang's poetry also. There is looniness approaching grandeur in these poems—however odd that may sound—and it gives Vogelsang great latitude in collating the quotidian familiars of his

speakers' lives. The voices in these poems are restless, ranging nervously
back and forth over experiences both lived and desired. On Vogelsang's
planet, the power to invent (that is, *to imagine)* is the power to transform and
invigorate. Sometimes, in his poems Vogelsang shows us several movies at
once—at times on split screens, at times overlaid. Whatever the pain and
darkness circulating in these poems, they convey too a stark, personal hon-
esty and a stubborn compassion for the world. Of the many highly original
and exciting poems in A *Planet,* here is a love poem I especially admire,
"Feeling That Way Too":

> It gets dark and I get scared.
> Dogs bark, stop, and bark continuously,
> The only sound
> As the plunging sun chars orange clouds
> In what seems to be Nevada.
> You are afraid too and go into the bedroom to sleep
> Clothed under blankets in corduroys and wool socks,
> Bare chest probably cool.
> Our cats blink at me, raise and let limp their heads.
> Disturbed too, you heave a little and rustle.
> The bed creaks and squeaks seconds after.
> I still sit still, monitoring the blood in my ears.
> And suppose, though shivering with fright, I should
> Dance in the pale dark, waving my pants
> Over my head, singing I've got bells
> That jingle jangle jingle or Pepsi-Cola
> Hits the spot? Or switch a light on?
> The mood fills up its ugly red cheeks as
> Silence comes down like a hunk
> Of gooey lead in the ear.
> And though a few seconds later you will say
> "Oh I feel so good, my bare skin feels so nice, like ice cream,"
> Now I hear you walking through the dark hall
> Then naked you step quickly through a white beam
> In this room then hurry to me in that six-foot wide shaft
> Of total blackness between the beam and me and
> My eyes tear and I really do reach for the switch.

In her second book of poems, *Erosion*, as in her much praised first collection, *Hybrids of Plants and Ghosts*, Jorie Graham is focused intently upon the relationship of the mind and spirit with the world of the external, the world of flesh and earth. Her method is discursive, but poetically not didactically so, and her impulses, even when considering the nature and implications of works of art, are invariably philosophical. Graham constantly questions the mind's influence upon "the real," and whether that influence is true or imagined, accomplished or desired; she questions the discrepancy between historical time and time as corrupted by memory; she questions how the spirit articulates itself in the world of nature and the world of art.

Graham's poems are often meditations upon themselves in process. The mind's multiple intersections with a subject or an occasion in turn create a moving locus for a poem, and the shifting play of images and ideas is held by what is their discursive authority. She distrusts, and rightly so, any rigid or fixed perspective, and the restless metaphors of her poems often signal the urge toward an abstracted verbal equation. Even at these times, when her "subjects" might seem most remote, the poems refuse the pull of circularity and the impulse to become reductive and enclosing. Instead, she allows her poems an appealing open-endedness, granting them a syntactical but not an intellectual closure. I suppose I'm making these poems seem much less earth-bound and substance-filled than they in fact are; yet, in looking at what are the desires for the abstract and philosophical in her poetry, I think we can see most clearly where Graham's great originality and vision rest. All of her poems exhibit grace and musical resolve, but here is the last part of one of the most subtly powerful poems in *Erosion*, the quiet and exquisite "Wanting a Child":

> Nothing is whole
> where it has been. Nothing
> remains unsaid.
> Sometimes I'll come this far from home
> merely to dip my fingers in this glittering, archaic
> sea that renders everything
> identical, flesh
> where mind and body
> blur. The seagulls squeak, ill-fitting
> hinges, the beach is thick
> with shells. The tide

is always pulsing upward, inland, into the river's rapid
argument, pushing
with its insistent tragic waves—the living echo,
says my book, of some great storm far out at sea, too far
to be recalled by us
but transferred
whole onto this shore by waves, so that erosion
is its very face.

In *Tar*, C. K. Williams' fourth book of poems, there is a muscular, prosaic density that invites us to see his poems as small novellas, or perhaps as parts of the greater novel that is the body of his poetry. Like his fine (and mysteriously undervalued) third book, *With Ignorance, Tar* presents us with poems whose nominal subjects include varying extremities of experience—extremities of sexual hunger and disease, of dissipation and neglect—that could easily approach melodrama. Yet it is the victory of these poems that the serious witnessing that becomes each poem's meditative action never spares the witness—the speaker, the poet—in its own self-examination. These poems are both testimony and testament. The nominal subjects of these poems might seem unpleasant and even grotesque, but it is the resilience of the human spirit that is the true subject of these poems. It is the activity of memory (of memory's reclamation and revivification of the past) that provides the speaker's faith—its depth and resonance—and that allows his spirit to *understand* and then to go on. It is the prosaic quality of the poems in *Tar* that makes possible their comprehensive descriptiveness. They offer their "realism" and ask to be seen as the poetry of nonfiction. But, in fact, at their cores these poems reflect again and again upon the nature of consciousness, the nature of sensibility and its transformations throughout a lifetime, especially a creative lifetime. The poems all hold to the locus of the self. The poet (his sensibility) is the lens that mediates the "reality" culled in *Tar*, and it is by its clarifying focus that the inner and outer darknesses of the poet emerge.

Let me say too that *Tar* is a book of great tenderness and compassion. "Waking Jed," a description of the poet's son coming out of sleep, is a dazzling and memorable poem. But perhaps the most moving poem is Williams's delicate elegy for James Wright, echoing one of Wright's own fine meditations on the spirit. Here are the last two stanzas of "On Learning of a Friend's Illness":

How cold it is. The hoofprints in the hardened muck are frozen
    lakes, their rims atilt,
their glazed opacities skewered with straw, muddled with the
    ancient and ubiquitous manure.
I pick a morsel of it up: scentless, harmless, cool, as dessicated as
    an empty hive,
it crumbles in my hand, its weightless, wingless filaments taken
    from me by the wind and strewn

in a long, surprising arc that wavers once then seems to burst into
    a rain of dust.
No comfort here, nothing to say, to try to say, nothing for anyone.
    I start the long trek back,
the horses nowhere to be seen, the old one plodding wearily away
    to join them,
the river, bitter to look at, and the passionless earth, and the
    grasses rushing ceaselessly in place.

Because I've written on them elsewhere, I've not included in the above round-up two of the year's (and any year's) finest books, both superbly written and both *essential* volumes for any serious reader: *Summer Celestial*, Stanley Plumly, and *Selected and New Poems*, Norman Dubie. Lastly, let me insist that everyone buy, steal, or borrow the two books that together make the publishing event of the year *The Complete Poems: 1927-1979* and *The Collected Prose* of Elizabeth Bishop. Bishop's prose divides into, on the one hand, her nonfiction reflections (on persons and/or places) and, on the other, her distinctively delicate fiction. Her prose, as does her poetry, shows her to be one of the most acute observers and effortless stylists in American letters; and her *Complete Poems* exhibits exactly what a life's work should exhibit—fierce integrity, genuine poetic invention, and inexhaustible verbal grace. These books belong on the shelves of every poet and every reader of poetry in America.

# Eugenio Montale's "Two in Twilight"

I have always been reluctant to discuss in print the work of Eugenio Montale. This is not because of any ambivalence I feel about his poetry, but because it has, for many years, been for me a place of sanctuary, a world of privacy I find consoling. Montale's work has always existed for me in a realm beyond the daily literary clatter of my life as a poet and teacher. Still, I am pleased by the attention Montale's work has received in this country, just as I'm delighted that he has been translated with such brilliance, in his poetry by William Arrowsmith and Charles Wright, and in his prose by Jonathan Galassi. Yet, what matters to me most about Montale is my own quite private relationship with his work, the intimacy I feel it can call up within me, and the influence I know it exerts upon my own sense of the emotional music within my own poems. All this said, I would like to consider a poem of Montale's that holds for me that intimate and elliptical architecture familiar to the best of his work, a poem that is, like many of his poems, a love poem, in this case a failed-love poem. It will not take an especially perceptive reader to find in Montale's poem a tenor and dramatic situation I have tried to make use of myself, which perhaps helps explain my long-standing attraction to this particular poem.

"Two in Twilight" appears in Montale's *La Bufera e Altro* (in the book's third section, entitled *Intermezzo)*. Though the poem was first published in 1943, G. Singh, in his critical work, *Eugenio Montale*, quotes Montale, from Montale's note on the poem, to the effect that, "a rough draft already existed as early as September, 1926. I recopied it, giving it a title somewhat reminiscent of Browning's 'Two in the Campagna' and inserted a few words where there were blank spaces or erasures. I also removed two superfluous verses. Thus I did what I would have done a long time ago, had I known that the draft could one day interest me." [1]

This comes, in fact, as no surprise; the dramatic situation of "Two In Twilight" echoes similar love poems from Montale's previous book of poems, *Le Occasioni*. In fact, one can imagine "Two In Twilight" in its first draft state as a kind of rehearsal for the final staging of, for example, the familiar concerns of Montale's "Mottetti," the latter being a more complex and sophisticated articulation of a similarly intimate yet metaphysically rich landscape. The core and axis of "Two In Twilight," as in many of Montale's poems, is the profound sense of the *other*, the lover to whom he speaks, about whom he meditates even while addressing. It is this intimate address in so many of the poems that allows us to be *held* to them, as if the poems themselves had reached out to their readers with a lover's immediate and casual intimacy.

In "Two In Twilight," the whole of the landscape (including the speaker and his companion) is caught in the distorting light of day's close. Like the waning day, the exhausted affair is at its end; the poem is in fact a coda to the relationship, a final meeting of the sort in which two people establish the unspoken final terms upon which they will part for good. At the beginning of the poem, every motion, gesture, or movement by either the speaker or his companion is simply a gesture cut off from any meaning, any substance. The two are held in an irreal, almost hallucinatory light—an underwater light playing over their faces as if they were the drowned. In the oppressive atmosphere of their meeting, they are sealed as within a bell jar. Yet, they are not only estranged from each other; the events implicit to the poem have occasioned a self-estrangement as well. The speaker's own voice sounds, even to himself, disembodied, wasted, and unsustainable. Then, confronted by the day's erasure, transfixed by his own spiritless and confused dissolution, the speaker is yanked back into the world by a sudden gust of wind in the valley below, and with this small cathartic frenzy (of wind, of spirit) to disrupt the stale and stilled atmosphere, he is once again able to regard *outward*, out of himself; he is able to notice again the particulars of the world, the first lights of evening sketching in the outlines of the piers in the harbor below. The final stanza, in William Arrowsmith's translation,[2] reads:

...the words fall lightly
between us. I look at you in a soft
quivering. I don't know
whether I know you; I know that never have I
been so divided from you as in this late
returning. A few instants have scorched
all of us: all but two faces, two
masks which, with a struggle, carve themselves
into a smile.

Now the speaker knows how separate and distinct he and his companion are, and will remain; he knows how little he knows her, if at all. There is no hope of any reconciliation, no possibility, it seems, of even a literal recognition, for *who is she, is she the someone I knew?* the poem is forced to ask. Their life or their time together has seared and scorched them in such a way that what was whole and complete about them as human beings has been reduced to the mere semblance of a life, of a person, of a face: they are again, at the poem's conclusion, portrayed as partial beings, as simply masks. In the small play which has been acted out in the course of the poem, the players themselves have been slowly erased by a past as failing as the light. All that remains is the brief relief of their masks, upon which a cruel knife of light carves a final, mutual smile of resignation and departure. It is this concluding image, the ultimate carving of the human mask, which, for me, lifts the poem out of its pathos and into the realm of the exquisite.

I find Montale's constant meditative poise, linked with his urgent intimacy, unfailingly appealing and convincing. If Montale's layers of verbal seduction are to some readers obfuscating, they are to me enthralling. Eugenio Montale has always been for me one of the few poets—like Yeats, like Stevens—I can return to repeatedly as a source of imaginative replenishment, as a source of mysterious delight.

1. G. Singh, Eugenio *Montale A Critical Study of His Poetry, Prose, and Criticism* (Yale University Press, 1973), p. 153.
2. William Arrowsmith's translation of "Two In Twilight" can be found in *Antaeus*, Vol. 40/41.

# Randall Jarrell's "Seele im Raum"

One of the most fascinating aspects of Randall Jarrell's stunning dramatic monologue "Seele im Raum" is the way we can see so many of Jarrell's life-long concerns embodied in the poem: his deep love of fable and folk tale; his knowledge of psychology and his close reading of Freud; his constant empathy with the isolate sensibility, so often a woman at odds with her world; his devotion to Rilke, two of whose poems form the underpinning of "Seele im Raum"; and his love of the German language itself, which provides the serious and motivating pun upon which the poem revolves.

In the notes to his *Selected Poems*, Jarrell explains, "*Seele im Raum* is the title of one of Rilke's poems; 'Soul in Space' sounded so glib that I couldn't use it instead." In Rilke's poem, the speaking "soul in space" considers both the body it has just left and the question of whether it will ever again enter such a worldly, flesh-bound "body" of constraint. It is a voice that echoes the same raw nakedness as the voice in Jarrell's "Seele im Raum." Yet there is another Rilke poem that stands even more wholly behind "Seele im Raum," a poem Jarrell had translated. The fourth sonnet in the second part of Rilke's *Sonnets to Orpheus*, based upon the famous tapestry "The Lady and the Unicorn," reads, in Jarrell's version:

> This is the animal that never existed.
> None of them ever knew one; but just the same
> They loved the way it moved, the way it stood
> Looking at them, in pure tranquility.

Of course there wasn't any. But because they loved it
One became an animal. They always left a space.
And in the space they had hollowed for it, lightly
It would lift its head, and hardly need

To exist. They nourished it, not with grain
But only, always, with the possibility
It might be. And this gave so much strength to it

That out of its forehead grew a horn. One horn.
Up to a virgin, silverily, it came
And there within her, there within her glass, it was.

M. Herter Norton's more literal rendering of the final line tells us that the Unicorn "was in the silver-mirror and her." In the second part of *Sonnets to Orpheus*, the fourth sonnet follows Rilke's previous meditations about "space," both exterior and interior space, and about the reflective (reflected) "image" (self) and the nothingness of space within mirrors. It is no accident that Jarrell had linked these two poems of Rilke's in his mind, nor that he chose to braid their concerns into the new fabric of "Seele im Raum." In the tapestry, the Lady holds a mirror, showing the Unicorn its own reflection. It is this same conjunction of self and Other, of self and the mirrored nothingness, that Jarrell exploits in his echoing of the Rilke poems.

The woman in "Seele im Raum" has, of course, her own attendant Unicorn—an eland that only she can see, the embodiment and reflection of her own unhappiness. In those same notes to his *Selected Poems*, Jarrell describes an eland as "the largest sort of African antelope—the males are as big as a horse, and you often see people gazing at them, at the zoo, in uneasy wonder." "Uneasy wonder" is a good way to describe how the speaker's family, and we, view her eland as well, as it becomes clear that the animal is an emblem of her soul's trapped, breathless terror. In her own self-doubt, in the erosion of her identity, the woman in "Seele im Raum" has posited an eland to stand for her soul, an objectified and palpable (if only to her) manifestation of her soul's distress. Hers too is a soul in space, solitary and remote.

After her eland has been "taken" from her, after she has been "cured," the woman stumbles upon the unconscious link that language has forged for her, she discovers the unwitting proclamation her eland has been: "Today, in a German dictionary, I saw *elend*/And the heart in my breast turned over, it was —//It was a word one translates *wretched.*" She goes on to express her tremendous ambivalence about this discovery, and about her companion of the past.

> And, truly,
> One could not wish for anything more strange—
> For anything more. And yet it wasn't *interesting...*
> —It was worse than impossible, it was a joke.

> And yet when it was, I *was*—

It's wonderful to now recall Rilke's own comment about his Unicorn, quoted from a letter: "In the Unicorn no accompanying parallel with Christ is meant; only all love for the not-proved, the not-tangible, all belief in the worth and reality of that which our spirit has through the centuries created and exalted for itself, may be praised in it."

In the whole of the second half of "Seele im Raum" the speaker considers exactly what the "worth and reality" of her spirit's creation, the eland, has been for her as she reflects upon her present "healthy" state. Her recognition that the raw, pure being—her soul's naked self-creation—is dead is absolutely harrowing. In the culmination of her meditation, she wonders:

> Yet how can I believe it? Or believe that I
> Owned it, a husband, children? Is my voice the voice
> Of that skin of being—of what owns, is owned
> In honor or dishonor, that is borne and bears—
> Or of that raw thing, the being inside it
> That has neither a wife, a husband, nor a child
> But goes at last as naked from this world
> As it was born into it—

> And the eland comes and grazes on its grave.

> This is senseless?
> Shall I make sense or shall I tell the truth?
> Choose either—I cannot do both.

The profound conflict in this passage, between her own emotional truths and with "making sense," creates one of the most poignant moments in all of Jarrell's poetry. Yet there remains something indomitable about her, something valiant, wise, and defiant.

> I tell myself that. And yet it is not so,
> And what I say afterwards will not be so:
> To be at all is to be wrong.
> >           Being is being old
> And saying, almost comfortably, across a table
> From—
> >      from what I don't know—
> > >                in a voice
> Rich with a kind of longing satisfaction:
> "To own an eland! That's what I call life!"

It is this unravelling of emotional self-truths, the baring of such searing pain, that always startles me when I read "Seele im Raum." The dualism that both Jarrell and Rilke saw as a necessary and vital aspect of life is, for most of us, an unresolvable tension. Perhaps the lesson is simply that one needs great courage if one is to try living like the panther of Norman Dubie's poem "For Randall Jarrell," leaping, and "Making it, which could mean,/Into this world or some other. And between." Certainly the woman of "Seele im Raum" is living in the held breath of that leap.

# Pablo Neruda's "Walking Around"

"Walking Around"was the very first poem of Pablo Neruda's I was lucky enough to encounter. Though I've told the story of this first discovery of his work before (in an essay entitled "Neruda's Wings"), I think it bears retelling in order to situate my responses to and my prejudices (I think it's one of Neruda's truly great works, from his strongest period) about the poem.

It was the spring of 1968, an astonishing time for those of us caught up in the delirium of what seemed to be the promise of great changes and even greater freedoms ahead. At times during those glorious spring afternoons, my poetry class—that is, the class in which I was a member—would meet outdoors, especially if our leader felt like it, and that spring Philip Levine often did feel like taking us out of our dreary modular classroom at Fresno State College and into the leering air.

I could have said "electric" air, or "revolutionary" air (especially given the time), but at eighteen years old I felt everything that spring was terribly sexy and leering. It was a rich, ripe, and often oppressively fecund world that seemed to be exploding all around me. It was, of course, also the dark, morose and somewhat embittered world of any eighteen year old, though whatever chip was on my shoulder seemed to me just to make my walk (swagger?) that much more memorable, yet I doubt anybody else felt that way. And that spring, my friends and I seemed to be doing a lot of walking around. Except for Larry Levis, who rode his very cool black motorcycle. While quoting Whitman. I'm not lying.

On one of those spring afternoons Levine, as he often would in class, read to us a few of his favorite poems, perhaps one or two that he'd recently come across in magazines and just published books, or others that were some of the poems he cared for most in the world, something from Wyatt or Shakespeare or Thomas Hardy or Elizabeth Bishop. That day he read to us Neruda's great poem, "Walking Around."

One could feel the whole class collectively holding its breath. I'd never heard anything like this poem. It embodied what I would soon discover were Neruda's many astonishing virtues: the understated, inevitable and almost "natural" surrealism; the explosive image making; the often deceptive calm of the tone; the richness of presence; the tremendous generosity and expansiveness of both poem and poet, their embrace of the world with all of its gorgeous paradoxes; the sensuality, sexuality and whiff of true magic; and finally, that sense of the world's own defiant resonance and inexhaustibility.

The opening of "Walking Around" continues to be haunting to me. The fatigue and irony, the flat, world-weary fierceness of "As it happens I am tired of being a ma..." and its repetition (at the end of stanza three) still startle me with each rereading. And I would guess that many poets of my generation can remember the moment he or she first saw or heard the phrase, one of Neruda's most famous, "like a felt swan/navigating on a water of origin and ash." It is a phrase that not only embodies the sense of passage through a life the poem wants to echo, it also slaps us in the face with the child-like memory of the felt swan pressed to the child's play board, collapsible and two-dimensional, fleeting as a handshadow on a bedroom wall, flat as a soft black mirror of the broken adult self.

It's this opening, with its catalogue of discouragement, that gives us first that kaleidoscopic experience of passage. The speaker's weary walk leads him into the tailors' shops and movies ("all shrivelled up, impenetrable"), until the huge dimension of his fatigue arrives: "The smell of barber shops make me sob out loud." Already on our way, as we walk hand in hand with the poem's speaker, the world seems a place too much for us, too overwhelming; its ordinariness and its bald pathos seem, simultaneously, impossible to accept. The speaker wants only the stillness of a kind of death ("I want nothing but the repose of either stones or of wool"), a stasis, a final *stop* to this moving around, this endless walking around of our pathetic lives.

And it is at this very moment, at the opening of the fourth stanza, where the lips of the speaker curl with the taste of revenge, "Just the same it would be delicious/to scare a notary with a cut lily/or knock a nun stone dead with one blow of an ear." One can see how these images of blows against propriety and official culture (and the culture of death the notary represents) remain so appealing to the adolescent within us all. It's no accident that the poem then spends its next two stanzas stating the speaker's defiance of that fate, the living death in which he finds himself, the streets of which he continually finds unrolling beneath his slowly shuffling feet.

It is the terror of this possibility, of this *being* the speaker's fate, that drives him on through his city, its shops and avenues appearing to him like images from a familiar Inferno ("There are birds the color of sulfur, and horrible intestines/hanging from the doors of the houses I hate..."). It is a landscape in which "there are mirrors/which should have wept in shame and horror," given what they've been forced to witness and reflect, as well as a world of "orthopedic appliances/and courtyards hung with clothes hanging from a wire:/underpants, towels and shirts which weep/slow dirty tears." This is a world in which even the intimate and ordinary clothes of men and women have reason to weep, and even those tears are fouled by the filth, pollution and waste they have been touched by. And perhaps the most violently lonely, most wickedly solitary image of this poem: "there are forgotten sets of teeth in a coffee-pot," an image that rivals anything in the young Eliot's highly celebrated annals of disaffection.

In looking back upon this poem, I think too that the poem's brilliant enactment of the *walk*, of its movement and passage, is a model that has held tremendous power for me throughout the years. Here, Neruda's (or the speaker's) restless, world-weary fatigue seems to me to be both Odyssean and Dantescan, yet startlingly personal, undeniably universal.

Whether at eighteen or at forty, I think most readers will feel as I do, that "Walking Around" is one of those rare poems that feels fresh, new, just written. It is a poem that, like its author, remains still an inexhaustible resource.

# SCRIPTS AND WATER, RULES AND RICHES

In looking over the many volumes of poetry and of prose by poets that appeared in 1984, the work of four poets seemed to me especially intriguing. Two of them, Donald Justice and Howard Moss, are well known to readers of contemporary poetry, and their younger companions in this piece, Roberta Spear and Craig Raine, certainly should be.

In Donald Justice's brilliant collection of essays and interviews, *Platonic Scripts*, we learn in a section of the book entitled "Notes of an Outsider," a gathering of journal and notebook entries dated 1962-1982, just why Justice has chosen this title: "I write or try to write as if convinced that, prior to my attempt, there existed a true text, a sort of Platonic script, which I had been elected to transcribe or record." For Donald Justice it is always the *poem* not the self, that commands the direction and force of one's writing. Again and again, in both his interviews and his essays, we come upon the fierce resolve of the craftsman as he explicates with astonishing lucidity what he sees as the importance of formal technique, the crucial place of metrics in poetry, and the essential relation between poetry and memory.

In his interviews, there is a measured quality to Justice's responses that may strike some readers, at first, as a guardedness, a cautiousness. Yet to anyone familiar with Justice's poetry, this will be recognized immediately as his modesty and his reluctance to pontificate in an age of pontification and self-aggrandizement. Justice's interviews are marked by his clarity and composure; like his poems, his responses often convey the delicacy of being "composed" in the musical sense of the word. And his composure, his grace and calm in the face of stupid questions, is greater than that of any poet who comes to mind. Justice's statements are always underlined by his sly wit, his charming restraint. These interviews seem a record not only of his philosophical (aesthetic) constancy throughout his poetic career, but also of the poetic integrity required to fight, or ignore, the many conventions of literary fashion. In an essay published in 1975 (and originally titled "Effacement of the Self"), Justice says:

> I haven't ever intended to put myself directly into the poems, not in any of the poems I've written. I've always felt it was an author's privilege to leave himself out, if he chose—and I so chose, contrary to the choice of certain friends and contemporarie...I am often speaking in some imagined or borrowed voice. I may be writing about things I know personally, even intimately, but to a certain degree I want to pretend that it is otherwise.

Later in the same interview, Justice says, "I'm just not that interested in imposing my sense of self, of my discoveries about the essence of life, on others. I don't like to think of myself as a propagandist or evangelist." The interviewers then ask, "In other words, understatement is to you, practically, a religious principle." And Justice quite simply responds, "Yes." How marvelous! And though Justice feels "nervous about fingering the self too much, or about others who do," his reasons for writing poetry strike me as always quite personal and likewise always candidly expressed. And why does a poet write? Why does Justice write?

> ...one of the motives for writing is surely to recover and hold what would otherwise be lost totally—memory or experience. Put very simply, so that one might not wholly die. Sometimes I think of poetry as making things. Common enough, surely. And I would like to have made some nice things, beautiful things. And in those beautiful things to have got something I would not like to have forgotten: probably involving my own experience, but perhaps that of others.

For Justice, "for the art of poetry itself, basic is some formal or technical interest." He adds, "there are properties which I think belong unarguably to poetry, and one of them is *technical virtue*....Without it poetry dies." The process of revising is central to Justice ("I myself am not sure that I would take as much pleasure in writing were it possible to commit the original idea with perfect spontaneity to paper"), and his concern is explicated in two marvelous essays about the writing of two of his best-known poems, "Anonymous Drawing" and "First Death." His essays are *all* instructive and precise, but perhaps the most eloquent discussion of his poetics occurs in the quiet but remarkable essay called simply "Meters and Memory." As these three excerpts show, the functions of meter are multifold for Justice, though they share a consistent purpose:

> The emotion needs to be fixed, so that whatever has been temporarily recovered may become as nearly permanent as possible, allowing it to be called back again and again...

> While the meters and other assorted devices may ultimately make the lines easier for an audience to remember, they are offering meanwhile, like the stone of the sculptor, a certain resistance to the writer's efforts to call up his subject, which seems always to be involved, one way or another, with memory. (Hobbes somewhere calls imagination the same thing as memory.) In any case, memory is going to keep whatever it chooses to keep not just because it has been made easy and agreeable to remember but because it comes to be recognized as worth the trouble of keeping, and first of all by the poet.

> ...meters serve as a neutral and impersonal check on self-indulgence and whimsy; a subjective event gets made over into something more like an object. It becomes accessible to memory, repeatedly accessible, because it exists finally in a form that can be perused at leisure, like a snapshot in an album. Memory itself tends to act not without craft, but selectively, adding here to restore a gap, omitting the incongruous there, rearranging and shifting the emphasis, striving, consciously or not, to make some sense and point out of what in experience may have seemed to lack either.

And so, for Justice, it is the cohesion of the technical virtues necessary to poetry, the gathering of sense with music, and the artful objectification of the subjective event that are all somehow melded in the mysterious act of writing. At the end of *Platonic Scripts* there is a brief but pointed admonition to all poets, a kind of echo of all that has come before, that one write: "Not forgetting rhythm; not forgetting truth." It is a resilient and resounding conclusion to a fascinating book.

Like her first book, the highly praised volume of poems *Silks*, Roberta Spear's new collection, *Taking to Water*, embodies all the virtues of graceful understatement. The poems charm us with their restraint, precision, and care. There is never the slightest egocentric gesture in this work, as Spear is an eloquent observer, not a self-congratulatory performer.

For Spear, it is the constant intertwining of the natural world with the delicate oscillations of human desire that commands her attention. She is a deft, subtle craftsman; where other poets would be flashy and brash, Spear is measured and calm. The effect is startling, as each poem gathers in authority from the earned authority of those poems that have come before. It is the poise of Roberta Spear's voice that convinces us, again and again.

*Taking to Water* is divided into two parts. The first contains poems that take as their settings the South, the Carolinas, where Spear lived for several years; the second is made up of poems of travel drawn from France and Italy. As in *Silks*, many of the poems have a fabulous quality; the magical quietly weaves itself into the events of the ordinary world until both the poem and its figures are transformed. In this book memory and its reclamations are less a concern for Spear than some reckoning with the present and, more importantly (because of the child she is carrying or who is newly born in many of these poems), some reckoning with the future. She says, "I am learning to love/what is coming as much as I loved/what was before." And in the book's final poem, Spear and her husband sit in an outdoor cafe, watching, or imagining, the one:

> with a message, the face
> of a gypsy child who has your eyes
> and plays a painted fiddle.
>
> In his dish, coins
> stamped with the names
> of the old world we're in,

and one with the name
of the new world in me.

Poems of travel are often simply diaries of displacement. Perhaps what's
most winning about Roberta Spear's poems is that, wherever she is, her
observations make her totally at home. This is a capacity that goes beyond
"sympathy" for a place or a people; it is the basic recognition and assumption
of the humanity common to all people, in all places. Here is one of the most
powerful of those poems, "Rue Madame":

When the light touches ground,
he's out shuffling under the chestnuts,
banging on the broken shutters.
His trousers inhale and flare,
finning the air behind him—
a fish out of water, they say.
The green bristles pool
under his chin and the aroma
of black Basque mussels escapes
when he walks too quickly.
From a family with too many
small fries to keep him.
But Marcel is his friend.
He pushes the water from the abattoir
to the curb with a stiff broom
and says that no man is a fish.
He claims he's more like the old
trotters sent into the city,
for he often rolls his head half-circle
to watch the sky end on a knoll.
And the boys who steal the cigarettes
Marcel gives him call him a frog.
Always, the warts on his nose,
the bubble of phlegm, the flies....
Once, I took you out for a stroll
in this city where they'd eat old men
if they had the right sauce.
And on that hard gray ribbon
that ties us together,

112

he crossed our path and grinned.
He knelt and rubbed his stain
across your eyes, whispering
*what a beautiful child*, as though
more than the memory had returned.
Before you're old enough to know
what made you laugh that day,
he'll be gone—and with him,
that staff of light,
those gentle creatures
who answer to any name.

*Rules of Sleep*, Howard Moss's new volume of poetry, is the third since his gathering of *Selected Poems*, which was awarded the 1972 National Book Award. Most readers of contemporary poetry know that Moss's poems are models of craftsmanship and that his urbane wit is without equal. Critics too have pointed to the elegant beauty of his poems and to the lucid ease that informs all of his work. What perhaps needs to be said again is that Howard Moss has also written some of the most powerful and moving poems of the last ten years. One looks back over *Buried City* (1975) and finds the poems: "Chekhov," "Sawdust," and the marvelous title poem. From *Notes from the Castle* (1980), one finds four more extraordinarily compelling poems: "Gravel," "Many Senses: Mexico City," "Stars," and the heartbreaking "Elegy for My Sister." The subtle orchestrations of emotion in these works is dazzling. If you haven't read these poems recently, go back and discover them again.

Early in *Rules of Sleep* we confront one of the book's recurring concerns in the poem "The Gallery Walk: Art and Nature" when the poet says, "I am only trying to teach you/What pleasure is, and also about/The end of things,/And how the two of them go hand in hand." The transitory beauty of the natural and the somewhat dumbly fecund pulse of nature can, of course, both find their embodiment in art. But for Moss the traditional conflict (of art and nature) is one best resolved by the many celebrations of the arts, as this lovely Yeatsian passage (from the conclusion of the poem just mentioned) shows:

And so it is better to look at the dancers,
Or these beautiful canvases of dancers dancing,

Or listen to music recreate the pulse
Of sounded, marvellous emotions caught
In the lines of the body, its grace and flights,
And to see on the wing of a violin
Nature soaring in, all green,
A tree, in which a bird will seek
Its habitation the summer long,
Singing its heart out, as usual.

What this passage doesn't show, however, is how the quiet undercurrent of Moss's sense of *ending*, his recognition of the mortality of all things, is a note that is sounded often here. I don't mean to suggest that the poems of *Rules of Sleep* are overly solemn—quite the contrary. These poems are all in some way meditations on the spirit, on the fierce necessity of the human spirit, and as such they are, like the end of the poem just quoted, celebratory and joyful, and often quite defiant of that inevitable ending. One of the most remarkable poems in *Rules of Sleep*, one of the many meditations on the human spirit, is the poem "In Umbria," which weaves together, as many of Moss's poems do, the forces of landscape and the forces of the spirit. In this poem, set in Assisi (and, at the poem's opening, the church of St. Clare), Moss wants also to consider the nature of the miraculous (and the miraculous in nature). Using a painterly approach and vocabulary (the poem is dedicated to the painter Daniel Lang, who lives part of each year in Umbria) in his consideration of the Umbrian landscape stretching before him, Moss finds the traditional religious potencies of *light* and *dark* playing out their drama over the hillsides he sees below and across the histories he recalls. Though the spiritual life and the more secular life of the spirit are not necessarily the same, Moss sees, in the oppositions of light and dark across the landscape, a familiar story: "The shades of Umbria are growing darker." The pun on "shades" being, one hopes, self-evident. The poem concludes in a startling passage that, like the best of art, both religious and secular, gives voice to the voiceless:

And what the dead have to say today
Is old, old as the hills, a phrase
Meaningless until one stares at these
Great slants of grave sites, reaching up
Always to the light, which the dead can't do,

Whose every particular is shelled to bone;
They say, "Our hearts, too, were full
Of sunlight once. Joy is in the shade.
Look at it. Look. It is beautiful."

As in all of Moss's work, the poems of *Rules of Sleep* are filled with unparalleled musical beauty; like Merrill and Wilbur, Moss is a master of verbal music. And, recalling Yeats again, Moss loves the colloquial in a formal context; finding the dailiness of speech flexing its muscles in a highly rendered poem is always one of the great delights of Moss's poetry. But perhaps the proper place to conclude any discussion of *Rules of Sleep* is with the mention of one of the most charming and poignant dramatic monologues of recent vintage, that of "Einstein's Bathrobe." That's right, the poem is spoken by none other than the great man's bathrobe, and the effect of this intimacy is both witty and terrifying. With the combination of play and forcefulness common to many of the poems of *Rules of Sleep*, "Einstein's Bathrobe" concludes:

At tea at Mercer Street every afternoon
His manners went beyond civility,
Kindness not having anything to learn;
I was completely charmed. And fooled.
What a false view of the universe I had!
The horsehair sofa, the sagging chairs,
A fire roaring behind the firescreen—
Imagine thinking Princeton was the world!
Yet I wore prescience like a second skin:
When Greenwich and Palomar saw eye to eye.
Time and space having found their rabbi,
I felt the dawn's black augurs gather force.
As if I knew in the New Jersey night
The downcast sky that was to clamp on Europe,
That Asia had its future in my pocket.

Though less well known in America than his friend James Fenton, Craig Raine seems to me the most consistently inventive and compelling younger poet to have appeared in Great Britain in years. Like his earlier two books,

*The Onion, Memory* and *A Martian Sends a Postcard Home,* Raine's new collection, *Rich,* is a dazzling sketchbook of verbal brilliance. In Britain, poets are now occassionally referred to as belonging to the "Martian" school of poetry, a name assigned not only in reference to Raine's second collection but also because of his unique ability to see the ordinary and daily objects of the world as if from afar, as if with the more objectifying eye of one from another planet; and some critics, finding schools convenient, have chosen therefore to lump any poet exhibiting any like tendency into this fictional "school." But the truth is that, though Raine may have imitators and sympathizers, there is no one at all remotely like him. His talent is individual and unduplicable. With his remarkable eye for resemblances, Raine exploits elliptical metaphors and shifting similes in order to allow us to see our world in a fresh and more powerful way. Yet, what is perhaps more difficult, Raine in the process also allows us to see language itself in a fresh and more (if oddly) precise way. As one might imagine, the combination is both startling and satisfying.

In *Rich,* the riches spoken of are not material, though they may be of the world and its beauty; the riches are of the heart and, most imperatively, of the imagination. Raine is a poet who relishes small tendernesses (see the poem "In Modern Dress," about his children); the intimate and its details are granted the status of the grand. His image making is always delightful and surprising. To take two such images almost at random from the book's title poem, there is "the Steinway,//her grinning grand/with its dangerous fin" and "the goldfish mouthing/its mantra." Because it is so easy to be captivated by the verbal intelligence of Raine's work, it is easy to forget how full they are of *people,* how laced with human dilemmas and emotions each poem is. His portrait of an old man in a hospital (or nursing home) in the poem "Again," as well as the amazing poem "Baize Doors," remain unforgettable. Here is the latter poem:

> She had forgotten the bellows again
> and the family was due back from church.
> Her mind was on the gardener's boy,
>
> who'd left her in the lurch
> the Friday before: without his reference,
> leaving only a collar stud behind
>
> at the back of a paper-lined drawer,

and that drawn length of linen blind
which curtsied gently in her hand

then vanished when she let it go.
She knew that she must be alive
by her breath on the window

when she deliberately adjusted
an hairpin, before going downstairs...
The bellows were kept in the kitchen

beyond the bottle-green baize
where the floral carpet stopped
and the stone steps started.

No one had ever fallen before.
The under-cook was broken-hearted
about the blood and slipped

a *Reynold's News* between her floor
and the opened skull. Morgan, the valet.
was dispatched for the doctor,

who turned the face to find
a phrenologist's head: the stop press
transferred backwards on the brain.

The gardener's boy was on her mind.
A pair of bellows prayed in the hearth.
The kitchen fire fell to its death.

The second (center) section of *Rich* is a prose memoir of childhood that is primarily a portrait of Raine's father who, in the thirties, the poet says, "had been a painter and decorator, plumber, electrician, publican and boxer, but, when I was growing up, he was a Spiritualist and a faith healer...." A bomb armourer and victim of an accident, Raine's father suffered "five major brain operations" in which doctors "removed part of his brain and inserted a silver plate." Raine's father emerges from this portrait as a figure of great charm and courage, a proud and generous man. He is so large a figure, in fact, that he appears also in two of *Rich's* finest poems, "Plain Song," about Raine as a child spying upon his father's Spiritualist activities, and "A Hungry Fighter," which recounts the story of the title fight, for the featherweight championship of Great Britain, between Raine's father and Micky McGuire. Because of an unfair punch, Raine's father loses.

Perhaps Raine's plainest account of himself as a poet occurs in the book's title poem, which is part love poem to his wife, part hymn to the Muse, and part celebration of the Earth's wealth. At the poem's conclusion, its speaker says:

> I am the steward
> of her untold wealth,
> keeper of the dictionary,
> treasurer of valuables,
>
> accountant and teller,
> and I woo her with words
> against the day of divorce.
> Mistress of death and of birth,
>
> she owns the trout
> tortured with asthma
> and this field in spring,
> threadbare with green.

In this subtle and moving book, one full of constant surprises, Raine also confronts the wreckage and sadness of his world. In his wonderful version of the Anglo-Saxon poem "Wulf and Eadwacer," we find a timeless yet somehow especially twentieth-century voice describing the tragedy of exile in its most human and personal terms. Listen:

> Nothing was said. Ever. Just stares.
> They would have wiped his face,
> as it is wiped now in any case:
> the shape of his lips, his tongue
>
> and the touch of it, are wrong.

Now I remember only the hairs
on the back of his slim hands,
holding mine at the edge of our lands
when we said that goodbye.
So vivid they seemed. So black.
I could not look him in the eyes.
When he promised to come back

for me, after winter, in the dark,
I knew that I could wait forever,
ill with every dog's bark,
each splash from the river.

I do not want him to return now.
I could never explain how
the other one I do not love
came every day and would not move.

A soldier. Nothing was said.
He watched me and the unmade bed,
his fist frigging the dice all day.
I missed you is so easy to say.

# MEMORY AS MELODY

The Sunset Maker, Donald Justice's first collection of poetry since his Pulitzer-Prize-winning volume of Selected Poems (1979), is the finest of all of Justice's very fine books of poetry. In many ways, The Sunset Maker is the culmination of all of the virtues of Donald Justice's work, just as his Selected Poems was the dramatic exhibition of those virtues.

Donald Justice has long been known among poets as a technical virtuoso, a formal master as accomplished as any poet, American or foreign, one might wish to name. His verbal grace has often been touched by a love of poetic games, and his masters have been, clearly, John Crowe Ransom and Wallace Stevens. Also, throughout his career, there has been the unadvertised (but quietly alluded to) influence of the poetries of Spain and France. Typically, Justice refused to claim a profound "brotherhood" and close kinship with those poets he admired and, most often in privacy, translated; instead, he simply allowed them to fulfill his work from within. The pleasure he took in the translation of twentieth-century French poets (some of the translations are available in Contemporary French Poetry, edited by Justice and Alexander Aspel) is visible in many of the poems in Justice's collection Night Light (1967). Equally visible in the book Departures (1973) is the rich, often dark mystery one associates with modern Spanish poetry, most importantly to Justice the poems of Raphael Alberti and Caesar Vallejo. Although Baudelaire, Kafka, and Rilke all serve as models or points of departure for certain poems in The Sunset Maker, the presiding spirit of this book is a figure a bit closer to home, the Master himself, Henry James.

*The Sunset Maker* is itself made up, by its own maker, of poems, stories, and a prose memoir. The formative experience of Justice's early instruction in and acquaintanceship with music offers the axis upon which the book turns; it is the education of a sensibility that first learns the lessons of art and beauty in a medium *other* than words. It is this delicate paradox that touches all of the poems in *The Sunset Maker*. Equally, the painterly qualities of light that command the stage of the book's title poem give us a companion example of the way that beauty is created—not "captured" or "re-created"—in yet another nonverbal form of art.

Like the flags of smoke from burning leaves tracing the air in late fall, an elegiac mist arises from the poems of *The Sunset Maker*. Justice has always cultivated a healing nostalgia in his poetry, one that he grants to the people and events of both a public past as well as a more personal past. Here, using a more expansive palette than ever before, Justice becomes the maker of memories, his own *and* others', as well as their chronicler. *The Sunset Maker* becomes not simply a kind of American Album (one of the poems is entitled, after James, "American Scenes [1904-1905]") but a family album as well, one in which the sketches and portraits of memorable places and people figure importantly. Part of this album includes the poems "My South," "Manhattan Dawn (1945)," and this gorgeous poem, "Nostalgia of the Lakefronts":

> Cities burn behind us; the lake glitters.
> A tall loudspeaker is announcing prizes;
> Another, by the lake, the times of cruises.
> Childhood, once vast with terrors and surprises,
> Is fading to a landscape deep with distance—
> And always the sad piano in the distance,
>
> Faintly in the distance, a ghostly tinkling
> (O indecipherable blurred harmonies)
> Or some far horn repeating over water
> Its high lost note, cut loose from all harmonies.
> At such times, wakeful, a child will dream the world,
> And this is the world we run to from the world.
>
> Or the two worlds come together and are one
> On dark sweet aftenoons of storm and of rain,
> And stereopticons brought out and dusted,

Stacks of old *Geographics,* or, through the rain,
A mad wet dash to the local movie palace
And the shriek, perhaps, of Kane's white cockatoo.
(Would this have been summer, 1942?)

By June the city seems to grow neurotic.
But lakes are good all summer for reflection,
And ours is famed among painters for its blues,
Yet not entirely sad, upon reflection.
Why sad at all? Is their wish not unique—
To anthropomorphize the inanimate
With a love that masquerades as pure technique?

O art and the child are innocent together!
But landscapes grow abstract, like aging parents;
Soon now the war will shutter the grand hotels;
And we, when we come back, must come as parents.
There are no lanterns now strung between pines—
Only, like history, the stark bare northern pines.

And after a time the lakefront disappears
Into the stubborn verses of its exiles
Or a few gifted sketches of old piers.
It rains perhaps on the other side of the heart;
Then we remember, whether we would or no.
—Nostalgia comes with the smell of rain, you know.

The impulse to memorialize is always tempered in Justice by, well, his temperament; it is a poetic temperament characterized, as poet Michael Ryan has put it, by a "passionate restraint." The reticence one associates with Justice's poetry, this passionate restraint, is precisely the counterbalance to the sentiment of memory. Time after time, Justice has sought to skate close to the edges of that sentiment as a way of teasing the reader into a startling poetic moment—for just one example, look back to the astonishing poem "First Death" in the *Selected Poems.* In *The Sunset Maker,* the urgency of memory seems always an essential interior pressure in the poems. Perhaps it is in the several fine elegies (two for friends, one for his mother) that the poet most starkly stands and bears witness to what *is* past. Here is the powerful and poignant elegy "Psalm and Lament":

> *in memory of my mother (1897-1974)*
> *Hialeah, Florida*

> The clocks are sorry, the clocks are very sad.
> One stops, one goes on striking the wrong hours.

> And the grass burns terribly in the sun,
> The grass turns yellow secretly at the roots.

> Now suddenly the yard chairs look empty, the sky looks empty,
> The sky looks vast and empty.

> Out on Red Road the traffic continues; everything continues.
> Nor does memory sleep; it goes on.

> Out spring the butterflies of recollection,
> And I think that for the first time I understand

> The beautiful ordinary light of this patio
> And even perhaps the dark rich earth of a heart.

> (The bedclothes, they say, had been pulled down.
> I will not describe it. I do not want to describe it.

> No, but the sheets were drenched and twisted.
> They were the very handkerchiefs of grief. )

> Let summer come now with its schoolboy trumpets
>          and fountains.
> But the years are gone, the years are finally over.

> And there is only
> This long desolation of flower-bordered sidewalks

> That runs to the corner, turns, and goes on,
> That disappears and goes on

Into the black oblivion of a neighborhood and a world
Without billboards or yesterdays.

Sometimes a sad moon comes and waters the roof tiles.
But the years are gone. There are no more years.

Twilight, sunset, a taste for endings. Justice's project in *The Sunset Maker* is a recuperative one. This Maker of memories, this Master of words, however aware he is of the relative constraints of the endeavor (as opposed to the possibilities of music or painting), still *composes* this album as a way to allow us to regard and share a history, a past that will become common to us all. And this is one of the healing, recuperative aspects of the poetry in this book. For Justice, it is the *recovery* of the past, of memory, that necessarily attends his search for an America that will remain vital to him; in this recovery is the poetic (re)creation of that America, that shared past. In *The Sunset Maker*, the creator is in some ways the Creator. Not only are worlds created, they are peopled with men and women and, of course, furnished with a few natural effects—sunrises, sunsets....

The desires and disappointments within lives often arise as the melodies in Justice's poems. Here, as we turn the pages of the album, we're given a catalogue of challenges and defeats faced by many of his figures, yet these figures are allowed to greet their fates with a winning, even transforming, grace. Justice has a profound understanding of the intoxicating power of the "glamours" of the world as only a writer who likewise understands the world's harsh grasp, its loneliness and poverty, can employ. Perhaps this is one of the reasons that, in *The Sunset Maker*, Justice's plainspoken and direct voice holds its astonishing authority throughout; even when the poet adopts the tonalities of Kafka or Rilke or Henry James, it is always the voice of Donald Justice speaking to us from the finely carved mouth of the mask. Here is the marvelous poem after Kafka, echoing a passage of *The Diaries*, entitled "Young Girls Growing Up (1911)":

No longer do they part and scatter so hopelessly before you,
But they will stop and put an elbow casually
On the piano top and look quite frankly at you;
And pale reflections glide there then like swans.

What you say to them now is not lost. They listen to the end

And—little heartshaped chins uplifted—seem
Just on the point of breaking into song;
Nor is a short conversation more than they can stand.

When they turn away now they do so slowly, and mean no harm;
And it seems their backs are suddenly broader also.
You picture yourself in the avenue below, masked by trees,
And, just as the streetlamps go on, you glance up:

There, there at the window, blotting out the light...!
Weeks pass and perhaps you meet unexpectedly,
And now they come forward mournfully, hands outstretched,
Asking why you are such a stranger, what has changed?

But when you seek them out, they only
Crouch in a window seat and pretend to read,
And have no look to spare you, and seem cruel.
And this is why there are men who wander aimlessly through
    cities!

This is why there are cities and darkness and a river,
And men who stride along the embankment now, without a plan,
And turn their collars up against the moon,
Saying to one another, *Live, we must try to live, my friend!*

The heart of *The Sunset Maker* belongs to music. It is his and the book's true love. The poet's learning of the intricacies of the piano and of musical composition (as hinted earlier, Justice's poems are always *composed* in the sense of both musical and pictorial composition) becomes the gravitational center for this book, in both poems and a prose memoir. The memoir, entitled "Piano Lessons: Notes on a Provincial Culture," is a recounting of the child's early encounters with a series of piano teachers, beginning with a Mrs. Snow. These materials are reshaped and performed upon a poetic keyboard in the poem "Mrs. Snow" (which precedes the memoir and acts as its prelude), as well as in the three poems that follow. Here is one of the latter poems, one of the many superb sonnets illuminating *The Sunset Maker*, entitled "The Pupil":

Picture me, the shy pupil at the door,
One small, tight fist clutching the dread Czerny.
Back then time was still harmony, not money,
And I could spend a whole week practicing for
That moment on the threshold.
                                        Then to take courage,
And enter, and pass among mysterious scents,
And sit quite straight, and with a frail confidence
Assault the keyboard with a childish flourish!

Only to lose one's place, or forget the key,
And almost doubt the very metronome
(Outside, the traffic, the laborers going home),
And still to bear on across Chopin or Brahms,
Stupid and wild with love equally for the storms
Of C# minor and the calms of C.

These poems and the memoir are concerned with an artistic coming of age, and they are all the more fascinating because we, as readers, know that the speaker's primary artistic focus has become, subsequently, poetry and not music. Companionably in tune with the work of this section are the story "Little Elegy for Cello and Piano" and what is called its "pendant" poem, the book's title poem, "The Sunset Maker." In this fictive reconstructing (much as a memory is reconstructed in a poem) of a brief phrase of music recalled from a concert in the past—from a composition supposedly by the speaker's dead brother-in-law, a composer for whom the speaker now acts as executor for the scores—Justice joins the temporal consideration of light and its passing (in the figure of the sun passing through palm leaves in Bonnard's *The Terrace*) with the passage out of life and into memory of this beloved phrase of music. Trust me, the story and poem are far more elegant and powerful than my brief summary might imply. Clearly, for Justice, these brief phrases of music or memory are all of memory that we will be allowed; these fragments of elegy recalled in music, words, or color and light are our only glimpses into a past we need to re-create as solace and as art. What has passed into the past is both natural and unnatural, it is both remembered and created; it is art. "The Sunset Maker" concludes:

                    And I agree
It's sentimental to suppose my friend
Survives in just this fragment, this tone-row
A hundred people halfway heard one Sunday
And one of them no more than half remembers.
The hard early years of study, those still,
Sequestered mornings in the studio,
The perfect ear, the technique, the great gift
All have come down to this one ghostly phrase.
And soon nobody will recall the sound
these six notes made once or that there were six.


Hear the gulls. That's our local music.
I like it myself; and, as you can see,
Our sunset maker studied with Bonnard.

In Donald Justice's poems, it is not simply the irony we recognize in that so many of his deeply fatigued figures or speakers have once had dreams and great hopes, it is also that we experience a sense of their courage, even a delight at their own self-awareness and good humor in the face of all. Perhaps the proper place to conclude a discussion of *The Sunset Maker* is with one of the poems gathered under the title "Tremayne." These poems display Justice's love of Weldon Kees, especially Kees's "Robinson" poems, and it's hard not to see the character Tremayne as an occasional stand-in for the poet. In any case, these poems have, in recent years, become signature pieces for Donald Justice, and rightly so. Here is the concluding poem of the sequence, "Tremayne Autumnal":

          Autumn, and a cold rain, and mist,
            In which the dark pineshapes are drowned,
        And taller poleshapes, and the townlights masked—
        A scene, oh, vaguely Post-Impressionist,
              Tremayne would tell us, if we asked.

          Who with his glasses off, half-blind,
            Accomplishes very much the same
        Lovely effect of blurs and shimmerings—
        Or else October evenings spill a kind

Of Lethe-water over things.

"O season of half forgetfulness!"
Tremayne, as usual, misquotes,
Recalling adolescence and old trees
In whose shade once he memorized that verse
And something about "late flowers for the bees..."

# WHERE THE ANGELS COME TOWARD US:
# THE POETRY OF PHILIP LEVINE

The publication of Philip Levine's most recent collection of poetry, *Sweet Will*, following by only a year his superbly edited *Selected Poems*, presents an excellent opportunity to consider the twenty years of work these two volumes represent.

Throughout his career, Philip Levine has looked for an American voice, a voice that could stand comfortably in the tradition of Whitman and William Carlos Williams. Levine's primary impulse is narrative, and his poems are often narratives of human struggle—of the particularly American struggle of the immigrant, and of the universal struggle of individuals ignored and unheard by their societies. Levine's poetry gives voice to these "voiceless" men and women who he feels have been too rarely recognized and honored in our literature.

Philip Levine's poetry, known for being urban and "angry," is also filled with great naturalistic beauty and great tenderness. His poems present a poetic voice that is both as colloquial and unliterary as daily speech and as American as jazz. Levine has always desired a relatively "invisible" and unadorned style, one that could allow the voices of his speakers and the details of their stories to fully command the reader's attention. Yet the technical achievements and the formal underpinning of his poetry are too often neglected. The *Selected Poems* makes clear that the metrical and rhymed poetry of Levine's early books, as well as his superb syllabic verse, remains some of the most highly-crafted and imaginatively powerful poetry of the time.

For Levine, poetry is almost always the poetry of witness. Here is his requiem for the silent fifties, and the title poem of his first collection, "On The Edge":

> My name is Edgar Poe and I was born
> In 1928 in Michigan.
> Nobody gave a damn. The gruel I ate
> Kept me alive, nothing kept me warm,
> But I grew up, almost to five foot ten,
> And nothing in the world can change my weight.
>
> I have been watching you these many years,
> There in the office, pencil poised and ready,
> Or on the highway when you went ahead.
> I did not write; I watched you watch the stars
> Believing that the wheel of fate was steady;
> I saw you rise from love and go to bed;
>
> I heard you lie, even to your daughter.
> I did not write, for I am Edgar Poe,
> Edgar the mad one, silly, drunk, unwise,
> But Edgar waiting on the edge of laughter,
> And there is nothing that he does not know
> Whose page is blanker than the raining skies.

The poem's speaker, with his refrain, "I did not write," was born—like Levine—in 1928, in Michigan. His name recalls, with a wry wit, one of America's more famous outsiders. Here are the elements of what will remain at the core of many of Levine's poems: a disenfranchised voice, often American, solitary yet resilient, self-ironic, accusing, compassionate, steadily proclaiming his or her role as observer from the harsh recesses of the working world. Since any real "power" to this voice, even in a democracy that promises the equal importance of *all* of its citizens' voices, has been neutralized, the speaker has seized instead the voice of this poem. In this way, in spite of the speaker's insistence upon his own silence, we find, in fact, that this silence has been *spoken*. That is, it has been written, and it is a silence that becomes both testimony and inscription.

"The Horse," another of the poems drawn from *On The Edge*, illustrates the moral outrage that will steadily inform Levine's work. This poem, dedicated to a survivor of Hiroshima, establishes two of Levine's recurring concerns—the earth's constant ravishing and destruction by man, and the capacity of the natural world to regenerate and renew itself. It is this same power of resurrection, earthly resurrection, that Levine finds and champions in the oppressed men and women who people many of his poems, one of the most memorable of these victorious losers being the boxer of the poem "A New Day":

> The headlights fading out at dawn,
> A stranger at the shore, the shore
> Not wakening to the great sea
> Out of sleep, and night, and no sun
> Rising where it rose before.
>
> The old champion in a sweat suit
> Tells me this is Chicago, this—
> He does not say—is not the sea
> But the chopped grey lake you get to
> After travelling all night
>
> From Dubuque, Cairo, or Wyandotte.
> He takes off at a slow trot
> And the fat slides under his shirt.
> I recall the Friday night
> In a beer garden in Detroit
>
> I saw him flatten Ezzard Charles
> On TV, and weep, and raise
> Both gloved hands in a slow salute
> To a God. I could tell him that.
> I could tell him that those good days
>
> Were no more and no less than these.
> I could tell him that I thought
> By now I must have reached the sea
> We read about, or that last night
> I saw a man break down and cry

Out of luck and out of gas
In Bruce's Crossing. We collect
Here at the shore, the two of us,
To make a pact, a people come
For a new world and a new home

And what we get is what we bring:
A grey light coming on at dawn,
No fresh start and no bird song
And no sea and no shore
That someone hasn't seen before.

The delicate and powerful syllabics of "The Horse" and the iambic tetrameter lines (with gorgeous variations) of "A New Day" provide supple examples of Levine's technical grace and of the coupling of formal exactitude with unfamiliar subjects that is one of his many gifts. Even with its wink at Keats, "A New Day" remains unforced and unliterary.

It was in his second book, *Not This Pig*, that Levine first brought to maturity the line that would serve as the basis for his narrative ambitions in the poems to come. One of the several poems of seven syllable lines in this volume, "The Cemetery at Academy, California," best represents this solidifying of voice in Levine's poetry. Here is the central stanza of that poem:

I came here with a young girl
once who perched barefoot on her
family marker. "I will go
there," she said, "next to my sister."
It was early morning and
cold, and I wandered over
the pale clodded ground looking
for something rich or touching.
"It's all wildflowers in the spring,"
she had said, but in July
there were only the curled cut
flowers and the headstones blanked out
on the sun side, and the long

shadows deep as oil. I walked
to the sagging wire fence
that marked the margin of the
place and saw where the same ground,
festered here and there with reedy
grass, rose to a small knoll
and beyond where a windmill
held itself against the breeze.
I could hear her singing on
the stone under the great oak,
but when I got there she was
silent and I wasn't sure
and was ashamed to ask her,
ashamed that I had come here
where her people turned the earth.

Levine loves to braid strands of narrative, visual, and meditative detail into a unified poetic whole. He often uses details of the present to stitch together fragments of memory, pieces of the past (both public and private histories), to give texture and relief to the surface fabric of a poem. This technique, which helps lend narrative unity and historical resonance to his poems, is one Levine will echo and refine throughout his career.

"Not This Pig," with its superb air of defiance, is often seen as the poem most clearly embodying the strengths of Levine's work of this period; yet I think a far more representative poem, one more indicative of the directions he would take, is the delicate and moving "Heaven." The poem reflects Levine's ever-present questioning of individual and society, of the relationship between conscience and law. The poem has a basis in Levine's own refusal to serve in the Korean War, but its central figure is not Levine; he is *anyone* with beliefs:

If you were twenty-seven
and had done time for beating
your ex-wife and had
no dreams you remembered
in the morning, you might
lie on your bed and listen
to a mad canary sing
and think it all right to be

there every Saturday
ignoring your neighbors, the streets,
the signs that said join,
and the need to be helping.
You might build, as he did,
a network of golden ladders
so that the bird could roam
on all levels of the room;
you might paint the ceiling blue,
the floor green, and shade
the place you called the sun
so that things came softly to order
when the light came on.
He and the bird lived
in the fine weather of heaven;
they never aged, they
never tired or wanted
all through that war,
but when it was over
and the nation had been saved,
he knew they'd be hunted.
He knew, as you would too,
that he'd be laid off
for not being braver,
and it would do no good
to show how he had taken
clothespins and cardboard
and made each step safe.
It would do no good
to have been one of the few
that climbed higher and higher
even in time of war,
for now there would be the poor
asking for their share,
and hurt men in uniforms,
and no one to believe
that heaven was really here.

One of the valid conventional wisdoms about Philip Levine is that he is one of the few urban—as opposed to suburban—poets. He is, certainly, our most gripping poet of the city. Perhaps this is because he sees the used and abused city, the working city, not the city of galleries, museums, and restaurants. He sees and records the workings of the ravaged and exhausted city; he witnesses the blood and courage of those who live and work within it.

Perhaps the most compelling aspect of Levine's poetry is the place that anger is granted in his work. One of the few sources of power left to many of his speakers is to touch their own frustration and rage, and it is that current that electrifies their presence in these poems. The daily injustices that build into a larger sense of outrage accrue in Levine's poems much as they do in his speakers' lives—slowly and inexorably. It is an especially clarifying anger that we find at work throughout Levine's poetry, an anger that grants us the perspective of the real, and not a literary, world. It is an anger that we experience as a relief, the same relief we feel when the lens of a movie projector finally comes into focus; it is the clarity of truth that provides our sense of relief. No other American poet so clearly acknowledges the place and necessity of anger—in our lives and in our country—and it gives Levine's poetry an energy and an unkempt integrity that is unique.

In Levine's search for an authentic American voice, we can see the influence of daily speech, as well as the echo of black speech. It's not simply Levine's empathy with the oppressed and victimized that gives rise to a poem like "They Feed They Lion." It is also his desire to unleash the full power that he sees latent in American speech, in *all* of America's voices. We can hear it crashing forward in this poem, along with echoes of Whitman, Yeats, and Christopher Smart:

> Out of burlap sacks, out of bearing butter,
> Out of black bean and wet slate bread,
> Out of the acids of rage, the candor of tar.
> Out of creosote, gasoline, drive shafts, wooden dollies,
> They Lion grow.
> > Out of the gray hills
> Of industrial barns, out of rain, out of bus ride,
> West Virginia to Kiss My Ass, out of burned aunties,
> Mothers hardening like pounded stumps, out of stumps,
> Out of the bones' need to sharpen and the muscles' to stretch.
> They Lion grow

One facet of Levine's special genius is that those "literary" influences are always an internal fuel for his poems, never an exterior decoration. "They Feed They Lion" concludes with this extraordinary verbal surge:

> From the sweet glues of the trotters
> Come the sweet kinks of the fist, from the full flower
> Of the hams the thorax of caves,
> From "Bow Down" come "Rise Up,"
> Come they Lion from the reeds of shovels,
> The grained arm that pulls the hands,
> They Lion grow.
> From my five arms and all my hands,
> From all my white sins forgiven, they feed,
> From my car passing under the stars,
> They Lion, from my children inherit,
> From the oak turned to a wall, they Lion,
> From they sack and they belly opened
> And all that was hidden burning on the oil-stained earth
> They feed they Lion and he comes.

Just as Philip Levine chooses to give voice to those who have no power to do so themselves, he likewise looks in his poems for the chance to give voice to the natural world, taking—like Francis Ponge—*the side of things*, the side of nature and its elements. And Levine is in many ways an old-fashioned troubadour, a singer of tales of love and heroism. Though it comes colored by the music of his world, what Levine has to offer is as elemental as breath. It is the simple insistence of breath, of the will to live—and the force of all living things in nature—the Levine exalts again and again. At the conclusion of his exquisite love poem, "Breath," he says:

> Today
> in this high clear room
> of the world, I squat
> to the life of rocks
> jewelled in the stream
> or whispering
> like shards. What tears
> are still held locked

in the veins till the last
fire, and who will calm
us then under a gold sky
that will be all of earth?
Two miles below on the burning
summer plains, you go
about your life one
more day. I give you
almond blossoms
for your hair, your hair
that will be white, I give
the world my worn-out breath
on an old tune, I give
it all I have
and take it back again.

The startling and memorable poems of *They Feed They Lion* first brought Levine to national prominence, yet it's his next book, *1933*, that most clearly reflects the realm of loss that touches all of his work. The title refers to a year of great personal loss (the death of his father) as well as to a world on the verge of radical change. It is a world seen from the perspective of innocence, the perspective of a child. The poems form a loose family album of portraits of people and events culled from memory and given a unified shape. The spirit—the emblem of the sparrow that inhabits these and other of Levine's poems—bears witness to these losses and to this changing world of industrial explosion, an ending depression, and a growing war. Each day brings only the barest hope, but hope exists. It is in this book that Levine, in confronting the vanished past and his father's death, first confronts the image of his own mortality. And it is, he says in one of his interviews, his "urge to memorialize details" that helps him to stay the loss of places and people.

In the poem "Goodbye," about the funeral of a child (seemingly a relative, perhaps a cousin, of Levine's), the poet sees in his own reckoning with this death (a feared, mirror-death for the child-speaker) that it is this occasion that enacts a shift from childhood to young adulthood. The sparrow—both messenger and angel—is seen here as the embodied spirit of the lost child. Notice the double meaning of the conclusion of "Goodbye":

In the first light
a sparrow settled outside
my window, and a breeze woke
from the breathing river,
I opened my eyes
and the gauze curtains
were streaming.
"Come here," the sparrow said.
I went. In the alley below
a horse cart piled with bags,
bundles, great tubs of fat,
brass lamps the children broke,
I saw the sheenie-man pissing
into a little paper fire
in the snow, and laughed.
The bird smiled. When I unlatched
the window the bird looked back
three times over each shoulder
then shook his head.
He was never coming back inside,
and rose in a shower
of white dust above
the blazing roofs
and telephone poles.

It meant a child
would have to leave the world.

Almost all of the poems of this volume become entries and notations of homecoming and return. The title poem, "1933," seems to me one of Levine's finest. Surreal, gnarled, emotionally charged, and—in some ways—collapsing under the pressure of its own intensity, the poem rises to an elegiac beauty that allows the poet an essential recovery of his childhood. It is also a profound declaration of loss. The poem brings together again the son and the lost father (as will the later poems "Starlight" and "The Face") in the most elemental of meetings. The voiceless father, whose voice arises in his son, the poet, and the details of their mutual loss will continue to thread their way through other of Levine's poems. It is the poem "1933" that freed

Levine to write two of his most astonishing poems, also poems of sons and fathers, "New Season" and "My Son and I." The poem "New Season" represents the culmination of Levine's work to this stage. It is personal and yet public; it concerns both the private matters of his life (the daily events in the life of one of his sons and the occasion of his mother's seventieth birthday) and the public past (the Detroit race riots that occurred when Levine was fifteen). In spite of its length, let me quote in full "New Season" in order to show the "braided" narrative movement the poem employs, a movement that occurs in many of Levine's best poems:

> My son and I go walking in the garden.
> It is April 12, Friday, 1974.
> Teddy points to the slender trunk
> of the plum and recalls the digging
> last fall through three feet
> of hard pan and opens his palms
> in the brute light of noon, the heels
> glazed with callus, the long fingers
> thicker than mine and studded with
> silver rings. My mother is 70 today.
> He flicks two snails off a leaf
> and smashes them underfoot
> on the red brick path. Saturday,
> my wife stood here, her cheek cut
> by a scar of dirt, dirt on her bare
> shoulders, on the brown belly,
> damp and sour in the creases
> of her elbows. She held up a parsnip
> squat, misshapen, a tooth pulled
> from the earth, and laughed
> her great white laugh. Teddy talks
> of the wars of the young, Larry V.
> and Ricky's brother in the movies,
> on Belmont, at McDonald's,
> ready to fight for nothing, hard,
> redded or on air, "low riders,
> grease, what'd you say about my mama!"
> Home late, one in the back seat,

his fingers broken, eyes welling
with pain, the eyes and jawbones
swollen and rough. 70 today, the woman
who took my hand and walked me
past the corridor of willows
to the dark pond where the one swan
drifted. I start to tell him
and stop, the story of my 15th spring.
That a sailor had thrown a black baby
off the Belle Isle Bridge was
the first lie we heard, and the city
was at war for real. We would waken
the next morning to find Sherman tanks
at the curb and soldiers camped
on the lawns. Damato said he was
"goin downtown bury a hatchet
in a nigger's head." Women
took coffee and milk to the soldiers
and it was one long block party
till the trucks and tanks loaded up
and stumbled off. No one saw
Damato for a week, and when I did
he was slow, head down, his right arm
blooming in a great white bandage.
He said nothing. On mornings I rise
early, I watch my son in the bathroom,
shirtless, thick-armed and hard,
working with brush and comb
at his full blond head that suddenly
curled like mine and won't
come straight. 7 years passed
before Della Daubien told me
how three white girls from the shop
sat on her on the Woodward streetcar
so the gangs couldn't find her
and pull her off like they did
the black janitor and beat
an eye blind. She would never

forget, she said, and her old face
glows before me in shame
and terror. Tonight, after dinner,
after the long, halting call
to my mother, I'll come out here
to the yard rinsed in moonlight
that blurs it all. She will not
become the small openings
in my brain again through which the wind
rages, though she was the ocean
that ebbed in my blood, the storm clouds
that battered my lungs, though I hide
in the crotch of the orange tree
and weep where the future grows
like a scar, she will not come again
in the brilliant day. My cat Nellie,
5 now, follows me, safe
in the dark from mockingbird
and jay, her fur frost tipped
in the pure air, and together we hear
the wounding of the rose, the willow
on fire—to the dark pond
where the one swan drifted, the woman
is 70 now—the willow is burning,
the rhododendrons shrivel
like paper under water, all
the small secret mouths are feeding
on the green heart of the plum.

This melding of the narrative line with present and recollective detail is a crucial feature of Levine's later poetry. The narrative voice, with its measured intelligence and quiet confidence, shares a kinship with the voice of "The Cemetery at Academy, California" and other earlier poems. It has been a natural progression from the seven-syllable syllabic line to the primarily three-beat "free verse" line that characterizes these later poems. The conversational ease of this voice is always remarkable, and Levine seems closest here to one of his ambitions—to bring forward a body of poetry that is accessible to *all* readers. It's instructive to look again at what Levine himself has to say about the development of this aspect of his poetry, in particular about his use of the three-beat line. In a passage from an interview with David Remnick, he says: "I think I developed that line from my favorite line, which is Yeats's trimeter line. I think it comes from an attempt to find a free verse equivalent. He can use it in a song-like way or mold it into long paragraphs of terrific rhythmic power. I was very early awed by the way he could keep the form and let the syntax fall across it in constantly varying ways, the way certain sixteenth-century poets could with pentameter. The short line appeals to me because I think it's easier to make long statements that accumulate great power in short lines. You can flow line after line, and the breaks become less significant because there are so many of them, and they build to great power."

It is equally important to consider the issue of Philip Levine's political beliefs, which he calls "anarchist" and which are, in fact, quite simple: he believes an individual human being is of more value than any government; he believes human freedom and dignity are the world's most precious resources (as opposed to, say, gold and oil); he believes that faith in the individual and the truthful (poetic) use of language are both political acts. In the preface to his book of interviews, *Don't Ask*, Levine writes: "When I refer to myself as an anarchist I do not mean to invoke the image of a terrorist or even a man who would burn the deed to his house because 'property is theft,' which I happen to believe is true. I don't believe in the validity of governments, laws, charters, all that hide us from our essential oneness. 'We are put on earth a little space,' Blake wrote, 'That we may learn to bear the beams of love.' And so in my poems I memorialize those men and women who struggled to bear that love. I don't believe in victory in my lifetime, I'm not sure I believe in victory at all, but I do believe in the struggle and preserving the names and natures of those who fought, for their sakes, for my sake, and for those who come after." And in an interview with Arthur Smith, he adds: "I think the writing of a poem is a political act. We now exist in the kind of a world that Orwell was predicting, and the simple insistence upon accurate language has become a political act. Nothing is more obvious than what our politicians are doing to our language, so that if poets insist on the truth, or on an accurate rendition, or on a faithful use of language, if they for instance insist on an accurate depiction of people's lives as they are actually lived—this is a political act."

Philip Levine has always written poetry that is also more overtly political, and much of the best of it in his *Selected Poems* is drawn from the volumes

*The Names of the Lost* and *7 Years from Somewhere*: "Gift for a Believer"; "On the Murder of Lieutenant Jose Del Castillo by the Falangist Bravo Martinez, July 12, 1936"; "On a Drawing by Flavio"; "Francisco, I'll Bring You Red Carnations"; and two exceptionally powerful poems of domestic politics, "Ask the Roses" and "To My God in His Sickness." In these poems, as always in his work, Levine is giving voice to those without, as he returns "names" and presence to those whose names have been taken from them or erased by history. There is often a barely restrained passion in these poems; for those who prize decorum above all else in their poetry, Levine's poems will seem ill-mannered in their fierce convictions and desires. Like few other American poets, Levine forces us to consider our own moral values and, more generally, the place of moral values in any body of poetry. Levine's ethics are often the true refrain of his poems.

Levine managed, in his book *One for the Rose*, to disconcert some of his readers and to delight the rest with the kaleidoscope of voices and the fragments of self given full stage there. There is an imaginative range to these poems that remains pleasing and surprising even after many readings, and a mad, rakish quality that is invigorating. Levine's humor is at its most relaxed and open: the characters in these poems are full of extravagant and playful gestures, impossible histories, and biting commentaries. A sampling of these exuberant speakers includes: the world's first pilot; "The Conductor of Nothing," who rides trains endlessly back and forth across the country; a man who believes he once lived as a fox (and behaves accordingly); and a foundling who may well be the embodiment of the Second Coming! They are the most appealing gallery of rogues and impostors and saints of any book of American poetry in recent years. Still, perhaps the most powerful works of this period are the more typically "Levine" poems, "Having Been Asked 'What Is a Man?' I Answer" and "To Cipriano, in the Wind." Both of these poems address the nature of human dignity. The former considers courage in the face of serious illness; the latter celebrates the fierce beliefs of man from Levine's past:

> Where did your words go,
> Cipriano, spoken to me 38 years
> ago in the back of Peerless Cleaners,
> where raised on a little wooden platform
> you bowed to the hissing press
> and under the glaring bulb the scars

across your shoulders—"a gift
of my country"—gleamed like old wood.
"*Dignidad*," you said into my boy's
wide eyes, "without is no riches."
And Ferrente, the dapper Sicilian
coatmaker, laughed. What could
a pants presser know of dignity?

In Levine's most recent collection, *Sweet Will*, he uses as an epigraph to
the book a passage from Wordsworth that concludes, "Ne'er saw I, never
felt, a calm so deep!/The river glideth at his own sweet will...." *Sweet Will* has
been seen by some reviewers as a transitional volume, a book that takes up
past concerns of Levine's poetry. Yet *Sweet Will* strikes me as an especially
autobiographical collection, more nakedly so than any other of Levine's
books. Like the river in the passage from Wordsworth, Levine glides ever for-
ward, carrying with him his own past. The poems here carry with them the
great freedom of voice won by the work of *One for the Rose*. It's my own feel-
ing that *Sweet Will is* both a reckoning with past themes and concerns and
also a sequence of highly personal and revealing annotations to those *Selected
Poems*. Levine addresses his own past in the most direct manner of his career.
Once again, he examines the current of politics in his poetry as it's expressed
in the context of the crushing American workplace and in the history of
European anarchism. But he announces most explicitly what he considers the
real continuity of purpose in all of his poetic works—that he is, first and fore-
most, a storyteller, a moral storyteller. The poem that serves as a centerpiece
for *Sweet Will*, "A Poem with No Ending," begins, "So many poems begin
where they/should end, and never end./Mine never end, they run on/book
after book, complaining/to the moon that heaven is wrong/or dull, no place
at all to be./I believe all this." And it's true that all of Levine's work can be
seen as being of a piece; like "To Cipriano, in the Wind," all of his poetry
seems, whether public or private, to revolve around the questions of human
freedom and human dignity. A poem that exhibits this force in Levine's
poetry as dramatically as any is the title poem of this volume, "Sweet Will."
A paradigm of the complex braiding of concerns that occurs in all of Levine's
work, this poem is another of the defiant celebrations of the individual that
distinguish his poetry. "Sweet Will":

The man who stood beside me
34 years ago this night fell

on to the concrete, oily floor
of Detroit Transmission, and we
stepped carefully over him until
he wakened and went back to his press.

It was Friday night, and the others
told me that every Friday he drank
more than he could hold and fell
and he wasn't any dumber for it
so just let him get up at his
own sweet will or he'll hit you.

"At his own sweet will," was just
what the old black man said to me,
and he smiled the smile of one
who is still surprised that dawn
graying the cracked and broken windows
could start us all to singing in the cold.

Stash rose and wiped the back of his head
with a crumpled handkerchief and looked
at his own blood as though it were
dirt and puzzled as to how
it got there and then wiped the ends
of his fingers carefully one at a time

the way the mother wipes the fingers
of a sleeping child, and climbed back
on his wooden soda-pop case to
his punch press and hollered at all
of us over the oceanic roar of work,
addressing us by our names and nations—

"Nigger, Kike, Hunky, River Rat,"
but he gave it a tune, an old tune,
like "America the Beautiful." And he danced
a little two-step and smiled showing
the four stained teeth left in the front

and took another suck of cherry brandy.

In truth it was no longer Friday,
for night had turned to day as it
often does for those who are patient,
so it was Saturday in the year of '48
in the very heart of the city of man
where your Cadillac cars get manufactured.

In truth all those people are dead,
they have gone up to heaven singing
"Time on My Hands" or "Begin the Beguine,"
and the Cadillacs have all gone back
to earth, and nothing that we made
that night is worth more than me.

And in truth I'm not worth a thing
what with my feet and my two bad eyes
and my one long nose and my breath
of old lies and my sad tales of men
who let the earth break them back,
each one, to dirty blood or bloody dirt.

Not worth a thing! Just like it was said
at my magic birth when the stars
collided and fire fell from great space
into great space, and people rose one by one
from cold beds to tend a world
that runs on and on at its own sweet will.

This poem, like the body of Philip Levine's poetry, makes one simple demand of us—that we read it by the light of human compassion. Quietly, dramatically, with growing power and beauty, the poetry of Philip Levine has become both the pulse and conscience of American poetry. He is one of our few essential poets, and in his eloquent voice he reminds us of the courage required to sing the most worthy songs.

# HOME AT LAST

In *Travels*, one of the most beautiful and moving collections of poetry of his career, W.S Merwin displays his narrative gifts (more familiar, perhaps, to readers of his elegant prose) to provide us with a book of deep historical resonance and luminous poetic grace. These new poems revolve around complex issues of passage through time's portals of birth and death, through experience, over the earth and through the natural world. In the poem "The Hill of Evening," a meditation on aging, Merwin says. "I was thinking again/ of age and of what in each season seems/just out of reach just beyond what/ is in front of us a kind of ghost/of what we see to which we offer up our days."

This is W.S. Merwin's fourteenth collection of poetry. With each new book we have been reminded why, for forty years, he has remained a pivotal figure in the literary life of this country. One of our most honored authors, our finest translator of poetry from other cultures, and a prose writer of immense range and power ("The Lost Upland," his most recent prose work, was one of only nine books selected for the *New York Times Book Review*'s list of best books of 1992), W.S. Merwin continues to earn his place as one of our most influential and compelling contemporary poets.

Those who know Merwin's poetry are familiar with its timeless, even mythic qualities. There is often an extraordinary sense of urgency to the language—the densely charged utterances of a Merwin poem—yet his work seems always to revolve around a deeply calm and spiritual gravitational center. An acutely attentive poet, he is invariably a startling and inventive maker of images, one whose spare lines and seemingly stark, unpunctuated stanzas tend to keep the reader off guard, allowing a poem's phrasings to convey a sense of constant surprise. It is an inspired tactic, as it serves to demand an alertness and complicity of his readers, one which entwines us in the narrative movements of his poems.

Yet Merwin's much-imitated and exhaustively discussed poetic style, forged in the seminal book "The Moving Target" and honed for the past thirty-five years, continues to be mildly revised and reinvented in each subsequent book. In *Travels*, he grants his storytelling impulses a greater freedom even as he continues a major focus of his earlier poetry, an investigation into the interrelatedness of humankind and the natural world. Merwin asks that we acknowledge and reflect upon our primary relationship with the earth. To this end, he sets us traveling through time and across geography to experience the aspects of passage he and the protagonists of his poetry—many of them naturalists and botanists—have experienced, that we might share their concerns and convictions.

In "The Blind Seer of Ambon," Merwin speaks as the 17th Century Dutch herbalist Rumpius (Georg Eberhard Rumpf), who lived most of his life in the East Indies. This ironic apologia could stand as Merwin's own:

> I may have seemed somewhat strange
> caring in my own time for living things
> with no value that we know
> languages wash over them
> one wave at a time.

From the outset, in his prefatory poem entitled "Cover Note," Merwin makes perfectly clear his purpose in *Travels*. Playing off "To the Reader," Baudelaire's famous prologue poem to *Les Fleurs du Mal*, Merwin addresses us directly:

> Hypocrite reader my
> variant my almost
> family we are so
> few now it seems as though
> we knew each other as
> the words between us keep
> assuming that we do
> I hope I make sense to

you in the shimmer of
our days while the world we
cling to in common is
burning.

Merwin's poems in *Travels* often bear witness to the pursuit or revelation
of nature's secrets, yet the wisdom borne by and born of these "secrets"
inevitably reflects one truth—that, after the travels we call our lives, we neces-
sarily return to our true and final home, the natural world. This seeking
after home—or the idea of home—drives many of Merwin's new poems. In
the marvelous piece "Rimbaud's Piano," we find the young poet-traveller
returning to his mother's house at Charleville, however briefly, before what
will be his self-exile to Africa. Having already abandoned poetry, Rimbaud
insists upon having a piano in the house, a somewhat desperate yet poignant
attempt to create some sustaining sense of self and home.

In the book's tour de force, a magical 19-page narrative, "The Real World
of Manuel Cordova," Merwin's title character is kidnapped in the upper
Amazon by a tribe that wishes to make him the heir to their dying chief.
They need an outsider, the tribe feels, who knows the intruding "alien"
forces of the white men in order to withstand them and survive. As he is
groomed to become chief, Cordova is initiated into the rites of the tribe,
including a drugged dream-travel in which he begins to discover the alchemy
of nature. Cordova is a man who walks along the cusp of the "civilized" and
"primitive" worlds until, at last fearing he'll collapse into the abyss that sepa-
rates the two, he escapes to his old "home."

*Travels* invokes many of these powerful voices, charting passages through
time-as-history, as well as time-as-aging. The landscapes here are both physical
and spiritual; for Merwin, the two are not divisible. Our choices and respon-
sibilities concerning one concern the other. In recent years, Merwin has
emerged as one of the most articulate spokespersons for ecological causes; his
work is filled with reminders of our failed earthly custodianship.

In an early stanza of the poem "Fulfillment," Merwin confronts us with
the harsh dilemmas of passage:

but what could we
do to prevent a day from ending
or a winter from finding
us how could we stop a wind

        with no home
from sliding into
our sleep or keep our parents
     from death
or ourselves from leaving.

The poem concludes with this solemn coda:

        summer is done and the last flocks have
vanished and from the sleepless
cold of the unremembered river that
one voice keeps rising
to be heard once once only once but there
is nobody listening.

Merwin continues to write, of course, in hope that we are listening. In his superb poem for biographer Leon Edel, "Writing Lives," he confesses:

        Out of a life it is done
and without ever knowing
how things will turn out
or what a life is for that matter
any life at all
the leaf in the sunlight
the voice in the day
the author in the words.

With the continuing benediction of his poetry, we as Merwin's readers are able to continue, perhaps more graciously and contentiously, along our own worldly travels. At the conclusion of "Cover Note," we discover the poet has armed us with

        words that I hope might seem
as though they had occurred
to you and you would take
them with you as your own.

Now, he seems to imply, it's up to us.

# Dark Harbor

The past thirty years have been good ones for American poetry. Never before have so many poets of true stature and lasting importance written so powerfully and beautifully, some addressing the urgent issues of social reckoning that presently face us, others exploring those timeless questions concerning the individual self and soul.

Mark Strand's stunning new book-length poem, *Dark Harbor*, comes to us as a timely reminder the great power and solace of American poetry at its very best. Across the landscape of the imagination, Strand sets in motion a familiar pilgrim of the self, a spirit, a seeker whose origins reside in Dante, Wordsworth and Leopardi.

In its forty-five parts (and opening "Proem"), *Dark Harbor* quietly unfolds "like pages torn from a family album," detailing the consolations of memory, the resiliencies of hope and the shifting of "a devotion/To the vagaries of desire." *Dark Harbor* is also a meditation on the speaker's longing—for both the refuge of the past and hoped for, if shadowy and death-darkened, harbor of the future. It is a book so deeply compelling, so heartbreaking, and so elegantly written that it arrives as the fulfillment of Strand's long and distinguished career.

One of our most recent Poet Laureates, a past MacArthur Fellow, and this year's recipient of the prestigious Bollingen prize, Strand has long been recognized as one of our premier poets. His translations (of Rafael Alberti and Carlos Drummond de Andrade) are essential contributions to Twentieth Century literature. Strand's writings on realist painting, in "The Art of the

Real," as well as his superb book on painter William Bailey (to whom *Dark Harbor* is dedicated), are models of contemporary art criticism; they also reflect a source for Strand's own painterly compositions.

Strand's poetry has often been discussed as a hybrid of the acutely perceived "real," as in the work of a poet like Elizabeth Bishop, and of the highly speculative and imaginative verbal pageants of a poet like Wallace Stevens. Strand himself has frequently acknowledged these poetic parents, yet never has their marriage seemed more apt than under the shaded arbors of *Dark Harbor*. The deceptive simplicity of Strand's lines and the exquisite eloquence of his cadences reflect an ease of intelligence unequaled since Stevens. In fact, in its abstract lyricism, *Dark Harbor's* most profound echoes seem to arise out of Stevens' gorgeous late poems, notably "Notes Towards a Supreme Fiction."

Many readers of Strand's early poetry (his *Selected Poems* appeared in 1980) are accustomed to work in which the self is predicated upon a renunciation of the world, or upon a recognition of the insubstantiality of all things. Indeed, it sometimes seems that the self is barely held by the sieve of these poems. Yet Strand's early work always desires to invent its own transparency, so that a more complex psychological life might be revealed.

These attempts to pare down the self to its own essentiality gave way somewhat in Strand's most recent collection, *The Continuous Life* (1990). Where once the quotidian was banished, the elements of daily life there found celebration. Now, in *Dark Harbor*, we find ourselves accompanying the poet along the course—the journey—of an artistic life. From the safety of home we begin what the speaker ironically calls "passages of greater and lesser worth," with the triple pun on "passages" of time, travel and poetry.

There is something resolutely personal and intimate illuminating the world of *Dark Harbor*. Out of the origins of childhood, Strand recognizes, we begin that simple passage toward oblivion. Constantly, Strand seeks to "embrace those origins as you would yourself," hoping to counterbalance "the weight of the future...." This is, after all, a poem of absolute departure, one which set us sailing toward a shore obscured by the indeterminate future. And, as in many great poems of departure, we find:

> ...if anyone suffers, wings can be had
> For a song or by trading arms, that the rules
>
> On earth still hold for those about to depart,

That it is best to be ready, for the ash
Of the body is worthleess and goes only so far.

At times, the delicately ephemeral and fabular quality of the writing seems
to lift us into the realm of dream. In Strand's poetry, dream and memory
often become the vehicles by which one traverses the harsh terrain of daily
life. Like the work of the great Italian writer Italo Calvino, there is also a
playful, even comic spirit stitched through the lines. The elegiac impulses of
*Dark Harbor* don't preclude this lighter touch; most often, we find a dry and
sardonic wit, though occasionally the humor turns broad, as in this passage
when:

A man who'd been cramped and bloated for weeks
Blew wide open. His wife, whose back was to him,

Didn't turn around right away to give everything—
The cheese and soggy bread— a chance to settle.

Early in *Dark Harbor*, the speaker asks every poets' question:

How do you turn pain
Into its own memorial, how do you write it down,

Turning it into itself as witnessed
Through pleasure, so it can be known, even loved....

This desire to understand the transformation of experience into poetry,
this yearning to experience that alchemical, Orphic equation stands at the
heart of this book. The poet's presiding fear, therefore, resonating through-
out the final passages of *Dark Harbor*, is that, like one's flesh, that other
body—of poetry—might also disappear. Near the conclusion of the poem the
speaker asks:

And after I go, as I must,
And come back through the hourglass, will I have proved
That I live against time, that the silk of the songs

I sang is not lost? Or will I have proved that whatever I love

Is unbearable, that the views of Lethe will never
Improve, that whatever I sing is blank?

As the speaker's profound sense of mortality rises, he fears the "truth is/
Soon the song deserts its maker." He imagines that the "measures of noth-
ingness/Are few. The Beyond is merely beyond,/A melancholy place of failed
and fallen stars." Yet, in the book's final section, a desolate version of the
afterlife that seems a playful combination of Rilke's angelic order and the raw
coast of Western Ireland, the speaker takes his place in a group—of other
departed poets, it seems—gathered around a fire. We're left with this image
of arrival and consolation as he looks into the distance, toward the hill:

Above the river, where the golden lights of sunset

And sunrise are one and the same, and I saw something flying
Back and forth, fluttering its wings. Then it stopped in mid-air.
It was an angel, one of the good ones, about to sing.

# MATERIALISM

The distrust between poets and philosophers is ancient, and like all disputes over turf and borders, each side usually views the other with deep and enduring suspicion. In her poetry, Jorie Graham has always stood a bit precariously on the narrow cusp of this barely civilized mayhem, siding with neither of the antagonists yet drawing her strength as a poet from them both. Graham's fifth collection of poems is a startling and commanding step forward for one of our most exciting younger poets. *Materialism* is a book-length meditation on the nature of the spirit and the nature of "matter in our material world"—concerns that echo throughout her work. The destruction of our body and the loss of our cultural selves are at the heart of Graham's poetry, as are questions about the future of the modern soul. Graham has always been an intensely philosophical poet, as abstract and "difficult" in her own way as John Ashbery; yet like Ashbery she writes with such passion, beauty and sensual love of language that she is able to rescue even the most highly abstruse of poetic passages. In her introduction, as editor, to *The Best American Poetry 1990*, Graham reminds us that poetry "implicitly undertakes a critique of materialist values." In fact, *Materialism* could have sprung from a question posited in a poem ("Who Watches From the Back Porch") from Graham's previous collection, *Regions of Unlikeness*, in which she asks, "Is it because of history or because of matter,/mother Matter—the opposite of In-/terpretation.../that we feel so sure we lied,/or that this, here, this thing/is."

*Materialism* is punctuated by a series of poems, all tellingly entitled "Notes on the Reality of the Self," which contain some of the book's most compelling and searing self-questioning. In one instance, the speaker says, "I put my/breath back out/onto the scented immaterial. How the Invisible/roils." Later, with both personal and poetic disquiet, this penetrating question follows, "Is there a new way of looking—/valances and little hooks—inevitabilities, proba-/bilities? It flaps and slaps. Is this body the one/I know as me? How private these words?" With *Materialism*, Jorie Graham has written many of her finest poems to date. The poem, "The Dream of the Unified Field" stands as one of her most dazzling accomplishments. Interleaved with these poems are passages drawn from what are described as some of "the great male voices of Western culture": Plato, Sir Francis Bacon, Emerson, Brecht, Wittengenstein, Jonathan Edwards, Walter Benjamin, Whitman, not to mention Leonardo da Vinci. Some are represented with selections as discrete as filets and others with whole slabs of philosophical beef.

The project of *Materialism* is both to offer and to challenge these voices, from the the perspective of Graham's own poetic female "otherness." Jorie Graham often has—to my ear, at least—the upper hand in these implied conversations, as her language is predictably more supple and sensual. Yet the sense of interchange is far more successful than one might at first imagine. And, having tuned her poetic satellite dish across time in this way, Graham makes it possible for us as readers to imagine we're overhearing those urgent whispers of thinkers and artists who can, she clearly feels, help to provide a kind of civilizing, meditative context for the brutalities and incongruities of our public and personal histories. For some readers, Graham's work has often seemed too laden with philosophical and artistic allusions, as if the poems existed in a kind of echo chamber of traditional Western culture, invoking both its best and worst aspects with equal—therefore suspect— aplomb. To my mind, this resonance has always been a great virtue of her work, a shrewd way of reckoning with and revising those many influences and traditions that any artist inherits.

Perhaps to more fully appreciate the power and accomplishment of her recent poems, it might be helpful to back up a moment and take a brief overview of Jorie Graham's poetry. Her first two books, *Hybrids of Plants and Ghosts* (which takes its title from Nietzsche) and *Erosion*, were also philosophically inclined, self-consciously involving the likes of Voltaire, Plato, Montesquieu and Bergson. Yet even in this early work, the constant counterbalance to these philosophical heavyweights was the powerful influence upon her poetry of the world's great art, especially the works of the Italian Renaissance. This combination of complex influences, as she moved from the more conventional stylistic gestures of her first two volumes to the far more expansive and discursive meditations of her next two volumes, *The End of Beauty* and *Regions of Unlikeness*, served to help unlock Graham and her poetry. With these latter titles, she emerged as one of our most highly imaginative and innovative poets.

Stylistically, Jorie Graham has always employed a highly cinematic sense of movement. Her poems are theatrical and gestural, even a bit talky. In the past, Graham has used a pocket tape recorder in drafting her poems, to help generate this conversational effect. It is important to Jorie Graham, as it has been for many other modern artists, that her work clearly reflect the act of its own making, its own fluid processes. In much of Graham's poetry, her speculative impulses, set free in self-conversations on the spiritual in nature and the nature of the spirit, are often posited against backdrops of Western religious iconography and classical mythology. In "Materialism," she chooses the male "mythic" texts of our philosophical heritage to serve the same purpose. In this way, she has been able to consider and revise those very myths and/or inherited ideas that have propagated our understanding of ourselves—or perhaps misunderstanding—across time. It is this revisionary ambition that stalks the poems of *Materialism*, allowing the hard, shifting edge of her lines to reflect the oscillations of a mind at work.

In "The Visible World," a poem that appears late in *Materialism*, the poet asks, "What heat is this in me/that would thaw time, making bits of instance/overlap/shovel by shovelful—my present a wind blowing through/this culture/ slogged and clutched-firm with decisions, over-ridings,/opportunities/taken?"

Jorie Graham's speculative and sensual poetry exemplifies the poetic hallmarks of the most powerful writing of the late 20th Century: multiplicity, simultaneity and polyvocality. It echoes an aesthetic and cultural past but is, truly, like nothing we've seen before.

# II.
## ROMAN NOON: AN INTERLUDE

It is noon. The sun is just starting to shift. All morning, it has drenched the tables of the outdoor café at one side of the Piazza della Rotonda, fronting the Pantheon. S is there, drinking espresso, writing. Soon the table where he sits will be in shadow; he'll rise slowly, gathering his cigarettes and books, scattering some stray *lire* for the waiter. Then, he'll walk a few dozen yards to the café on the other side of the piazza where, he knows from fifteen years' experience, the sun will be good for the whole afternoon. He settles himself. Without having ordered, he is brought an espresso. Everyone knows his routine.

Just up the way, on the Camop Marzio, C is up in his apartment, his serene white apartment, writing an article or book review for *La Republica*. Or perhaps he's working on the lectures he is meant to give, in the coming year, in America. Words love C; he is their Magus. They hover on the terraces of his apartment, waiting to be called. The view from these terraces is superb, the words acknowledge, a panorama of Rome; yet it is never as remarkable as the view through C's eyes. It is *his* vision, *his* touch, that they desire. It is the dream of words to be issued upon his breath, delivered upon his tongue. He will die before even the first sentence of the first lecture is given—the sentence he has just written, a moment ago—yet they will survive; they will be tended, his words, with his own rare humor and reverence. They will survive. Like history, like Rome.

If C had risen for a moment, to stretch or walk over to the window, he might have seen me stepping out of a bar after a quick espresso, on my way to lunch with a friend, at Il Buco perhaps, where I'll sit late into the afternoon, a little drunk, sipping *Vin Santo*. Or I might be headed, instead, up to the Piazza del Popolo, to sit outside at Rosati, admiring the parade of *ragazzi* and the more refined lunch crowd. There is a man near where I am sitting;

161

he's standing just at the edge of the tables, clearly waiting for someone. Looking left, looking right. A cab pulls up in front of the door to Rosati and pauses, motor idling. No one gets out at first. I can't see if anyone is inside; the reflection of the sunlight on the windows has turned them an impenetrable silver, like the mirrored sunglasses the waiting man is wearing. Abruptly, a woman steps from the cab and turns slowly until she sees him. She is in her early forties, and she is shining. Her hair is the color made of a mist of champagne mixed with sepia, a shimmering that collects at her shoulders where, even in this heat, her elegant fur coat begins, falling in dark shadows to her ankles. She is so beautiful that every eye follows her as she breaks into a run (expertly on high heels) for the whole length of the cafe; she throws her arms around his neck and holds him to her. It is theater. It is opera. It is thrilling. She means, I can tell, every bit of it, too, from the bottom of her exquisite heart. What can he feel but love? And what do these old lovers discover after all these years? That he is moderately successful (I hear him saying, for they've taken the table beside mine), but nevertheless discouraged by life, especially by love. And she...she works in film now, a former actress turned producer, spending most of her time in America, in Washington, D.C., where she has a lover so famous she cannot, for discretion's sake, actually name him. He is married. He is, to her world, the Anonymous One. And she too is discouraged, especially by love. I finish my Campari and leave, walking across the Piazza del Popolo, to the steps leading up to the Pincio and its view of the city. I look back once, briefly. They are still not yet holding hands. Not yet. Almost....

After I climb to the Pincio, I might take a walk through the park of the Villa Borghese. In the *galoppatoio* aristocratic girls are beginning their noontime riding lessons, backs stiff in the saddle, lovely mouths set in a pucker of slight surprise, eyes fixed on some unknowable horizon. Oaks and umbrella pines. They can hear, from the soccer field not far in the distance, the shouts of boys who have gathered slowly in a pick-up game, each having stopped on his way home from a half-day's work or school. They've piled jackets and book bags at each end of the field to mark the goals, and the silver-and-black soccer ball ricochets back and forth across the field like a smooth, silver ball bearing in a pinball machine. I'm watching, sitting on a green bench, happy, but also wishing I were in Trastevere, having a lazy lunch at der Belli, my favorite trattoria, named for the poet who lived in the quarter. I love it there; I love the food and the sardonic Sardinians who run the place. Who was it who said there's nothing like a café named after a poet to make you think the world is just and good?—especially if you can eat and drink cheaply there.

Where else might I be during a Roman noon? On the terrace outside my writing studio, a converted potting shed that is built right into the old Aurelian wall. There, the legions of lizards who guard the studio will appear for me to inspect them, green or silver, glistening in the heat. I praise their good work. They crawl up the legs of the table to touch their heads to the cool bottle of *Frascati* I've placed there; they are awaiting their next orders. But I'm busy, writing you a letter about the *scirocco* that hit Rome two days ago, mixing the pollen of the cypress and umbrella pines with the red dust of Morocco—the oppressive blasts of the hot winds shouldering their ways along the street until, by its end, an inch-think crust of dust had been laid over the city. The roofs and walkways all streaked with yellow pollen and powdery, red Moroccan dirt. On an old Lancia parked on the street leading into the Piazza del Gianicolo, someone had drawn a message—*Giulia te amo*—and as the couple ahead of me passed it, they nodded in grave approval of such testimony. Then, from the overlook there at the Garibaldi monument, at the top of the Gianicolo, where the view of Rome is more spectacular than any other, the couple—older than I'd at first supposed—stood quietly, occasionally pointing out to one another a familiar church or monument. They were Roman; they loved watching over their city. The man slipped his hand out of the crook of his wife's arm and patted her ass briefly, right where the line of her grey cardigan sweater met the black of her skirt. I turned and started walking back toward one of the long stairways leading down into Trastevere, the *scirocco* over the city pulsing. On my way, I stood for a moment by the Fontana Paola, the water of the fountain as loud as a river's rapids, the cool mist blowing wildly, settling the dust around me. I stood there, imagining how I might write you about my own place in it all. Stairways and fountains, dust and stone. A man alone in the Roman noon.

# III.
## INTERVIEWS

# RENAMING THE PRESENT

This interview was conducted by Rick Jackson for *Poetry Miscellany*.

POETRY MISCELLANY: *Hush* is particularly interesting for the conception of language that operates throughout the book There is always something elusive. As Heidegger would have it, there is a presencing that does not presence, or arrive. The character in "Coming Home" is always in the process of doing just that, always being deferred. The elusiveness is manifested in your repeated use of words like "something," "or," and "perhaps"—there is a subjunctive or "undecidable" cast, to borrow from Paul De Man, to this language. And yet, this very language of absences can provide a Derridian "supplement," as in "Naming the Unborn," where the lost son is named as if to presence him. And in the poem for Peter Everwine there is a similar presencing, here of a whole world, the son, the field that will be spoken in silence. There is an elaborate gathering of signs, of "traces," if we want to keep this terminology from linguistics and philosophy, that makes a presence of absence in "Hush." The poem becomes, as you say to your son, "The dark watermark of your absence, a hush." Words become not so much denotative signs but signifiers; a poem is made of "some few words that sound like music and the sea." Perhaps, in this context, you could begin by sketching your sense of your language and how it has changed.

DAVID ST. JOHN: These things that you mention have always been for me the

most important aspects in poems. The episodic detail in all the poems is cru-
cial to the way I want the poems to move, crucial to the texture of the lan-
guage. I think of "Gin" as a kind of *Ars Poetica* with its fragmented newspa-
per account of murder at the beginning, the business of the friends complain-
ing that "Even your stories/have no point, just lots of detail," and the other
"disguises of omission" that occur. The false causalities, the positing of con-
gruent alternatives through a poem are ways, for me, to describe through
those "tracings" some area of concern. I'm not interested in trying to name
something with one name because I don't believe whatever I'm discussing
has one name. To name something in a fixed way involves a fallacy for me.
In my poems there is that kind of "sliding of signifiers" that Jacques Lacan
describes, the verbal texture that Barthes is describing in "The Eiffel Tower."
What I mean is that there is a great deal of difference between the subject or
sequence of subjects that a poem takes on and what I would call the "move-
ment." I do believe in this context that poems are models of consciousness,
and I think that's their value. Exploring or experiencing a poem has to do
with exploring a progression of consciousness about an area of concern. This
is why the episodic detail is so important; I try to allow the poems to propel
themselves through narrative details that are distractingly specific yet have
enough commitment to a beginning and an end so as not to prove merely
frustrating.

Yeats' statement, "I seek an image of the modern mind's discovery of itself,"
seemed to define poetic activity in the early part of this century. For me,
there's been an enormous revision of that; I seek the movement or progres-
sion of the mind's discovery of itself. That's an enormous distinction,
because it takes the sense of the imagistic construct, which is necessarily and
implicitly fixed, and suggests a more kinetic grammar of poetry.

POETRY MISCELLANY: There's a subversion of simple simile and metaphor. "A"
is not simply like "B," but rather "A" suggests "B," which in turn conjures
"C," and so on—Lacan's chain of signifiers.

DAVID ST. JOHN: Exactly. It's the movement that is important, not just A, B,
and C themselves. I think that the experience throughout the twentieth cen-
tury, after the lesson of *The Waste Land* and fragmentation had been
learned, is that as experience grows more fragmentary and disjunctive, we
need a model of consciousness that's more fluid and capable of absorbing
those jagged experiences. A set, structured model of consciousness seems to

me simply too vulnerable to suit contemporary experiences. Perhaps that is why the "deep image" seemed out of date so quickly, for however deep those images were, they were also fixed and static. On the other hand, James Wright's great value was not his reliance on that imagism, but his humanity and compassion, his enormous lyric gifts, his sense of the flow of things, of language.

POETRY MISCELLANY: This movement you have been describing tends to suggest a non-referential poetry. At least, the poems are often self-referential. A poem is always also about itself. And yet there is always a reference to an implicit "you"—Wright has this in a very different way—an "Other," as Lacan calls it, that provides a vague, even absent center. I've been reading an essay by Susan and Leslie Brisman that talks about the way all lyric poetry is implicitly an appeal to a supremely responsive auditor.

DAVID ST. JOHN: The poems in the latter half of *Hush* are enormously self-referential. That's also the reason why so many of the poems use the second-person address. It is a way to create tension, not only in the fact that the poems are to some extent also a self-address, but because with the second person I can evoke a kind of accusation of the reader as well. All the tension of the Lacanian Other is necessary for me. In most regards, in writing the poems I try not to be conscious of it in a pragmatic way, but the tension of the I/You address has always been crucial to the movement of the poems. In "Slow Dance" the conception of the "you" is probably the most difficult of any of the poems in *Hush*. It floats in and out of being more and less specific; there are times when it is very directed, times when it seems self-referential, times when it seems very general. Of the poems in the book it's probably my favorite because these kinds of maneuvers are done with as much grace as any of the other things I've done there. Now, I've tried to make the poems in *The Shore*, with the unavoidable exception of "Of the Remembered," less self-referential. But the others maintain the fiction of a specific Other, a specific "You" to which there's a specific relationship. That provides, I suppose, a more apparent and available surface. But what interests me is still the subterfuge, the maneuvers, the ways temporalities can be fragmented and superimposed, that tension between the namings and the mis-namings, the verbal texture, the positionings of the "you."

POETRY MISCELLANY: What holds all these things together is *voice*. As this trace movement progresses, as the poems radiate out, often leaping dramatically, as does the opening poem in *The Olive Grove*, for example, the voice provides a coherence, a believability. It allows the "stew," as you call it in "Gin," to disguise its origins without the loss of a base; it allows the poems coincidentally to "bloom/In such false directions."

DAVID ST. JOHN: Yes, to involve the kind of duplicities, the kinds of false presencing that goes on in the poems requires the necessary paradox of the strong presence of the voice. If the poems have any sense of authority at all, it's a sense of conviction that the voice presence enacting those poems is, if not to be trusted, at least to be heard. I feel that if I can maintain that and still accomplish the kinds of things I want to do beneath the surface, then that's as much as I can ask now. I like some of the poems in *Hush* to read as self-betrayals; the vulnerability is great in a poem like "Gin," where the details are given up, admitted by the voice. That's also true of poems in *The Shore*, though the narrative axis is more specific. The poems in *The Shore* were very single-mindedly thought out in terms of that voice presence. The riskiest poem is "Of the Remembered" because it generates multiple presences; the character of the voice changes from section to section as if the whole poem were a sort of autobiographical hologram that could create a sense of space in which I wanted to move. The presence in poems like "Blue Waves" and "Until the Sea Is Dead" is more consistent, a presence which is willing to posit an aura in a way the poems in *Hush* are unwilling, that they were in fact resisting. When I teach, the thing that concerns me most with young writers is that they recognize that poems are voice presences. It seems to take a very talented young writer about six years of trying on voices and masks to find the voice that most closely approximates the self or the idea of the self that they want to occur in the poems. It's this more intimate kind of persona poetry that interests me. I try to ask young poets to question themselves, to ask themselves: "Who's in that poem?" and "What presence, what self is being portrayed in this language?"

POETRY MISCELLANY: On a nuts-and-bolts level, voice can be strongly given in the line. This has to do not just with the ways disparate items can be held in one line, but with the ways sentences and fragments interweave in the lines, play off against them. How has your sense of the line changed with your sense of voice?

DAVID ST JOHN: In the last part of *Hush*, especially in "Slow Dance," when I began working in longer lines, I was able to work a verbal suspension that the more specifically imagistic, short-line poems that I had once written simply couldn't hold. The longer line enabled me to create a more sophisticated verbal imperative. I could push a reader through a line and then drop the reader to the fragment or line following in a way that would, I hoped, accomplish that false causality, that suspension, and even more important, that sense of movement in which the poem continues to propel through the details and extensions of rhythm that mark a consciousness, a voice. In *The Shore*, particularly in "Until the Sea Is Dead," I began working with a shorter line again and found I was able to continue a kind of narrative movement, a kind of fragmenting of temporalities, but with a much more measured pace, with a less wild movement through the poems.

POETRY MISCELLANY: We've been edging toward a more direct discussion of the nature of narrative. A kind of Nietzschean genealogy seems to lurk behind what you've been saying. "The River" describes history as "taking every irrespective turn against the grain" and then "How/The sand is taken, only to be put down later." History becomes a matter of chance. Could you sketch out a little more fully your sense of narrative in relation to this sort of history? I'm thinking of section IX of "Of the Remembered"; there you talk about history, myth, and making up a story only to admit: "I've only taken pieces of several/To make one story I love, one chord/I hear most." These details give a sense of the poem emerging out of its own stuff.

DAVID ST. JOHN: Yes, that's what I want; I want the poem to arrive out of itself, to discover itself. The sense of chance is very important to me. I first tried to deal with it in the poem "Four O'Clock in Summer: Hope," which describes in the first section the painting by Yves Tanguy and the chance way the elements of the painting fall into place and out of place, could be one thing or another. There *is* a sense of randomness in the way the future passes back into the past. It was, in a sense, the falseness of drawing those distinctions that I wanted to talk about. The narratives of most of my poems are in fact dis-narratives: they exist by taking fragments and joining them as invisibly as possible so that the reader has the sense of a whole story controlled by the voice or voices that speak it. This seems to me a very realistic notion of how things work; just as in daily life our attention goes in and out of focus, we preserve a continuity in terms of our temporality. It parallels the way

171

memory invades a present or the way dreams and desires, just other names for the future, invade the present. All of these invasions, these disruptions and eruptions, are very important to talk about. Unless we acknowledge them, they can be enormously threatening, even overwhelming. Unless you can maintain a narrative line in a poem that has as many scenes, sequences, and emotional temporalities as "Slow Dance" does, you'd get stopped at every point, swamped. The narrative has to create a movement strong enough—like the movement of the river itself, even accumulating not so important details—to keep the poem going.

POETRY MISCELLANY: "Until the Sea Is Dead" intermingles the Russian trader story, inserts a voice into it at the beginning, adds a sense of the real past in the story of the two, and in the last few pages produces that sense of the undecidable we were discussing earlier. The whole thing makes a complex web, a "supreme fiction," as Stevens would say.

DAVID ST. JOHN: There are two anecdotes that have to do with *The Shore* as a whole which deal specifically with what you're saying. The poems in the volume contain a lot of autobiographical detail, but they aren't in themselves autobiographical. They're fictions. After reading the manuscript, a very close friend of mine asked me how much was truly autobiographical, how much fiction, and she was shocked to find that only certain details were true. A great deal had been invented to duplicate the movement in types of situations, kinds of emotional concerns. The other anecdote is that when I received the proofs back from *The New Yorker* for "Until the Sea Is Dead" someone in their checking department had written in it that the story about the Russian trader was unknown to anyone who could be reached in Fort Ross. It seemed wonderful to me that someone just assumed the story was true. I realized that part had been successful.

POETRY MISCELLANY: How did the poem originate?

DAVID ST. JOHN: I wanted to include a very defined story within a story. I knew when the poem began what the story was going to be in terms of the metaphor, the trader, the woman, and how I wanted it to return later on. Initially, the episode that now ends the poem was set earlier on, and then a friend who read that version said that the episode should end the poem. As soon as she said that, everything fell perfectly into place and I was able to end it in a few weeks. What I had tried to do was bring the poem to another climax before the end, but that violated the meditative movement of the last forty lines.

POETRY MISCELLANY: You've mentioned the notion of temporality several times here, especially in connection with the narrative movement of pieces. Your sense of time is one of the most sophisticated in contemporary poetry. Earlier, in *Hush* say, in "Six/Nine/Forty-Four," there is a juxtapositioning of space and time. In "The Color of Salvation," the character's last friend lives in moments that are comprised of other times yet hold "all of life." But what I have in mind here is the more complex vision that informs *The Shore*. The past exists always as a fragment as in "Hotel Sierra"—at the beginning it is a "place without a past for us," but by the end the fragments have been so presenced by the voice that a past has been created. In fact, the two have all they can do to break away from it, to "travel in their own time," at the end. "The Shore" itself is an attempt to break away from the tyranny of the past, which gets repeated in gestures like the watching of the scene below the peo ple in the poem. "Elegy" attempts to create its own future. And even the past becomes futural in "Until the Sea Is Dead":

> If you had been beside me, sleepless
> Or chilled by the sudden violence
> Of the winds, maybe you'd have walked
> Here with me, or come after
> To see what kept me standing in the night.

It's part of the structure of deferrals that motivates so much of your work.

DAVID ST. JOHN: I'm often amazed how rarely the problem of temporality gets talked about. It's true, I think, that the basis of my poems is elegiac exactly in the way you're saying. The poems exist in the subjunctive and conditional, the futural, and this seems to me to be the true state of experience. The passage that you refer to is where temporalizing occurs most dramatically. I wasn't sure whether I'd be able to get away with it or not, and it was the one passage I wanted most to get away with. There's a sense of being able to falsify a temporality and yet necessarily recognize the condition, the fact, of the present. There's an attempt to distort that present with the future and with whatever weight the personal past can bring.

POETRY MISCELLANY: And the distortions are owing to the traces, conscious and unconscious, the fragments in language. In "The Boathouse," you say, "I believed I'd take/What came, a life with no diary's/Hieroglyphics,/Only the crooked arc of the sun." But this pure presence soon evaporates into "habit," even when the past that informs it seems lost: "Every voice I hear/Within my own *(of the father/The mother)* remains a saying so/Lost to its history."

DAVID ST. JOHN: And in that sense the temporality finds its way into the naming, the pattern of the naming. So in that way, to try to defy the temporality is to try to find other ways to name. It is to take the naming out of the frozen plane of a limited temporal orientation. In "Of the Remembered," the third section, with the epigraph from *The Wind in the Willows*, I wanted to talk about this sense of language, and in other sections of the poem the violations which that sensibility suffers.

POETRY MISCELLANY: Section VI of "Of the Remembered" begins with "now," a word you will repeat a couple more times and also subvert time in the way you've been discussing. The "now," the fragment, is seen as part of a web, layered as it were, like the whole poem. By definition, the whole thing has to be incomplete—"*blossoms in every last region of delay*." It must continue on the way Derrida says in his essay on Shelley. But how did it come to be written?

DAVID ST. JOHN: I'd been wanting to write a section like VI, the italicized broken section, for a long time in order to talk about that "scripting" which occurs in language and which you've so accurately described. In fact. I had been wanting to write the whole poem for a long time, and it wasn't until I went to England, out of my daily literary routine, that I was able to make much headway. I had been carrying sections of it around for a couple of years. Originally, the poem was in thirteen sections and had a very symmetrical design. Once I realized the fallacy of that type of unity, I could begin to see that it was necessarily partial, as you say. I settled for the present ten-part structure. The whole thing involves the play of forces, voices, against each other. I wanted the flatter, more prosaic sections to act as a kind of balance to the more heightened, lyrical sections—the italicized section, for example. I think the flatter sections are the more autobiographical ones. When I was finished with it, finally thought I was done with it, I wasn't sure it had been worth it, though I feel much better about it now. I wanted it to be so good, my ideal of it had been made so present, that when I looked back on it, on the ways it had exhausted me, I doubted its value. I think finally that the poem is an interesting failure that doesn't cohere the way I hoped it would. But there are kinds of things I did in the poem that were, at that stage, crucial and necessary for the development of my work. At least I hope it proves to be.

# I VS. YOU:
# THE ROMANTIC AMBIVALENCE OF SELF

This interview was conducted by D. W. Fenza for *Telescope*.

"Let us go then, you and I,"—so begins T.S. Eliot's "The Love Song of J. Alfred Prufrock"; that form of address—the writer speaking as if addressing someone as you—is an old convention, as old as the love song or prayer. Who the "you" is in Eliot's poem is ambiguous, unclear. Is it Prufrock's better conscience? An alter ego? A lover? A friend? The reader? Merely an allusion to Dante? Or all these? It is, perhaps, an interesting irony of modern literature that, while Eliot and Pound were advancing theories of the "objective correlative" and Imagism—their insistence on concrete images in poetry to communicate emotions and ideas—one of the swan songs of their age is "Prufrock," in which the second person pronoun emerges as an ungrounded and enormously complex abstraction, far removed from being a concrete image. This form of address has become widespread in contemporary poetry. With hopes of gaining some insight to the reasons a poet adopts this convention, we asked David St. John a series of questions concerning its use. David St. John is the author of *Hush* and *The Shore*. His poetry has also appeared in *The New Yorker*, *Antaeus*, *The Paris Review*, and *The American Poetry Review*. The interview was conducted on September 17, 1982 at *Telescope*'s offices in Baltimore, Maryland.

TELESCOPE: In many ways, *The Shore* is part love song, part dirge. The poems appear confessional and often addressed to a lover, ex-lover, or someone long lost; the poet speaks in the first person, intimately addressing someone in the second person. It seems that most modern and post-modern poets take for granted that this *I-and-you* lyrical structuring of a poem is acceptable and significant. Why has this form of address become so prevalent in this century's poetry?

ST. JOHN: Well, I can't speak for all of the poets in the Twentieth Century, but I can take some guesses; and one of the things I think that's happened is that, with the sense of self-enclosure of a first-person poem, the feeling of indulgence and limitation became so profound that poets began casting about for solutions. In an interview with Richard Jackson, Marvin Bell said that he tried never to use "you" to mean "one."—that he always had someone specific in mind, whether it was his son, a friend, or whoever; in that way the you-address can lend an intimacy to the poems that is engaging. But for other poets, the second person address has been a means to involve themselves in a more complex dialectic, a dialogue of consciousness that, otherwise, they would be unable to enact in their poems.

The wittiest answer I've ever heard to this question is John Ashbery's. When asked why the pronouns in his poems seemed to shift so maniacally at times, Ashbery said that it was because he just didn't have a very strong sense of self; that is: he really didn't have much sense of who he as an *I* was. There's an implicit paradox in his answer, however, in that any successful poem using the second person address, like one of Ashbery's, demands a strong, internal I-presence, regardless of how much the *you* is evoked. The force of the perceptive consciousness in Ashbery's poems has such conviction and presence that a tension emerges significantly within that *I-and-you* axis.

TELESCOPE: The kind of dialogue you're discussing seems to involve old philosophical considerations of identity, personal or otherwise—that in order for there to be an identity, there must first be a difference; and those differences are most clearly dramatized when one entity is contrasted with—or challenged by—another entity.

ST. JOHN: Yes, it's a way of self-definition, self-explication that, with some luck, doesn't have the indulgences of a poem spoken solely in the first person. In my own case, I've used the second person address for various reasons. In *Hush* that address was less specifically directed; it was a way to make the poem more intimate, more immediate—and to involve the reader in the dialogue. It was important to me in those poems to have a quiet confrontation with the reader.

TELESCOPE: As did Baudelaire in his work. "Reader, you know this squeamish monster well,/—hypocrite reader,—my alias,—my twin!"

ST. JOHN: Right, I wanted to make the reader complicit immediately in the situation, even in those poems which seem directed to a more specific other, as in "Dolls," where the design is an attempt to envelop the reader in the same relationship, the same tensions in which the speaker is caught.

TELESCOPE: Do you usually have one person in mind for your poems to address?

ST. JOHN: Not usually—very seldom, in fact. But even if one were to say that the you were a specific other, it seems to me a fallacy because any particular other is always a plurality of selves. One's ability to know another is always shaped by one's own precedents of past misunderstandings and understandings of others. I take the *you* to mean simply that which is not myself. I don't feel the need to define in very exact terms who the you is—just the need for the *you* to appear as *someone*; so the reader will at least know the *you* is not a small wire-haired terrier, for example. The *you* might be the reader, as well as my self, as well as a more generalized sense of that other, which is not me. The point is: the poems must become the field of mediation between the self and what is not the self; and it's on that field, in that arena, where the problems of experience—of dreams, desires, perceptions—can be confronted.

TELESCOPE: Many confessional poets, like Robert Lowell and Richard Hugo, admit to changing biographical details for what they hope is a better, more truthful poem. As Melville says, "It is not down in any map; true places never are." What do you think are the poet's responsibilities to autobiographical fact and fiction?

ST. JOHN: I'll let the poem present whatever facts and fictions it needs to make itself more interesting and true to the reader. In the poems of *The Shore*, the poems adopt the fiction that the *you* addressed is someone more specific, but, in fact, that *you* is a composite persona, just as the first person speaker, which has the illusion of being an autobiographical *I*, envelops and collates any number of fictive details in order to present—in a more engaging way, I hope—the emotional condition of the poem, the situation of a relationship and how the dialogue charts the course of that relationship.

TELESCOPE: If the *you* is a composite of the poet's lovers, friends, and imaginings, isn't there a danger that the *you* becomes, not ambiguous, but merely vague—that the personal mode of address becomes an empty mannerism?

ST. JOHN: That is a danger, surely. The use of *you* has often become a contemporary cliché in poetry. It became very fashionable to write the second person poem and to have the *you*, in fact, mean only *I*; but when that's the case, there is no prevailing tension, there is no dialectic, which seems to me entirely self-defeating because the whole point is to have that dialogue, a voice tempered by its antithesis. To forfeit that antithesis is to forfeit any interest I might have had in the poem.

TELESCOPE: Perhaps it was bound to become a worn-out convention, since that form of address is one of the oldest and most popular. The troubadors used it back in the Eleventh and Twelfth Centuries; and of course, it's *I-and-thou*, the form of prayer, which is ancient.

ST. JOHN: Right, that's important because what I've looked for in the second person address is a sense of both seduction and supplication. I think those are essential elements of poetry. Poetry should provide models of consciousness; and the I-and-you form is a way of exacting the basic maneuvers of the self. On the one hand, the self wants to appropriate whatever it is not, for the sake of power, or love, or whatever—that's where the seduction comes in. On the other hand, the self is often so bored or trapped within itself that it wants to be delivered by some other, stronger will into a more inclusive and thrilling life—that's, of course, where the supplication comes in. I should mention, though, that the poems I've been writing since *The Shore* are almost exclusively first person poems; they don't evoke the second person. Some of those poems are dramatic monologues. I felt I needed to write some poems that focused more on the illusion of an immediate speaker. What I found in writing these poems is that although I'm pleased with some of these poems, "The Swan At Sheffield Park" and "The Man With the Yellow

Gloves" in particular—the first person cuts down one whole aspect of mystery that I want to effect in my work. In a solely first person poem, one has to maintain a kind of immediate believability all the time; there are fewer opportunities to set up the kind of false causalities that I think, for example, make Ashbery's poems so beautiful and exciting.

TELESCOPE: Why insist on false causalities rather than true or logical causalties?

ST. JOHN: We don't always think in terms of logic, of course. When we think about ourselves or others, our meditations are always disrupted by the past, desires, the present, dreams, and various contradictory interpretations of them all. False causalities can be very true, in so far as they are how the self turns to face its world. One person I know who uses the first person monologue and still accomplishes that meaningful discrepancy of temporalities and psychic boundaries is Michael Burkard. He creates a self-dialogue in a first-person declaration that has real freedom and real horror, which is what happens when the self is let loose upon itself. After I finish the dramatic monologues I'm working on now, I plan to return to something more along the line of the poetry in *Hush*—poems like "Slow Dance" and "Gin."

TELESCOPE: More lyrical poems?

ST. JOHN: More lyrical, yes, and less dramatically narrative; and returning more to episodic details that do not rise from a single setting or plot, like a relationship breaking up or whatever. The kinds of things Ashbery does in *Self-Portrait in a Convex Mirror* seem to me exemplary of what I have in mind. I seem to be coming full circle, moving from lyrical, second person poems to dramatic, I-centered monologues, back to lyrical poems that evoke the other again. I hope that what I've learned along the way is how to establish a much stronger first person voice so that I can use that strength to engage in what will be an even fiercer dialogue. I did another interview in which I tried to describe my work for *Poetry Miscellany*; in an interview in the same issue, Marvin Bell describes my work as having a "fierce intimacy." It seems he said in two words what I had been trying to encircle for six pages.

TELESCOPE: Yes, that seems to be an appropriate way of describing your work, especially if one considers how much antagonism and violence there is in those poems—the trader's suicide in "Until the Sea is Dead" or the bitterness of "Song Without Forgiveness" or "Scarves." Why so much antagonism?

ST. JOHN: It has to do with the fact that the *you* to whom the poems are addressed is not simply a beloved object. I think my poems rebel against the notion of a beloved object, especially if it implies that the object is passive. In both *Hush* and *The Shore*, the *you* of those poems is far more actively engaged in the world and striving for a self-definition—far more actively engaged, in fact, than the speaker of the poems. That paradoxical reversal of roles, where the speaker is passive and the one-spoken-to is really active, is quite important to those poems. What's also important are the effects of psychic violence, whether it's interpersonal or the fragmentation we feel working and living in any urban environment. For me, since poems are models of consciousness, the trick is to find a way of recovering from that disjunction and fragmentation.

TELESCOPE: It seems urban life for man is an odd paradox. We go through routines and habitual work weeks that bore us into senselessness, while at the same time the city conceals so many unpredictable atrocities that we're frightened at the same time.

ST. JOHN: Absolutely, and it seems to me that the more frozen and static the consciousness is, the more in danger it is of being shattered. The more fluid, the more supple, the more capable of absorbing those jagged bits of experience, the more successful that sensibility will be in persevering. I want a poem to have that same fluid capability of absorbing bits of episodic detail, bits of psychic violence, even disheartening memories or the disorienting fears of new encounters. My poems since *The Shore* include more and more various kinds of violence. Lately I've been working on a poem about a murderer, a terrorist. That poem and the others are, for me, just a natural response to the condition of the world we live in. And it's absurd to discount one's own bitterness at having constantly to deal with this world; and yet if a poem is able to talk about it and absorb it and still emerge with some sense of wholeness—that seems to me at least some kind of victory.

TELESCOPE: As we were saying earlier, the *I*-vs.-*you* dialectic is also the form of prayer, but many of your poems are hostile to the old archetypal patterns of myths, prayers and faith. Your poem "The Boathouse" complains "Even the sea sings one octave in the past"; and in "Of the Remembered," section nine, you say you want to speak in the present and "not in any/Postscript of prayers." It's another aspect of that antagonism that often rises in your voice— a subversion of the conventions of prayer.

ST. JOHN: I hope that my work does, as you say, both exploit and subvert the conventions of prayer. The manuscript of poems I'm now working on once had the working title *No Heaven*, which is now the title of one of the poems. It's not as nihilistic as it initially sounds; it merely indicates a preoccupation with the stripping away of illusions. Poets have always wanted to take some kind of romantic humanism to their hearts; I, too, wanted to believe in that goodness, that humanism; and that's certainly apparent in both *Hush* and *The Shore*. I didn't understand why many of the post-modern French critics often reject that humanism, which has its origins in the Romantics, and I resisted the impulse to make that rejection myself for a long time. But in my recent work, I've found that my beliefs about that humanism and goodness were really assumptions I had to test; and if they held any validity, any reality, those beliefs would survive my tests, and they would be recovered in such a way as to show their vitality, and not merely their status as being the assumed or obsolete humanism of a previous age.

TELESCOPE: That recent French criticism you refer to discusses the duality of self and other as the basis for all modes of consciousness. The dialogue between self and other becomes an allegory for the self's own intercourse between ego and id, reason and intuition; one dialogue obscures or reveals the other. Which texts of such criticism have been useful to you?

ST. JOHN: When I was at the University of Iowa, I took a class on Yeats, Mallarmé, and Rilke taught by Gayatari Spivak, who is the translator of Derrida's *Of Grammatology*. I didn't know it at the time, but in that class I was being introduced to Derrida's methodology, which Spivak administered in a totally painless fashion, with her wit and brilliance. Her lecture on the ninth and tenth *Duino Elegies* were as spectacular as anything I've ever read or heard on poetry. Shortly after that, my temporary roommate, another poet, Larry Levis, was reading Lacan's *Ecrits*, the whole thing in French, for his Ph.D. comps; and late at night, Larry would put on the Rolling Stones and spill over with all those theories as he tried to come to terms with them. I also read Susan Sontag, who introduced me to Roland Barthes—and

Barthes in turn introduced me to Foucault.

These modes of criticism have been entertaining to me, and they have provided notions against which I can form my own values about language and the ambivalence of self. Section six, for example, in "Of the Remembered" is where those values are most fluently articulated. Finally, poems are made of language, and as Foucault says, "Language always seems to be inhabited by the other, the elsewhere, the distant; it is hollowed by absence." Poetry is an attempt to use language with that hollowness and to reach beyond those absences—the gulf between you and I—and to invite the reader to bridge that emptiness.

TELESCOPE: So these modes of criticism have influenced you as a poet?

ST. JOHN: Yes, but I should qualify that with the following paradox: although such criticism is useful to me as a poet, I don't think it has very much to do with the actual writing of the poems. Each poem comes out of a matrix of consciousness that is far larger, more complex than any critical faculty.

TELESCOPE: Derrida makes a very complex pun that we can relate to this I-and-you structuring of a poem, especially a confessional love poem. *Id* is Latin for *it*, which in French is "*ça*"; throughout his book *Glas*, Derrida uses the contraction SA for *savoir absolu* (absolute knowledge), but as Goethe says, "The eternally feminine draws us beyond," and Derrida plays on the fact that *sa* is also, in French, a possessive pronoun which takes a feminine object. Truth and knowledge have been feminized. To seek the truth, then, is to seek the feminine through all the quandaries of our own subjectivity, the *Id* or *Ça*—which is similar to the seeking in your poems in which the narrator tries to define his world in discord or concord with the *you*. A feminist critic would argue that this is the old trap: the female is typecast as the intuitive one beyond language—she just smiles while the poet does all the talking—as was the case with Wordworth's Nature, Dante's Beatrice, Faust's Helen, Alastor's vision of love, and so on. Do you think the feminization of knowledge, a poem addressed to a vaguely feminine *you*, is sometimes self-defeating, that it obscures real women and real lovers with sometimes mystical and personalized philosophical quests?

ST. JOHN: To some extent, yes, of course. But a lot of the poems in *Hush*, for instance, are not addressed to a feminine *you*. In *The Shore* there are more often indications that the poems are addressed to a female *you*, and sometimes I even consider that to be a weakness of the poems. One of my ambitions has always been to write, not a poetry of androgyny, but a poetry in which the limiting and adamant gender-identifications of the characters is not given the opportunity to occur, because that kind of identification often only obscures the real shared and deep psychic strains in a dialogue. Possibly, in my best poems, there is the sense that the *you* being addressed is simply one aspect of wholeness in the poem, and that aspect could be either masculine or feminine. There's always a feminine and masculine aspect in the poem, and neither is significant without the other.

The names and genders of the minds speaking or spoken to are immaterial to what those personalities say and think and how they interact. Sometimes the poems work simultaneously as a self-address and an address to an other. It seems to me those poems can be read in a masculine or feminine voice; to me that's a very important condition for the poems.

TELESCOPE. As Derrida says, "Man and woman change masks, *ad infinitum*."

ST. JOHN: Absolutely. I don't see knowledge or truth as feminine, nor do I wish to. I have no interest in having a Muse of any kind; that strikes me as an archaic and insubstantial idea, and one that leads to self-indulgence.

TELESCOPE: Those theoretical works we mentioned earlier, those by Lacan, Derrida, Barthes, and Foucault, all are preoccupied with unnaming, with showing how false the fixities *of* language can be—how language represses, omits, and always fails to transmit experiences, emotions, and self-definitions in their totality. In another interview in *Poetry Miscellany*, you said, "I'm not trying to name something with one name because I don't believe whatever I'm discussing has one name. To name something in a fixed way involves a fallacy for me." This seems to be indicative of a great deal of contemporary poetry—a poetry that in many instances belittles words and oftens favors silence romantically, as if silence could re-embody what words fail to say. It seems as if contemporary poetry is sometimes a bizarre re-enactment of *Last Tango in Paris*, in which each leading man and each leading lady refuse to learn the other's name. Do you ever worry that this poetics of indeterminancy or unnaming has become artificial, as artificial as that relationship between the main characters of *Last Tango in Paris?*

ST. JOHN: To a certain extent, any naming or unnaming is artificial, just as any mode of social discourse is artificial, just as any mode of even vaguely civilized behavior is artificial. The question is: what values does one enact in that naming or unnaming, and are they values that address us in both a realistic and humane way? In *Last Tango*, for example, Marlon Brando plays a character whose refusal to name is his refusal to become complicit in what he feels will inevitably be a lie; in that character's previous relationship with his wife, his life was full of names, the talk that gave him the illusion that he really knew his wife; but after she dies, he finds that she had a lover and countless other habits he never imagined. He realizes that he didn't know her and that the naming was false. In his new relationship, he wanted a discourse that admitted how little we really know about one another—how little the *I* knows about the *you*; so in this instance unnaming has to do with values that try to exact a greater truthfulness and humility, but on the other hand, unnaming has simply to do with one's idea of freedom. The attempt to "live up to a name" is seldom glorious, but more often limiting and self effacing. Take the movie *The Passenger*, for instance, which is what lies behind my poem "The Boathouse," although it's not at all necessary for the reader to know that. The character Jack Nicholson plays assumes the name of an other, another man's identity, and he begins to live out that other's life because it's a deliverance from the enclosure of self, from his previous name, from the boring and limited creature his *I* had become. It's a spontaneous act on his part; the occasion presents itself and he simply does it; he naturally takes what he hopes will be freedom. One could make the argument that not to name is childish and that to name and accept the strictures and structures of language is to be an adult.

TELESCOPE: Right, that was Adam's first responsibility in the Garden: to name things.

ST. JOHN: Yes, but look how often our names are wrong—simple words like *man* and *woman* don't signify, in their full connotative sense, what they did decades ago—let alone the relationships between them. The names must necessarily be unwritten and rewritten again to keep up with changes in those relationships and changes in our understanding of them. One of the responsibilities of the poet is to make sure the language doesn't petrify, and to keep entertaining various possibilities of naming in an attempt to keep the language alive. It's not simply an attempt "to purify the language of the tribe." I don't like the idea of purity there because it invites the notion of rarity, and I think it's just more important to keep language alive, vigorous and connected to human impulses, emotions, and despairs. Basically, all I've ever wanted to do is write the most beautiful poems I could—that they be rhythmically gorgeous, that the language be of a high order. My intention is to write about a psychological condition that, by its definition, is not a static state; what each line, each cadence, each image serves to do, I hope, is act as a sequence of tracer bullets which illuminate different aspects of that condition. I have no desire to name any human condition with any fixity.

TELESCOPE: The unwillingness to name is an old conceit in poetry, especially love poetry—all those laments that words don't really describe one's love for another. The troubadors often refused to disclose the identity, the *you*, to whom their passions were addressed, as if dressing love in a name, a mere word, would make that love profane. And, of course, in Western and Eastern religions, God is the unpronounceable, the unnameable, the unknowable.

ST. JOHN: Personally, I've found that words usually far exceed or obscure whatever real emotion there happens to be. This may sound like a parody of Jerzy Kozinski's fable about himself, but there was a period in my life, when I was just turning eighteen, when I found it useful not to talk. I had the recognition that language necessarily lied, and I found it impossible to reconcile myself to that fact. Perhaps it wasn't an unusual pose to assume in the '60s, because many felt the same shortcomings of language, especially when one tried to describe any psychedelic experience. The gulf between the description of the experience and the experience itself is enormous—the words are so obviously *not* the experience itself; the words even seem feeble in comparison to the power of that experience.

TELESCOPE: Howard Nemerov says that poetry, like acne, is a secondary characteristic of adolescence. That statement puts poetry on a simple and down-to-earth plane, reminding us that poetry is basically a fall from innocence, the result of our knowledge that there's a distance between ourselves and others, ourselves and language. That statement reminds us that poetry—no matter what some critics will say about a poet's debt to the history of literature—is...

ST. JOHN: Hormonal. (laughter) Probably poetry does owe something to the body and to the distance each poet feels from it at times; and although there's a degree of flippancy in Nemerov's remark, there's real truth to it in that adolescence is a similar act of self-confrontation, self-definition. In good poets, the poems remain constant acts of self-confrontation, and that's where the defiance of repetition comes in.

TELESCOPE: Do you think that the *I-and-you* structuring of a poem is useful because it helps to summon the constant anxieties of love, self, and a fall from innocence?

ST. JOHN: Yes, that dialogue, I think, is the weaving of some rope you cast up from the chasm to pull yourself back up after the fall. Probably the only proper response to any contemporary relationship is one of simple despair; but that is so debilitating that it's pointless to allow that. I feel the need for some endeavor of reclamation—to pull back from that repetitive, continual fall, and that despair—to avoid self-immolation. I think a lot of poetry has climbed aboard what Michael Burkard once called the "self-referential express." What I look for in poetry is a sensibility that uses the inescapable condition of that self-referentiality to incorporate other, larger issues, to confront the *you*, the other. If the poet fails to include those larger issues, if the poet fails to avoid self-repetition, then the poetry is merely like one of those snow-domes that you can shake up and watch the snowflakes swirl around, the motions of the self's multiplicity; and that becomes quickly boring. I hope, of course, that my own poems don't become locked in that little snow-dome.

TELESCOPE: You keep referring to the necessity of defying repetition—could you explain a bit more why that's so important?

ST. JOHN: Repetition invites complacency. The physical repetition invites mental repetition that is not liberating the way the refrains of old religious meditations once were. And the more complacent you are, the more unwilling you are to engage yourself in any difficult questioning. Everyone lies to themselves with such skill so constantly that it takes a severely realistic and flinty character to turn back on the self and say, "Okay, who am I hurting, to whom am I lying, what am I not doing or saying?"—all these are questions that must also come up in the poems.

TELESCOPE: And perhaps it takes an equally realistic and flinty other, or *you*, to make sure the poems raise those questions?

ST. JOHN: Certainly. Unless the reflective surfaces of the poems present an other, a you, that is capable of calling into question the speaker's own assumptions and complacencies, it seems to me that a slackness and self-indulgence in the poems results. I imagine that's why poets often return to their best poems and re-read them in periods of slackness, or in dry spells—not to feel smug, not to be comforted, but to be chastised, instructed, and provoked.

# An Interview with David St. John

This interview was conducted by David Wojahn for the *Seneca Review*.

*The following interview took place in Baltimore, Maryland, on September 13, 1984.*

DAVID WOJAHN: In one of his essays in *The Dyer's Hand*, Auden draws a distinction between the Ariel poet and the Prospero poet, the former being in essence a poet of style, and the latter being what one might call a poet of content. Which of those two categories would you say you're most closely aligned with?

DAVID ST. JOHN: Well, it pains me to say it, but I think I am probably an Ariel poet. I find inseparable from what I say the style in which I say it. What's important in every poem is not only what's contentual about the poem but what makes the perception individual and original, and one hopes it is either new or, if not new, instructive in some way that is unfamiliar. It's a question I'm a little touchy about because I find the content of my poems to be often reduced to something I feel it's not. It would be easy, say, to look at my work as an investigation of relationships, whereas it seems to me it is an investigation of the psychological dynamics between people. More and more, that's what interests me; more and more, what I find provocative is the idea of poetry as a model of consciousness. In that way, then, the style of what's said is essential in reflecting the manner of perception. Unless one is able to present in the poem some model of consciousness or model of perception that allows the reader some way to frame and absorb an experience, then the poem hasn't done its work. It seems to me that content is not simply material; the content is process, so that the process of reading a poem, the experience of reading a poem—which is an experience of not only material but of style and perception—is an essential, and to me the most important, element of poetry. I suppose what I'm trying to say is that a poem potentially can introduce to a reader an experience of thought unfamiliar to him, and that seems a way of introducing the future to a body of readers. Also, I think every poem has to be alert to history, both the history of literature and the history of the world. Every poem has to be conscious of the culture in which it is framed, though that doesn't mean that every poem need exhibit an argument about topical matters. It seems to me the most interesting poetry is poetry that investigates the way the human mind performs and responds to history and experience.

DAVID WOJAHN: One of my reasons for asking that question is a sense I have in your work that artifice is seen as the force that defines our universe, that mitigates our existence, and that prevents our experience from being tragic and overwhelming, and I sometimes feel that that very kind of needful embrace of artifice is what allows you to achieve success with strategies and stylistic techniques that in the work of other poets might seem strained or mannered.

DAVID ST. JOHN: Well, I hope that's true. The idea of artifice is important to think of in even simpler terms, as the idea of making; in that regard, one of the few defenses we have is to *make*, to *create*. For me, it's been the most useful way of providing form to experience, as well as the most useful way of trying to understand, what I imagine the experience of one's future might be. In other words, it's important to me that poems try to push beyond what seem to be the limits of poetry. I don't mean this in any artificial avant garde way. I simply mean that the ways in which people think and talk tend to become constrained by their circumstances, and it seems to me an obligation of poetry to push the possibilities. I think that the sense of craft that's in my own poems, which is very important to me, is necessary to balance their basically romantic impulse. In the new poems, it's my hope that the rawness of sensibility both comments upon and deflates much of that sense of Romanticism.

DAVID WOJAHN: I guess one of the things that would distinguish an Ariel poet from a Prospero poet is that a Prospero poet seeks to order the world he views didactically, to impose an ethical value on it, but an Ariel poet seeks to either praise this world or to acquiesce to it. Do you think those last ideas, praise or acquiescence, are important ones in your work?

DAVID ST. JOHN: First, the problem of an ethical code is a fascinating one, because unless one's convinced that poetry should have a certain didactic element, no one would confess to wanting to impose any code upon any readership, although there are some poets who would argue that, no, in fact, that *is* their purpose and duty as writers. I think few American poets would really admit to that. But I think many poets have strong ethical codes that are embodied and exhibited in their perceptions, in their work. I find in the poems of many poets I love that a strong moral and ethical sense is exhibited as a function of style, as a function of the manner of their perception, so that the lens, in other words, through which their world is seen is every bit as much a function of their code and their personality as with a Prospero poet. As for the second part of your question, I think my poems are often poems of praise, even though they're also poems of loss. Their tone is basically elegiac. Poetry offers consolation in a way few things do. I believe that very strongly. I don't mean that poems on cards of condolence offer any consolation, but I believe poetry itself does. I've seen it; I've seen it work. I've never felt my poems were poems of acquiescence; I think, if anything, they're poems of revolt. Especially the poems of *No Heaven*. They're all poems about characters in conditions begging for revolt, a revolt that will become an affirmation. The movement through the book establishes that what seems to be a negation—"no heaven"—is in fact an affirmation; there is "no heaven but this," and that can clearly be read two ways. These characters, all of whom are existing at the margins of their lives, find a way to proclaim themselves to and for themselves. And, as these fragments of narrative are enacted throughout the book, they construct the sense of movement leading to the final poem, the final affirmation.

DAVID WOJAHN: One of the reasons I asked that last question is because I frequently see a tension in operation in your poems, particularly between the goal of richly and sensually rendering the physical world and the goal of identifying a kind of ideal metaphysical realm. A realm of experience continually torn between an allegiance to one of those opposites.

DAVID ST. JOHN: I think that's absolutely accurate. I think it's exactly that tension that would be called in some works a "fallen" state, and, for me, the project of the poems of *No Heaven* was to discover for myself what my own idea of one's recuperation in these circumstances might be, what reconciliation of those tensions was possible, what forms it all might take. A friend said that what he thought was both fascinating and dangerous about the book, in terms of a response to the poems, was that what was in fact a critique of a kind of decadence would be misunderstood as an embrace of decadence.

DAVID WOJAHN: The sense of opposition that we're talking about seems to manifest itself repeatedly in everything about the poems—the landscapes and the details, the narrative, and sometimes even the diction of the poems. You return again and again in all of your books to bridges, harbors, shores, to elements of the landscape that seem to signify for you that opposition. At the end of the title poem of *The Shore* you write, "In that dream we share, there is/one shore, where we look upon nothing/and the sea our whole lives;/ until turning from those waves we find/one shore where we look upon nothing/and the earth our whole lives."

DAVID ST. JOHN: Exactly. For me, that's the fascinating territory, those (seeming) lines of division and demarcation which, in fact, are illusory; every shore is in a sense a false shore. There is the constant interplay of land and water— its own yin and yang—but nothing is fixed and everything is twinned, doubled, in its own way. The regard of the outer, the regard of the inner, the regard of the one shore that's beyond the world, the regard of the one shore that is of the world—those energies are always twinned and entwined; that seems to me just a fairly descriptive way of presenting the tensions of a daily life. Those tensions are articulated in more and less extravagant ways, depending on one's temperament. Say, in the temperament of the speaker in *The Shore*, certain of those tensions find their articulation and embodiment in the form of a relationship. The characters of *No Heaven* are finding those conflicts almost everywhere they step into the world and in a variety of landscapes.

DAVID WOJAHN: But it does seem that this element of opposition in your work is underscored dramatically in your poems about love relationships. So many of those poems, in *The Shore* particularly, seem to be about a gentle collapse of the relationship between the speaker and the beloved—"Hotel Sierra," "The Avenues"—they seem to focus on couples who must resign themselves to never achieving that pure lasting intimacy that they so long for. In "Hotel Sierra," the speaker comes to the realization that he and the beloved have to be like those photos that she takes of the coast line, "only a few gestures/placed out of time."

DAVID ST. JOHN: I think one of the things that I now find less appealing about the poems in *The Shore* is, in fact, that sense of resignation, and it's one of the reasons why I think the new poems are poems of greater violence. They seem to me more accurate. Certainly the poems of *The Shore* are poems of a quiet disintegration and poems of repeated attempted reckonings, and those reckonings are always asking and seeking a particular equilibrium that will allow the speaker to continue. I find now that sense of resignation, even acquiescence, disquieting. It's not that I don't find the poems emotionally accurate. I'm sounding harsher about those poems than I mean to be; "Hotel Sierra" is a poem I still like a lot, as is "Until the Sea Is Dead," in which I found a violent episode to echo more dramatically and, I think, satisfyingly, the rupture between the characters. So the restraint of the poems of *The Shore* appeals to me in that I like what's happening in the writing, but I don't particularly like what it allows the figures in the poems to become to each other. That's looking back after five years, so it's easy to second guess myself now. At the time I didn't have that problem at all or I wouldn't have written the poems in that way. I think it's also a part of the attempt of the sixth section of "Of the Remembered," to somehow put those other poems in a different kind of focus.

DAVID WOJAHN: The issue of the impossibility of lasting intimacy between two people is also a large concern in *Hush*; it seems especially in that book having to do with its strikingly delineated poems about the relationship between fathers and sons. I'm thinking of the title poem, where the son and father only communicate sporadically, "sometimes he asks about the world," writes the speaker of his son, "sometimes I answer back." In fact, the speaker and the son seem removed from one another in such eerie and poignant ways that sometimes when I read that poem I think it's being addressed to a son who is geographically removed from the father because of separation, while at other times when I read the poem I think it's addressed to a son who is actually dead and the father is attempting a kind of discreet form of elegy that will allow him to mourn the death of the son without again feeling overwhelmed by his sorrow.

DAVID ST. JOHN: I think in any situation of a divorce, where there's a child involved, whether this situation exists with the father or the mother, aside from the geographical distance, there's no question that a minor death occurs and that mourning is the only proper response. It's the same in any relationship that ends, mourning is the only proper response because it's not an illusory death, it's a real death, and in the case of this poem I think the poem is, in fact, an effort to find an adequate voice for the mourning in the hope that the attempt will, for the speaker, help him to attain some equilibrium about his own dilemma, about his own guilt and sadness. But it's also a poem of a *son*, and I think that's an important part of it. And it's in some ways related to the Keith Douglas poem and to section nine of "Of the Remembered."

DAVID WOJAHN: In an earlier interview, published in *Telescope* in '83, you discuss at length that whole issue of the I and You as a principal axis around which your poems revolve. Yet you say your speakers use this "I versus you" dichotomy in an almost philosophical sense; the pronoun you is meant to be specific and intimate but it is not meant to represent actual persons, be it a lover or a son. Instead, the "you" is meant to be a composite of sorts, an amalgamation, to some extent, of many real lovers and friends. What prompted you to adopt that strategy? Is the blurring of the "you," the you's identity, simply a device that allows you to transcend the merely personal and confessional when you sit down to write or does it stem from a more metaphysical notion, that the "you," the other, can never be fully understood?

DAVID ST. JOHN: I would say some of each. In practical terms, it's an address that's always appealed to me because it's implicitly accusational. It's also a demanding address; it's saying *you* and *you listen*. And so, in a very under-handed way, I wanted to grab the reader and say, "*Listen*, you're in this poem, you're my lover, watch out, let's see what happens here." And I wanted to be able to be confrontational in that way; I wanted to be as demanding of the reader as I felt I had a right to be. I also wanted to be, then, gentle and sympathetic to the reader. I wanted to invite the reader into a more intimate conversation, and there are some poems, like "Gin," for example, where it's more clearly a self-address. The place in my own work where I find the technique working most successfully is in "Slow Dance," where the "you" weaves its way in and out of identification. It, I think, most successfully absorbs the reader into the fabric of the identity of the you. In *The Shore* there's no question that the "you" is more clearly identified as another person, a lover, and a definite other. In the poems of *Hush*, it's something I found attractive in Ashbery's work. The thing to remember is that in 1972 and '73 there weren't that many people yelling about Ashbery; outside of New York he was a fairly well-kept secret. I happened to have a number of friends who, like myself, admired him tremendously and felt that what he was writing was some of the most exciting poetry we'd ever seen. The poems in *Hush* are highly influenced by Ashbery. Obviously, there are a lot of other poets whose work has influenced my poems, both before and since. I think, in terms of admiring what Ashbery was able to get away with in using the second person address, I wanted to be able to pull it off myself, in a less abstracted way.

DAVID WOJAHN: In a poem like "Gin" the "you" obviously becomes a substitute for the speaker and it's not meant to be a separate character the speaker addresses. The "you" is used that way by a number of post-war American poets, Hugo comes to mind, Jon Anderson comes to mind. In writers like Ashbery and Michael Burkard, that issue becomes even more complicated because the pronoun often shifts without warning from "I" to "you," sometimes even to the third person, until we're uncertain if the speaker's using the "you" to refer to himself or to represent a person or reader being addressed. Why do you think our poetry has adopted that sort of pronoun blur in the last twenty years or so?

DAVID ST. JOHN: I think I would explain this shift in the usage of the "you," this usage of free-floating pronouns, not as a reflection of lack of identity or a sense of insecurity of identity on the part of the poets but, in fact, just the reverse. It's an attempt to expand the identity, to be more inclusive, to find a way of taking the traditional "I" beyond an opposition of self and other, a way of absorbing this opposition, of saying it's an illusory opposition and that human consciousness is capable of becoming the other, of *being* the other. It seems to me that that act of imaginative sympathy is what's always the most important aspect of art. One of the things that makes art a mitigating factor in society is that it demands and initiates a sympathetic imagination in order for an audience to enter into a relationship with it—whether it's painting, sculpture, music, or literature. There seems to me a false argument in recent years about the over-abundance of the "I," of first person poetry, of post-confessional first person poetry. Phil Levine tells a wonderfully funny story about his first book, *On The Edge,* having to be held up in the middle of printing because the printer, Kim Merker, had run out of capital I's. What I'm trying to say is that, since the Romantics, the problem of a strong first person in a poem has been constant for the poet at work. Solutions to that problem are as various as poets, but one of the most interesting and complicated solutions is the way in which a *second* person address has been used. At this point, what's disturbing is to see how quickly it's become a cliché, and to see the poems in which it's so misused as to be foolish, as to sound foolish.

DAVID WOJAHN: You grew up in the San Joaquin Valley of California, and yet I don't think that landscape figures as prominently in your poems as it does in the work of a number of other poets of your generation who grew up in the same area. I'm thinking of Larry Levis and Gary Soto, for example, and of some of Frank Bidart's early work. I'm also intrigued by the fact that all four of you are to a large degree poets of recollection, poets of memory, and yet their work harks back quite specifically to their youths in California, while your poems seem little concerned with any sort of Wordsworthian evocation of childhood. Can you talk a little bit about that and your upbringing?

DAVID ST. JOHN: For me, except in "Of the Remembered," the landscape of the San Joaquin Valley has never been as important to me as the landscape of the northern California coastline. It was there that I found the real embodiment, in the landscape, of what seemed to me dilemmas related to my life. Let me try to explain. Poems have real subjects, there's no question about it, and they have real figures, even if those figures are invented; yet, for me, poems aren't *about* their content, they're about the ways in which the perceiver—the writer, the figure, whether or not the figure is the same as the writer—comes into relation with whatever experience is at stake. It's that process of observation, reflection, and imagination that seems to me the substance of the poem. Even in "Of the Remembered," which is an attempt to write a more Wordsworthian kind of poem, there's always something else working against that; there's always section six or there's the last section with its little collation of the Tibetan Book of the Dead and the Egyptian Book of the Dead; there's always a tension fighting the simply remembered landscape.

DAVID WOJAHN: "Of the Remembered" is divided into ten sections, each essentially different in its approach and concerns, but what appears to unify the poem's sections is its ambivalence towards that entire process of recollection which alternatively seems both burdensome and solacing for the speaker.

DAVID ST. JOHN: And that's the problem of trying to name not only experience, but the more difficult process of trying to name memory. For me, memory exists as a piece of music, as a melody, and that's the function of the thread of melody that runs through that poem. To name one's memories—that is, to *fix* them in time—can be an act of constraint, a false definition. Of course, it's impossible to stop oneself from engaging in the act of memory. Memory serves the function of recuperation, of recovery, in a very real sense, but I find memory enormously untrustworthy. I have an excellent memory—at one time I had nearly a photographic memory—so that's not my point; my point is that the function of memory is to help shape experience and that memory is its own artisan; we have to understand and appreciate that about memory. If we indulge in memory, in poetry, and engage our selves in that process, we have to be artisans equal to it. We can't be slack about naming memory, because that naming is, in fact, renaming that allows memory to exist with both its names, its first names and its later names as well.

DAVID WOJAHN: One of the things that seems clear about the way recollection is viewed in your poems is that your speakers never seem to come to terms with the process of memory beyond acknowledging its obsessive hold on them. As in Cavafy's poems, the speaker reconstructs events from his past with the conscious knowledge that this reconstruction might bring him solace but might also cause him to relive events which are painful to him. It's this receptivity towards the past that seems to give the poems their character and gravity.

DAVID ST. JOHN: I would like to think so, yes. It's what I wanted to try to achieve; it's what remains important to me when I go back and look at "Of the Remembered." One of the poem's possibilities is solace, and yet it's not necessarily going to be solace. Again, it is that tension between the pain of the memory and its *potential* for solace—one can't enter into a state of recuperation or recovery without bringing these jagged bits of experience back up into consciousness, and it seems that the form of a poem can allow pieces of jagged, painful memory to be enfolded and absorbed, to be reckoned with.

DAVID WOJAHN: Are we to read "Of the Remembered" as a long poem in ten sections or as a sequence of interlinked and related poems? Or is the distinction important?

DAVID ST. JOHN: I think the distinction isn't that important. I see it as one long poem with discrete sections. The idea of a long poem in sections in many ways violated a certain aspect of my own aesthetic in that I was interested, in *The Shore*, in the process of the long, unbroken poem. In *The Shore*, I quit using stanza breaks because I wanted continuous motion. I wanted the breaks to be made to occur in other ways. "Of the Remembered" was originally structured as a thirteen-part poem with a certain symmetry, the action rising towards the seventh section and then working down from there. What happened was that three of the sections simply weren't very good and, although they had done exactly what I had wanted them to do as sections, in terms of the poem as a whole, they weren't satisfying. So then I put it together as a ten-section poem and found it was functioning the way I had first imagined it might. I find sectioning to be artificial, and I don't like the idea. I like other people's poems in sections; I just don't like my own poems in sections. Still, in "Of the Remembered," I wanted the sections to create certain tensions among themselves and to talk back to their speaker, as well as to the reader.

DAVID WOJAHN: One of the things that I frequently notice in reading the manuscript of *No Heaven* is that while many of the poems such as "Woman and Leopard," and "The Swan at Sheffield Park," or even "The Man in the Yellow Gloves" are relatively straightforward and maintain traditional narrative structures or traditional monologues, others such as "The Lemons" and "The Day of the Sentry" seem much more telescoped and compressed in their narrative strategies; again and again they seem to shift in person with relative impunity; characters appear without much introduction, curious "he's," "she's," and they's."

DAVID ST. JOHN: Well, it's those poems that matter most to me because they're enacting a kind of grammar of narration that I find most interesting. I think that many readers will find it troubling that the poems are so vulgarly presesentational, and what I hope is that readers will begin to see that the "he's," the "she's," and the "I's" all share something in common, and that they are all sisters and brothers, in some very troubling way, all part of a "family" that is coming apart at the seams. The kind of narration that's employed in the poems of *No Heaven* allowed me, I think, much more latitude in establishing some logical climates in the poems; that's what I wanted to try to effect. I wanted the tensions to carry over from poem to poem, and I hope the little echoes will be there as the reader reads through. One of the things that is a little worrisome to me is that the poems will be seen as the poems of the decay of elegance, when in fact it's a more universal dilemma of history. It's crucial to me that the importance and impulses of history be recognized in those poems, because I think they're poems of social and cultural dilemma; I don't think they're poems of fancy.

DAVID WOJAHN: I suppose one of the reasons people might have that interpretation is that many of the poems in *No Heaven* refer to European landscapes and that few of the poems in the collection, or in any of these collections, seem to use locale and place as anything but a backdrop to the events that take place. I sometimes feel that your work, say, unlike the work of many of the poets of the generation before yours—like Wright, Levine and Hugo or even people in your own generation like Plumly and Levis and Matthews— refuses to admit that there is a nurturing sense of place; in your poems I see no abiding locale that functions like Plumly's Ohio or Levine's Detroit, no place we can come back to in order to confront again our first experiences with transcendence and loss. Instead of embracing a locale, your poems, particularly in *No Heaven* seem to embrace the act of travel itself.

DAVID ST. JOHN: I think that's not only accurate but an important factor in the poems of *No Heaven*—that sense of there being some final and true homelessness. The characters in *No Heaven* aren't wanderers by choice, they're wanderers in search of their own homelands, and one of the symptoms of the malaise is that rootlessness, that sense of traveling over the surface of things, even the surface of the land, in a very literal way. A poem like "The Boathouse" tries to talk about that in a different way, that quality of looking for some rootedness, looking for a place that has the capacity to give rootedness, and being to a large extent disappointed. Now, this is very much, I think—to shift into a more autobiographical mode—absolutely related to the fact of growing up in California where the history of the land was pretty much the history of the latest mall. Even though Fresno is an agricultural area with vineyards, orchards—and they're beautiful—I really felt, especially in my adolescence, the poverty of any roots, any long standing historical or cultural associations. It's one of the reasons why I'm much more comfortable living in the East, and it's one of the reasons why I'm fond of New England. I think that it's a problem of my own, a problem in my own history, that I find necessary to address. Obviously, friends like Larry Levis don't feel this way. Also, I happen to like to travel; I find travel easy and comforting. I mean, traveling is hard work, as everyone knows, but I find it for my own temperament a very realistic way to live. I don't know quite how to explain it, but I find movement and travel suits my nervous system in some ways.

DAVID WOJAHN: One of the reasons why the act of travel seems so important in *No Heaven,* and in a lot of the other poems too, is that again and again your work presents a speaker whose responses are essentially passive, who works to not see the world aggressively. I sometimes feel that your poems strive to see the world with the same sort of wry curiosity in which one views the landscape from a train window; it's not like, say, Levine or the poems of James Wright in his *Two Citizens* period, that relate to the experience of travel in a way that is very aggressive and very fatalistic; your poems instead seek a kind of receptivity that defies somehow any aggressiveness, any of that sort of fatalism.

DAVID ST. JOHN: I think the poems of *No Heaven* are trying to be representative of states of concern—psychological states of concern and emotional states as well—and yet not be passive and resigned in the way that the poems and sensibilities of the speakers in *The Shore* were, and yet be responsible to the figures of the poems. It's interesting; I find it convenient to speak of the speakers, the figures, in the poems of *No Heaven* as characters because in fact they're all drawn on real characters and figures, and yet they're functional for me as fictions in that they're enacting states that are states of concern for me, and they're states that I want to see considered in a poem, in a particular way, from a particular perspective; in that way all of the poems seem to me latent with implied decisions, implied actions that will postdate the poem. So there's a certain tension that's being created by that that I hope begins to be resolved by the poem, "Leap of Faith." At the same time, I think there's much more humor in these poems—though whether many readers will find what I find humorous to be so is a question, especially since there is a certain amount of black humor at work. But I think humor is a necessary and useful tool in trying to consider these complicated states of emotional and psychological distress.

DAVID WOJAHN: One of the things that strikes me as particularly true of *No Heaven* but also true to some extent about the other books, is that while the speakers and protagonists of your poems very often strive for that kind of enlightened passivity that we've talked about, the female characters in your works, like the prostitute in "Six/Nine/Forty-Four," any number of the female characters in *No Heaven*, like the countess in "Meridian," seem very different in their passivity. They're almost trapped by it; they seem to exhibit a sort of depraved passivity, one that's hurt and vulnerable, but one that's *never* innocent.

DAVID ST. JOHN: I think, if you go back to *The Shore*, one of the things that you'll find is that the active party is always the "you" of the poems, nominally the female figure in the transaction. That may just be my own historical entrapment, in that, in most of the situations I see around me, the vital active parties have been the female figures in relationships. One of the reasons that's so is that they better understand their own entrapment; they better understand their own enslavement to convention, and so they're quicker to realize the necessity for revolt. It's why, for example, with the woman Clare in "Meridian," her entrapment is a multiplicity of entrapments. It's not only the collapse of the certain history that has to do with an aristocratic background, a certain sense of privilege, it is also an entrapment like that of the figure in "Black Poppy"—of drugs. It's a kind of self-imposed constraint and enslavement that I find being enacted very commonly around me. For me, it's not only a phenomenon of great sadness but one that's important to try to understand; it's important to try understanding what function that activity is serving for people who are smart, in many cases tremendously talented, and yet determined at all costs to destroy themselves. Of course, the more traditional way for writers has always been alcohol. Someone once asked me why there's such a prevalence of drugs in my poems and the answer is very simple: it's around me, in the ways I've seen people grant drugs a place in their lives. It seems to me an important thing to talk about. But, getting back to "Meridian," Clare is also feeling a sense of entrapment that has to do with her relationship with the speaker of the poem. It seems to me, in the poems of *No Heaven*, nothing is more killing to the figures than that sense of stasis. It's one of the reasons why a response to distress takes the form of travel, physical movement. There's no question that travel relieves personal distress; the danger is that a person begins to use that to avoid difficulties rather than to stand and confront them. In any case, these are all concerns that I think are present and active in the poems.

DAVID WOJAHN: The whole issue of passivity, too, seems related, in some degree, to the level of diction you employ in the poems; the tone you speak in is generally conversational but at the same time your language strives always for a kind of elegance, for a diction that I think some readers would say refuses to admit any brutality, any excessive use of vernacular.

DAVID ST. JOHN: I prefer writing poems that I find to be beautiful poems. I feel that I have to give the reader an entry into the poems before I can involve him with the kinds of psychological violence that seem to me the important points of discussion. The elegance of some of the poems, their demeanor, takes on more subtle gradations than in others, and there are poems that, in their syntax and their diction, seek purposefully to be disorienting. *No Heaven* begins in a syntactically aggressive fashion, as a kind of announcement. The poems want to disturb the reader's expectations, and it seems to me important that the first two poems do that.

DAVID WOJAHN: How would you respond to the charge which some readers and reviewers have made that in terms of their language, in terms of their forms, your poems move toward the mannered despite the incredible violence that sometimes occurs in them. For example, in "The Man in the Yellow Gloves," the speaker seems very adamant towards the end of the poem of defending himself against the accusation that by wearing the gloves he may be a fop or a dandy.

DAVID ST. JOHN: Well, that poem's both a good and a bad example, It's a good example in that what's under discussion in the poem is, of course, the way in which tragedy is masked by beauty, the way in which the violent is gloved by the elegant. And so, the speaker's defense is in some ways my own defense, that I have no particular desire myself to rip off those gloves. On the other hand, I think I could be damned much more completely by picking a poem that wasn't a persona poem. I think you could pick a poem like "Meridian" as being a poem of its own particular manners. And it's one of my favorite poems in the book, one of the key, central poems. I really in all honesty have no response to that question. If people find the poems mannered and elegant, fine. I have no complaints with people preferring to read other kinds of poems; they're just not the kinds of poems that I'm interested in writing. I'm interested in writing the poems that are in the book.

DAVID WOJAHN: More generally, how do you decide on a poem's form? Your work ranges from all sorts of vanguard pyrotechnics, unpunctuated poems that sort of follow Olson's composition-by-field esthetic, to a poem in traditional meter, form. Several of the poems in *The Orange Piano* are sonnets.

DAVID ST. JOHN: It's always pissed me off that it seems to be taken for granted that most young poets know nothing of traditional prosody. Here at Hopkins, I teach a course in traditional poetic forms every year. Both Phil Levine and Donald Justice were teachers of mine who emphasized traditional prosody in their teaching and it's always been important to me. Also, I found that any number of poets who are my contemporaries, or have been my students, find poems in traditional meters, poems with rhymes, to have a central place in their consideration of what poetry is. Just because they don't write sonnets doesn't mean they don't know the craft. It seems to me not only unfair but clearly untrue that young poets don't care and don't know about traditional prosody. As a way of keeping my ear tuned, I've always written poems in forms. Often I will do formal assignments for myself when I give assignments to my classes. But imposed forms do interest me less than a poem that discovers its interior form. That's what I find exciting. The activity of poetry has everything to do with finding a form for consciousness, for perception, and it's in that sinuous entity—of form—that I find the attraction, the appeal, of writing in the first place. In regards to craft, I find writing formal poems tremendously satisfying; yet what I see as the ambition for my own poems doesn't find its articulation in the formal poems that I write. The two sonnets in *The Orange Piano* I like a lot, and I'm very happy with them, but they seem to me to have ambitions that the poems in *No Heaven* don't share. The poems in *No Heaven* have their own ambitions and their own forms of suspension and satisfaction. In the poems in *No Heaven*, especially in, say, a poem like "The Swan at Sheffield Park," there are a lot of jarring enjambments, a lot of purposely roughening line breaks. In spite of the elegance of the poems, there are any number of moments that I think the readers will identify as jarring and disturbing; that's what I was after. I want to keep the reader alert, to occasionally disorient the reader so that I can exploit other moods later on. I do feel though that young poets have been unfairly accused of being "metrically illiterate." I think there's no question that most of the poetry that's being written is unmusical, but I wouldn't exempt formal poetry, highly metrical poetry, from that. Metrics and music are clearly different issues.

DAVID WOJAHN: Well, it seems like there's more formal work being written by young poets today than there's been in the last 30 years or so. Why do you think that is? Why do people of your own generation and even probably a younger generation go back to traditional form so extensively?

DAVID ST. JOHN: I think traditional poems carry with them the kind of consolation that form provides, a recognizable satisfaction of the known, and of working the known in a demanding way. I find Donald Revell's poems interesting; I'm most engaged by the poems of his that are in forms. Molly Peacock has an entire book of formal lyrics that try to use the form to work with a different kind of subject matter. Gjertrud Schnackenberg is a poet whose poems have a fluid interior form as well as, often, a traditionally metrical and rhymed external form. Trudie [Schnackenberg] is probably the best example of a young poet who's employed form in a way in which the form seems an essential element of her own voice rather than an imposed constraint.

DAVID WOJAHN: You followed *Hush* with *The Shore* in 1980, and one of the things that seems so remarkable about *The Shore*, and what happens in *No Heaven* compared to *The Shore*, is how much it strives to depart from the concerns and methods of your earlier poems. The staccato, fugue-like movement of poems in *Hush* like "Gin" and "Slow Dance" appears less frequently. The poems of *The Shore* follow more linear narrative patterns and make use of a flatter diction. How did you seek to change your style after the publication of *Hush*? What kind of process did you go through?

DAVID ST. JOHN: After *Hush* I really wanted a style that was seemingly more available, that had a more available surface for a reader. I wanted to try to enact the same kinds of movements, shifts, and departures that existed in the poems of *Hush*, but more underneath the surface of the poems in *The Shore*. I wanted to create the illusion of a calm, fluid surface while, in fact, being equally manipulative of the reader. Yet there's no question that the style itself was a definite shift. I was reading a lot of Elizabeth Bishop, whom I love, and her poems had tremendous influence on that book. After *The Shore* I wanted to do something very different and I wasn't sure what. I became more and more dissatisfied with the poems I was writing, which seemed adequate and interesting, yet not distinctive enough. I felt that, in the poems I was writing, I wasn't pushing what I sensed as my own limitations. I also felt that the poetry I saw around me, both in books and in magazines, was so complacent and so dull that I felt in revolt against that. I wanted to try to push the language in some other way. That's really what spurred my need to try to find the new manner, new voice, the new aspect for the poems of *No Heaven*.

DAVID WOJAHN: You're going to leave the States this week in order to spend the next year as a Fellow at the American Academy in Rome. What sort of projects do you plan to pursue during the coming year? What plans do you have for future collections?

DAVID ST. JOHN: I have a number of long poems that I've begun. I have three I intend to work on. I've written parts of a novel off and on over the years, but my fiction writing tends to be extremely slick and not terribly interesting to me. If I could find a style in which to write fiction as appealing to me as the styles I seek out in poetry, then it would be worthwhile to me to do. As of yet, I haven't. I've also been writing a good deal of prose about poetry in the last couple of years.

DAVID WOJAHN: If there were a time period, and a place you would choose to live in, when and where would it be?

DAVID ST. JOHN: Well, I like living in this time; I'm very comfortable in this time. I think it's a politically infuriating time, but it's hard to imagine a time that hasn't been politically infuriating. I like being an American; I have no desire to be anything other than American, but that doesn't mean I don't enjoy living and traveling in other parts of the world. In many ways I'm perfectly content to be living in this time and place, this world. For the most part, it makes me happy, and I love being able to write poems. It's the only thing I've ever really wanted from my life, and maybe this will seem to be a small expectation, but I'd like to write half a dozen really beautiful poems. If I can do that I'll be pleased, really pleased. That seems like a worthwhile endeavor for a lifetime.

# THE POETICS OF LIGHT

This interview was conducted by Suzanne Lummis for the *Denver Quarterly*.

SUZANNE LUMMIS: In your poetry you often make great use of the narrative; you have your own form of storytelling. Can you talk about how a poem develops in your mind and to what extent reality is transformed Do most of your poems have a basis in some event or are they totally invented?

DAVID ST. JOHN: Most often they're totally invented. The psychological situation or emotional context will be accurate to a real experience, but the details of the situation will often be completely invented. In terms of the narratives, even the poems that appear to be straightforward narratives are most often dis-narratives. By that I mean that they are fragmented pieces of narrative that are hung upon a liquid, rhythmic movement. Telling pieces of stories interests me much more than telling a whole story, because I think the pieces then begin to reflect something that's more three-dimensional within the experience of the poem. In a book like *The Shore*, my second book, all of those poems talk back to one another. In that way they're linked because they chart the dialectic of a relationship as it unravels. But in *Hush*, my first book, and *No Heaven*, the most recent, the poems are much more located around gestures and fragments than a true narrative.

SUZANNE LUMMIS: Your method reminds me of what David Hockney was working for in his collages. Have you ever heard him talk about his work? He feels that a photograph doesn't represent what life really looks like because it's a single, flat image, while in fact in any given moment there are all kinds of overlapping impressions happening at the same time.

DAVID ST. JOHN: Absolutely. In fact, I feel extremely close to Hockney's ambition in those photo collages. It was really extraordinary watching the PBS special on his photo collages; I thought his project had a great deal in common with the work of many poets I admire.

SUZANNE LUMMIS: In other words, you don't see life as linear and therefore you're not interested in telling stories through a linear narrative.

DAVID ST. JOHN: I think a linear reading of experience is a false reading because it posits the illusion of sequential unity, and it's my feeling that experience is disjunctive and fragmentary. What the poem does is to enfold those disjunctive and fragmentary moments of experience, thereby making them into a single fluid movement of consciousness. And that's an enormous difference from telling a story with a beginning, middle, and end. Obviously, poets aren't the only people who do this; playwrights and fiction writers also do it. Maybe the best way to approach this is to think of it as a cinematic grammar, because the grammar of film probably has more in common with how poetry moves than with what we traditionally think of as the conventional narrative arc of a short story or novel.

SUZANNE LUMMIS: With that in mind, what would you say to someone who had not read much poetry and was hearing yours for the first time in order to help them to know what to look for and how to experience it?

DAVID ST. JOHN: Certainly with my poems, or with the poems of someone like John Ashbery, perhaps it's best to think of them as word movies for the ear, and to experience the poems the way you might experience a piece of music—then their "meaning" will begin to yield and make itself present. Or, encounter the poems the way one encounters—or "reads," as we say—a painting. It's the same problem as when people first begin trying to make sense of abstract expressionism. Their previous methods of "reading" a painting hadn't equipped them with the vocabulary of understanding necessary to respond to what was happening  within the canvas. But any new vocabulary of understanding is assimilated so quickly that now anyone in a shopping mall in Dubuque can see a copy of a Rothko or a Jasper Johns and not be terribly troubled by it. That artistic language has entered the vocabulary of the culture. I think that another good piece of advice is to look for that human voice in the poem, the voice that speaks to the reader. The poets who I most admire bring a voice to their poems that has that dynamic human resonance, a kind of pressure in the language that is truly compelling.

SUZANNE LUMMIS: And who are they?

DAVID ST. JOHN: I think that Norman Dubie's a terrific poet. John Ashbery is an extremely elliptical but remarkable poet; his poems are both beautiful and consoling. They're some of the most musical and elegant poems around. I also think that Charles Wright is one of the most luminous and exacting poets now writing.

SUZANNE LUMMIS: All of these poets you mention have a certain calm in their work and draw more from the intellect than emotion. At least, the emotion in their work seems somehow muted or transformed or not directly accessible. You don't read one of those guys and go "Wow, he's really mad!" or whatever. So...I don't know what my question is exactly...how do you feel about emotion in poetry?

DAVID ST. JOHN: Well, there are poets who I'd consider to be tremendously emotional, like Galway Kinnell or Phil Levine, who I admire as much as any living poets. There are also poets who I won't name who are, I feel, exaggerated, in terms of the emotional figures that exist in their poems. I think they're trying to exploit the reader....

SUZANNE LUMMIS: Oh, I can think of somebody....

DAVID ST. JOHN: I think it has a lot to do with the poet's temperament. I certainly think that my own poems have an overtly dramatic element that, say, the more cerebral poems of Stevens and Ashbery don't desire.

SUZANNE LUMMIS: Are the really good poets being recognized?

DAVID ST. JOHN: I think that there are always poets who aren't appreciated as much as they should be; it's always a matter of degree. Look at a poet like

Charles Wright, who is extremely well-known and yet, in my own opinion, is not regarded as highly as he should be. I think he's really one of the most distinguished and distinctive poets writing. On the other hand, there are a lot of poets who are tremendously well-regarded who I think are totally inconsequential and dull. There are also poets who are *thought* to be something I feel they're not. Consider a poet like James Merrill who was once thought by some to be overly decorous and fanciful. In fact, he's disproved all of his critics repeatedly. In my view, Galway Kinnell was once under-regarded, though certainly in the past fifteen years, especially after *Book of Nightmares*, people have realized how terrific he is.

SUZANNE LUMMIS: How come no women are on the list here?

DAVID ST. JOHN: I think that the best writing in America is being done by young women. There's no question about it. Among the senior figures, who is there—Mona Van Duyn. I think Adrienne Rich is one of the great American poets. Louise Glück is a really superb poet who's charted her own course. There are a lot of terrific young women poets.

SUZANNE LUMMIS: Is that because women are suddenly finding their voice, or because there's a changing attitude about accepting women's work and more interest in what women have to say?

DAVID ST. JOHN: I think a lot of it is cultural. I think that poetry itself has needed the voice of women. Aside from the willingness of the literary community to hear the work of the young women—I think there's a genuine eagerness there—young poets like Jane Hirshfield, Roberta Spear, Karen Fish, Mary Karr, Lynn Emanuel, Brenda Hillman, Ann Lauterbach. and Jorie Graham have emerged as exceptional voices. Also, Gjertrud Schnackenberg, Ellen Bryant Voight, Tess Gallagher, and Carolyn Forché. Forché is clearly the best known of any of them, because she's taken a political position as well and that's aways a magnet for recognition. But there are dozens of young women working in relative obscurity who I think are so powerful, and who have such strong voices.

SUZANNE LUMMIS: Have you at any time dealt with political issues in your poetry?

DAVID ST. JOHN: I think that political issues arise in my poetry all the time. They're embedded there. I think that poems that want to take up the issue of consciousness and the ways in which consciousness performs always are...well, maybe "radical" is the right word. I think that the best poems reinvestigate ideas about consciousness, and I think that's a political act. Norman Dubie is an example of someone who's an extremely political poet. His poems concern themselves with junctures of consciousness—in terms of the history of consciousness. The history of ideas. And in his dramatic monologues, his *personae* are often voices speaking at those very junctures. Dubie seems to me to be a poet with an intellectual scope and historical perspective that is truly singular in contemporary American poems.

SUZANNE LUMMIS: I hear about Norman Dubie, but I don't see him around much.

DAVID ST. JOHN: Dubie is an interesting case because he chooses not to give readings and not to have a public presence in that way. He's decided that whatever reputation he has should come from the work and not from his own self-promotion. It's an ethical decision on his part and one that was made at the very beginning of his career.

SUZANNE LUMMIS: Oh boy, let's talk about that—the role of promotion and mentoring, all of this superfluous—or what should be superfluous—stuff that ends up having a big impact on poets' success. What region the poet is living in, what writing program they're affiliated with, whether some senior poet is recommending them; all this has nothing to do with the work. But don't you feel those things often play a big role?

DAVID ST. JOHN: I think there's no question that there are literary politics and that there is a literary network that exists, both in poetry and in contemporary fiction, the latter of which also involves agents and publishers who are publishing novels at big stakes. In poetry, there is no money involved except for the occasional grant. In the last ten years, I think the NEA has been remarkably equitable. There's no question that literary power is still centralized in New York. But in poetry, as trade publishers have slowly ceased to publish poetry, once again university publishers have picked up the slack. In other words, it's certainly less centralized for poetry than it is for fiction, although in terms of prizes the power is still heavily weighted towards the

East. Reputations are made in New York, not in Iowa City, regardless of what anyone thinks. They're not made in Washington, D.C.; they're made in New York. I'm talking about reputation as *reputation*; I'm not talking about the quality of the work, because I think *those* reputations will take care of themselves.

SUZANNE LUMMIS: You're coming to Los Angeles from Johns Hopkins University, in Baltimore, a place far removed from Los Angeles. Are you discovering any interesting things happening in L.A. poetry?

DAVID ST. JOHN: I think there's a lot of excitement and energy. I haven't seen enough work by people in Los Angeles to be able to generalize. I think that Los Angeles, like San Francisco, like Missoula, Montana, like Tempe, Arizona, are places where serious writers are doing serious work. As someone who has lived for fifteen years in the East, I can say that certainly there's a recognition by other poets *there* that the East Coast is not the only place where poets are writing well and writing seriously.

SUZANNE LUMMIS: I want to back up and talk about your own creative process. Where does a poem begin for you?

DAVID ST. JOHN: For me a poem begins with a piece of verbal music. Often, I find that if I go into a poem knowing "what I want to say" or what the poem is going to be "about," I can write—because I'm experienced—a perfectly decent, well-written, competent, maybe even interesting poem. But, the point is, I will have discovered nothing in the course of that poem; for me, it's absolutely essential to be able to make some kind of discovery as I become involved in the writing of the poem. I don't want to know where the poem is going to lead me necessarily. I may have a general sense of what the poem is going to address, but I try to allow language to guide me. Then I begin to discover what the focus and the architecture of the poem will be. Often, in fact, I will have a general sense of what the architecture and movement of the poem will be, but I don't have any of the details. And that's the real excitement for me. That's what I love to discover.

SUZANNE LUMMIS: We've been talking about your interest in exploring consciousness; is poetry more suited for these kinds of explorations than other art forms? A while back you said, "Poetry does it with language."

DAVID ST. JOHN: Language and words are the only means by which we have to understand ourselves or to talk about ourselves to each other, or, even more basically, simply to ourselves. And if our understandings of language and our understandings of how language performs and is enacted are constrained and basic, then so too will be the ways with which we try to understand ourselves. The more complex and resonant our understanding of language, the more sophisticated and accurate the ways with which we'll be able to understand and talk about ourselves. This is one of the things poetry helps to allow us.

SUZANNE LUMMIS: How did you come to poetry? Was there a specific moment when you decided you were going to be a poet?

DAVID ST. JOHN: I started writing as a teenager, but then I also started playing in rock and roll bands. My family had a lot of books around and I always read a lot as a kid. But I think that the turning point came when I was eighteen and I met Larry Levis, who introduced me to Phil Levine. This was in Fresno, where I was born. At that point I was still playing music. My grandfather had been an English professor and Dean of Humanities at the college. But I had been raised to be a tennis player. My father was a tennis player. Still, by the time I was eighteen, I had settled on poetry. And my temperament...even though I had written fiction and enjoy writing fiction, I find my own fiction to be too predictable and too slick. I really much prefer the stories and pieces of stories I can tell within poems.

SUZANNE LUMMIS: And now you're teaching here at USC. Let's talk about that, since teaching is the way most serious poets have chosen to make a living. Is that good for poets—that academic world—or would it be useful to have a few more poets out there racing cars, building bridges and...I don't know...getting drunk and falling off their bar stools.

DAVID ST. JOHN: I think poets live the least secluded lives of anyone in the academy. Certainly the poets I know who teach in universities live as complicated and raucous lives as the poets who don't teach. And there are also poets who do not teach who live as quiet, formal, and "academic" lives as the poets within. I don't think it has anything to do with whether the poet is in or out of the university; I think it has everything to do with the poet's own choices and temperament. I could point to half a dozen people teaching in universities who could give Bukowski a run for his drinking money. The point is that teaching allows a lot of poets the chance to talk about something they love, whereas there's very little other opportunity in America to talk about poetry with love and a depth of understanding. It's also important being around young writers; the enthusiasm and energy of young writers, I think, helps keep older writers young. It's invigorating. Poets teach not simply to make a living but because they draw on that energy. It's also an extremely expensive activity, of course, in terms of your time and creative energy. But most of the people I know still seem to feel it's a reasonable trade-off. Perhaps you can't teach forever. I think that there comes a point when poets should allow themselves to devote their energies simply to their own work, if they can afford to do so. But isn't that for each poet to decide? I have my own time picked already—but I'm not telling.

# REACHING TO TOUCH MYSTERY

This interview was conducted by Julius Olusola Sokenu
for *Hayden's Ferry Review*.

JULIUS SOKENU: David Kalstone in *Becoming A Poet* said of Elizabeth Bishop that she seemed to be searching for a place she'd never been—almost like longing for a connection with a place or people. Your work like hers deals with searching and travel as a means of self analysis; the poems in *No Heaven* come to mind specifically. What function does travel play in your aesthetic?

DAVID ST. JOHN: One of the things that has been a constant in my poems is the attempt to deal with a sensibility in process, in movement, and it's present in the poems of *The Shore* as well. Its two primary figures, both the speaker and the "you," are often in a state of movement and travel as they consider the process and progress of their relationship. In *No Heaven*, as well as *Terraces of Rain*—whose poems are all set in a limited locale, Italy—one of the things I'm trying to do is to create a sense of a moving backdrop. With the kind of displacement that I like to talk about, it seems to be useful to the poems to allow that displacement to occur physically as a component of the particular landscape. I suppose it's because I believe that poets are all to some extent talking about a kind of homelessness, about a kind of exploration that might lead them to some "true home." Different poems have different means of doing that. Some poets, as we know, are tremendously located in a particular place, whether it's a place in which they've lived, an imagined place, or a place from their past. For me it has been more urgent to find locales, whether unnamed American locales or European locales, to establish this sense of a moving backdrop, in what I hope is a cinematic fashion. Again, it is to emphasize that sense of displacement, that sense of necessary reckoning for the figures.

JULIUS SOKENU: You mentioned *Terraces of Rain* as your first book with a specifically identifiable locale; it is also the first time locale is used not just as a backdrop but as part of a sense of the poems. What's the attraction Italy holds for poets, especially young poets today, and people as disparate as Lawrence and Byron?

DAVID ST. JOHN: One of the things I wanted to do was to work against the convention of the tourist poem. What I wanted was more in the tradition of Goethe and Henry James. Once again, I wanted to set my figures, set my characters in motion against these particular settings. There were also certain conventions of that literature that I wanted to play against, to exploit in terms of watching the progress of the relationship that exists in many of these poems. I chose Italy not only because I had been living and traveling in Italy over a period of a year and a half, but because of this literary inheritance that I could play off of, and because of the sense of theater—even opera—inherent to Italian life itself. I wanted the figures who turn up in the poems to be set free in this landscape and I wanted to see what might happen to them. All of the poems are acts of discovery; I am as curious to find out what the figures might do as anybody else. I've been talking about these figures as if they were characters in a narrative sense, and though the poems may have some implicit narrative context, they are obviously not linear narratives. They are pieces of stories meant to reflect the larger fabric of some other story.

JULIUS SOKENU: In talking about *Terraces of Rain*, the poem "The Doors" seems to chronicle a relationship that seems coded. Could you explain how you came to the poem and the symbolism of the piece? And more specifically the use of the door.

DAVID ST. JOHN: The doors that are mentioned are in fact literal doors on the Church of San Zeno in Verona. These doors have set into them a series of bronze panels. All of these panels depict Bibilical scenes, and these doors became the object of pilgrimages. Religious travelers from all over the world would come to Verona to see these famous doors. One of the things that's happening in the course of the poem is that the male figure, who also appears in the other poems in these declensions of relationship, finds himself at San Zeno before these doors and begins to imagine himself as if he were one of the participants in these scenes. Whether it's the scene with Abraham and Isaac, or that of Noah and the flood, or the scene of Adam talking about Cain and Abel. The poem then resolves as he fixes upon one of the bronze panels that depicts the story of Salomé and John the Baptist. And so the whole pun on St. John and that element begins to play in it as well. The doors stand as portals to something beyond, some other possibility of access, of knowledge, even of a future. It's an archetypal image for us, that sense of not only what is beyond but also what is being withheld from us.

JULIUS SOKENU: The poem "The River," and other poems in *Hush,* seem to originate from the mytho-poetic; more recently the poems in *Terraces of Rain* seem to evoke the metaphysical. The characters in "The Doors," "Ecologue," and "Photograph of V" not only transcend space but (as in *No Heaven)* the use of pronouns such as you, he, she suggest that the mundane has become sacred, and that indeed we create our own heaven. Is this an accurate assessment of these poems and would you comment on the use of the mytho-poetic in your writing?

DAVID ST. JOHN: I think that all of the poems from *Hush* to the most recent share the same ambition of trying to touch mystery. Many of the poems, however situated they are in a particular landscape, often revolve around relationships and what happens between men and women, which seems to me some of the most fascinating material that exists. It's also true that they all do share this desire to unravel the daily, the visible, and the mundane in a way that will make accessible something that is more remote, more mysterious, that could bear the name of the sacred. It seems to me a poet's job is to unname the world. At this point in our history we understand that the many languages we have inherited provide us with structures of constraint, not structures of freedom. It seems to me one of the functions of a poet is to take the names that we've inherited from our cultures—the names we've been given by our cultures, our teachers and our families—and to explode those names and then to find ways of renaming that world in a more accurate, supple and subtle way. This seems to me absolutely basic in terms of the poet's occupation; unless we are able to do this as poets and as people then we are really condemned to speak with someone else's voice. Whether it's as Adrienne Rich says "the language of the oppressor" or simply, in a more insidious way, the language of the familiar. For me, my ambition as a poet more and more seems to run contrary to every major current in American poetry. It is, as I see it, for a poetry that will have the appearance of being, I'm happy to say, increasingly hermetic. And which will, in fact, seem to be exploiting values that one could associate with Mallarmé and the symbolists. As Americans we fear eloquence, we fear a complicated statement; we are afraid of those "foreigners" out there and their educations and their elaborate language and we find this in our literature as well as our politics. American poetry has become the Gary Cooper school of poetry. The less elaborated a poem, the more genuine it must be. What this has led us to is a poetry of reportage, simple reporting on events or emotions. I don't believe that's what poetry is; I believe poetry is a verbal enactment. Poetry has to do with the activated imagination in exactly the way that Stevens "stages" a poem in his poem "Of Modern Poetry." Ashbery's poetry has taken that notion of the stage and recreated a cinematic kind of screen. He's set the stage in motion and that has been tremendously exciting for American poetry. Unless we understand that a poem is not an object, unless we understand that a poem is an experience, then we can't recognize the failure of so much of American poetry. Unless we can recognize that the experiential quality of a poem is one of its greatest attributes then we are still condemned to be voyeurs of each other's worlds.

JULIUS SOKENU: So in creating a poem that is more mythical, with its own sense of place, and creating its own universe you are providing an alternative to what is considered "acceptable" in American poetry?

DAVID ST. JOHN: I think there are a lot of poets who are trying to find their way toward this kind of access, toward materials that seem to me the most precious, most mysterious. It's an old idea of poetry and one that has been unfashionable throughout much of the 20th century. What's relevant about this idea now is that poems provide architectures of the imagination. What a poem provides is the experience of another person's consciousness and the way in which they encounter a particular experience or a particular sequence of perceptions. What a good poem is able to do is to allow us to share the experience that's been offered by the poem. But I want to make a distinction;

by experience I don't mean the content of the story. By experience I mean the process of a poem, the style, the movement, the enactment of the poem; it's the enactment of a poem that is most crucial. It's experiencing that enactment which allows us to share in the empathies of the poet or to recognize and quite literally experience those concerns. In other words, every poem of reportage, every poem that draws its conclusions for us, is a dull poem. Unless we as readers are allowed to draw our own conclusions and make our own judgments the poem has failed, because it's imposed something upon us. This seems to me a crucial issue because so much of the poetry I see is concerned with the minutia of revelation, the tiny domestic details of experience.

JULIUS SOKENU: Given what you've just said what do you think of confessional poetry?

DAVID ST. JOHN: I think that confessional poetry has labored under a lot of misunderstanding. I still don't understand why Berryman is so undervalued in this country. I think Lowell is a fascinating poet and after his death his reputation suffered a tremendous reaction. I also think that poets like Randall Jarrell and Delmore Schwartz are terribly undervalued; I think that Sylvia Plath is a dazzling poet. Don't forget that those poets we call confessional poets came to maturity at a time in our culture when we were suffering a kind of national nervous breakdown. These poets articulated in their poetry and, unfortunately, at times in their lives, the manifestations of that breakdown.

Poets have traditionally spoken to and of the issues of the future at every turn of literary history. There is an important reason for this, and that's that art quite literally makes possible the future. What art intends to do is to create those structures of understanding—whether it's in painting, music, poetry or fiction—that we as a culture will need in those futures to come. This might sound grandiose to some but it seems to me quite literally true. If we look back at the history of modernism and the way in which the question of fragmentation is dealt with by Eliot's "The Waste Land," we begin to see how these are the very issues that we've had to address throughout this century. Or, look at Cezanne and the way in which he introduces a multiplicity of perspective into a single canvas, then how Braque and Picasso take this and run with it and we have the multiple perspective of Cubism. These are the things that make American poetry what it is today: multiplicity, simultaneity and polyvocality; many voices, many perspectives happening at the same time. In this century, as experience has become more and more accelerated, and as the fragmentation of that experience has become more pronounced, we as a culture have responded first in terror of this disintegration and then by embracing all of these fragments of the culture. It's one of the aspects of what has come to be called post modernism, that is, the way in which many fragments can be culled together into one text, into one fabric. It is very much what the poetry of John Ashbery tries to do. What Ashbery's poems make clear to us is that we as individuals are capable of a consciousness that can absorb these jagged pieces of experience and yet not be terribly threatened, that can *continue*, much in the way that the current of a river after a flood contains the debris and the wreckage of that flood and yet continues onward. So these are the issues that seem to me to be at stake.

JULIUS SOKENU: You mentioned the French Symbolists earlier. I have a sense that the French Symbolist poets are very important to your work. Do you see yourself continuing that tradition? In terms of this could you explain the poem "Merlin," included in *The Best American Poetry 1991*? It is different from most of your elegies in its tone and metaphysical associations.

DAVID ST. JOHN: Absolutely. You are right in linking your question to that poem. That poem was written at a time when it became clear to me that my own ambitions in my poetry had to do with an investigation of something quite mysterious and obscure. The poets I began returning to were the poets of mystery, the poets whom we associate with a kind of decadent occultism: Baudelaire and Mallarmé, to Celan, Dino Campana, Gérald de Nerval. These are the poets who, in the last few years, have emerged for me as central to my own ambitions. The evidence of this new chapter in an old orientation in my work hasn't been seen by people yet. The poems that are beginning to reflect this most profoundly are still unpublished. So far, the poems that most address this aspect of mystery are the poems of *No Heaven*. It's there that the poems come closest to touching what we might call the magical, mystical, and ephemeral. Saying these things will get me into endless trouble with many poets because one is no longer allowed to talk about the mystical, but I've decided that this is nonsense. I have both masked this impulse in my work and articulated it in the past in, I hope, interesting ways. Now that I've been writing for almost twenty-five years I don't feel that I have anything to prove. I am writing simply to please myself and two or three friends. I am writing to discover what I hope is to be discovered and I have no idea what that might be.

JULIUS SOKENU: So was "Merlin" an exercise in discovery?

DAVID ST. JOHN: "Merlin" was an important poem to me. It was meant to honor the memory of Italo Calvino, who seems to me the real magician of language of our century. He is the Magus to me; he is the Merlin of our time. I was lucky enough to get to know Calvino while I lived in Italy. His presence as an individual had a profound influence upon me, an influence I would count as equal to that of his work. There is simply no writer whose work I love more and no writer whose intelligence and investigative imagination I respect more. As everyone knows, his death was extremely sudden. I had left Rome only a few weeks before his death. I had seen Calvino and his wife, Chichita, the day before I left and we had made plans to get together the following fall in Cambridge, Massachusetts, where Calvino would be living. I was sitting in my apartment in Baltimore one afternoon and for no reason at all I went out to get the daily New York Times, and in it was Calvino's obituary. One thing about the poem "Merlin" is that nothing "happens." It's just the speaker's reckoning with the furniture of mystery while trying to sketch some absent space of who or what had been that mystery.

JULIUS SOKENU: Talking about imagination, Charles Simic is quoted as having said of contemporary poetry and poets, "What is curious to me is that we are no longer astonished at being alive. Wonder is getting to be a rare emotion." The poems of No Heaven and Hush in their ways seem to wonder aloud about the human condition. Poems like "Wedding Preparations in the Country" in Hush, "Waltz" and the title poem from The Orange Piano, and "Eclogue" from Terraces of Rain do the same. Do you agree with Simic and if so, do you agree that this ability to wonder makes you a Romantic in the tradition of Rilke? How do you sustain such romanticism in these trying times?

DAVID ST. JOHN: I think there's still a lot of that Romantic legacy we all work with or against. What interests me about Simic's observation is that American poets do seem to me tremendously presumptuous about the world they live in. We assume a kind of oddly masterful, even colonial attitude toward the people and things of the world, including I think the natural world. What good is the poet who is incapable of awe and wonder; that poet might as well be a politician. Unless a poet can be surprised, unless a poet maintains an extraordinary innocence in the face of all the horror we know, then we are again condemned to poems that will simply tell us what we already know. It seems to me crucial that a poet not only be able to see afresh but then to say afresh that which has been seen. It is the way a poet has said whatever has been seen that makes it live newly within us as readers. My own poems have been referred to as having a kind of decadence and one reviewer (of *No Heaven*) spoke of it, in fact, as a critique of decadence. I'll happily admit to every decadent aspect in my poems, but they also contain a kind of awe and innocence that one does not traditionally associate with the works we call decadent. Also, I think what's happening stylistically in my poems, especially the poems of *No Heaven*, is meant to be the real point of those poems. Anyone who looks to the content of the poems has missed the point. The narratives are there to serve the particular function of distracting the imagination; it's the engagement and the enactment of the process of the poem itself that is the real "meaning."

JULIUS SOKENU: Your books seem to develop around a particular theme or vision, and the tensions carry over from poem to poem. For example the Éluard epigraph, "*Are we two or am I all alone*" from *Hush* sets the tone for the book. Is this a conscious decision or a by-product of the process?

DAVID ST. JOHN: It's a conscious decision. Early on in working on the poems of *Hush* I realized that many of the poems I was writing had particular things in common. Although *Hush* is more of a collection than a book written as a book, I think from the poem "Four O'Clock in Summer: Hope" on, the book is very much of a piece. *The Shore* was written obviously to be a book. The poems talk back to one another, they refer to one another; there is the progress of a relationship within the book. Clearly, *No Heaven* was written as a book and in many ways I think of it as a book-length poem. That is why the interludes serve as quite literal interludes to the whole. *Terraces of Rain*, again, was written to be a book with the poems talking back to one another. I don't have much interest in writing individual disparate poems. Obviously I've done it and a lot of it and I've also published three limited edition books: *The Olive Grove*, *The Orange Piano*, and one is forthcoming called *The Unsayable, the Unknowable and You*. These limited edition books served as collections in that they've become repositories for individual poems that did not fit into the idea of the book that I was writing at that time. When I set out to write a new book it helps me to think of it as a whole book rather than just a series of individual poems. This may be a great disadvantage, and might make the books seem much less various than they might be, but that is what I have to live with, and that's the way I work best.

JULIUS SOKENU: In the poem "Iris," with the image of the train and the young boy bidding his grandmother farewell, one senses that the poem springs straight from your childhood. Can you comment about this poem and what it means to you?

DAVID ST. JOHN: As it happens, I just wrote an essay about that particular poem. One of the things that I don't want to do is talk about the poem in a way that I become reductive. In the essay I'm referring to, I labored long and hard to remain as vague as possible. But, let me say that the grandmother for whom the elegy is written, her favorite flower in the world was the iris, and she raised huge iris beds. Details of her own biography sort of emerge in the course of the poem, but I wanted it to be this imaginatively transformative act in response to the grief. What the speaker and the child within the speaker both respond to is this kind of twin image of the iris as this emblem of beauty and this emblem of grief. I think grief in some ways reduces us all to children, and in the elegy the speaker of the poem feels himself a boy again, and it's why the boy in the poem must die for the grandmother to be allowed to pass on. And that's why he's left standing on the platform at the end.

JULIUS SOKENU: Is your muse male or female? How do you explain your poems in light of recent feminist criticism which suggests that male writers, in casting women as objects of desire, contribute to their identity problems?

DAVID ST. JOHN: What's been interesting to me is that, on a first reading, I think it might appear to people that the female figures in my poems exist as conventional objects of desire. And yet, what women who have written about my work have discovered is, in fact, that the poems are consistently addressing the ideal of a dialectic. In other words, the poems are always about equality and the dialectic between the male and female principles. The whole premise of the book *The Shore* is that the relationship there is a dialectical process. One could argue that the speaker is given a greater empowerment, and yet there's nothing in particular that would force the reader to see that speaker as particularly male or female. I think the speaker of those poems could as easily be female as male. One of the reasons I've often liked using the second person in my poems is to allow for a more androgynous sensibility to arise from the speaking voice. The poems of *No Heaven* could initially be seen as more starkly masculine and feminine, that the figures are very much concerned with male and female roles, and *that*, I would have to insist, is the point. Those poems want to address the whole nature of male and female masks and role playing, and the specifics of the enactment of those roles on our daily stage. What's been gratifying to me is that the poems, even a poem like "Last Night with Rafaella," have not been misread. I think the whole point of a book like *No Heaven* is the attempt to subvert conventional roles, conventional ideals, and ideas that have to do with male and female relationships. Certainly it's been a constant ongoing concern in all of my work.

JULIUS SOKENU: Would you say that the muse is male at times, and female at other times?

DAVID ST. JOHN: I think my muse is a cross-dresser and I still can't tell if my muse is singularly sexed or not.

JULIUS SOKENU: You mentioned "Last Night with Rafaella," and it seems to me, and with most of your poems, the women are quite strong. They're not passive women. If anything, it seems that the speaker takes things in a much more passive manner.

DAVID ST. JOHN: I think this is an important point; it is without question precisely the situation of the poems of *The Shore*. The female figure is almost invariably the activating character. The speaker tends to be more tentative, more passive, and the function of that is very, I should confess, premeditated. It's to give the female figure the kind of presence in the poems that I hoped, and continue to hope, would run contrary to this whole contention in which the poems are clad.

JULIUS SOKENU: Jean Valentine in a recent interview with Michael Kline in *American Poetry Review* stated that a poem is a way of speaking to an audience. Speaking implies listening, and hopefully being heard. What are you saying and who do you see yourself addressing?

DAVID ST. JOHN: I think if one imagines that one has a large audience there's the instant danger of being tempted to make proclamations. I think when one thinks of one's audience it should be a very discrete audience because we constantly have before us the example of poets who seem, to me at least, to be behaving as if the world were hanging on their every whim and utterance. I think poetry, contrary to what people may complain about, has an enormous audience. I hope my poems address certain issues that have relevance in regard to the dilemmas of contemporary life, to the kind of psychic wreckage we often find ourselves confronted with (either in ourselves or in friends), the dilemmas of male/female relationships which seem, to me, crucial to our time. I would hope the poems also provide the experience of music and beauty. I believe profoundly in the idea of Art; I'm tremendously old fashioned in that way. I believe art is one of the most transformative experiences that a human being can have. I mean painting, I mean music, sculpture. I don't want to separate poetry from any of the other arts. It seems to me absolutely urgent that what poetry does and can do be seen in the context of what art as a whole can do. At the same time, the vocabulary of how any particular art functions changes from century to century, decade to decade. I certainly feel myself to be a poet of this time. Even though I feel that a lot of my values are very similar to Symbolist values, the ways in which I choose to accomplish those values, I would hope, are completely contemporary, and quite different from how poets of the late 19th century would choose to enact their poems. I think it's this idea of enactment that's quite different.

JULIUS SOKENU: Your poems are populated with visual artists. Some of your most striking poems, like "The Avenues," in *The Shore,* have been about artists or paintings and photographs themselves. There seems to have been an abundance of painters in your life. What influence have they had on your work?

DAVID ST. JOHN: The other arts are central to how I think about poetry. One of my aunts was a painter. I was an enthusiastic but terrible rock and roll musician myself, but music of all kinds—classical, jazz, rock—have always been a big part of my life. Cinema has been important for me. Also a lot of the figures who intrigue me are figures who are themselves contending with the imagination and the realm of what is artistic. They exist in the poems because they intrigue me in the world as well. It would be hard, I think, to overestimate the influence of painters, film makers, even musicians on my work. So, my values about what a poem is and how a poem works and exists in the world have very much to do with non-linear arts. I think the biggest mistake that poets make is to believe that poems exist in some way divorced from the other arts. Certainly a poem seems to me to have much more in common with a painting or a film than it does even with a story. A poem is not linear; or at least my idea is that a good poem is not linear. One could argue that a good story is not linear either. I think people get confused because they think they understand how language works and so they think they should "understand the poem." They don't get it–that a poet uses language as his *material*, in a way that a sculptor uses stone or wood or clay, and a painter uses paint.

JULIUS SOKENU: You mentioned film; which specific film makers influence your work or interest you?

DAVID ST. JOHN: Obviously, Pasolini is someone who interests me, who, even though he's best known in this country as a film maker, is a tremendous poet. And as a temperament and sensibility he interests me. Film makers who I found really dazzling are many of the obvious ones, but I would name Bertolucci first. And maybe it's no accident that his father was an extremely famous poet. He himself began working in cinema alongside Pasolini and at nineteen published a book of poems. There's something poetic in what he thinks of as being "cinematic." Bergman, Truffaut; I'm also a huge fan of Eric Rohmer. I think Rohmer is a sensational film maker. I envy the way in which he is able to envelop that kind of wit in his movies, as well as great passion, in a very seemingly offhanded way. But, the Italian neorealists fascinate me for the sense of struggle and texture in those movies. Other influences who are more contemporary would be Wenders, who in his friendship and close workings with Peter Handke shows that same poetic impulse that I admire and envy.

JULIUS SOKENU: Do you use seduction and sensuality to make the unpalatable grief and inability to connect of the characters in your poems palpable?

DAVID ST. JOHN: The simple answer is yes. I hope the poems do in fact function as seductions to the reader. I think the sensuality of the poems is one of their most important attributes. I want the poems to be rich and sensual. I want that to act as a kind of realm of awe and pleasure for the reader. At the same time, as you suggest in the question, the particular psychological land-scape of one of these poems might be fairly desperate, fairly harsh, even though it's joined to a kind of sensuality. The two seem to me absolutely companionable, both in experience and poetry. It's a tension that I think we don't often see. Think of Bertolucci; there's this kind of visual richness and sensuality, and yet the particular scene or concern of the film at that given moment might be tremendously severe, even harsh. I think that's something similar to what I'm looking for in these poems. I suppose that, given what I've said about the sensuality, the opulence, the extravagance, the decadence, of my own poems, someone unfamiliar with them would go expecting to find Oscar Wilde. It's simply against the landscape of contemporary poetry, I think, that my poems do stand out in that regard. I'm not sure this is good or bad; certainly to many poets this would be bad. It's one of the things I like most about my own poems.

JULIUS SOKENU: What disturbs you most about contemporary poetry?

DAVID ST. JOHN: The idea that language is simply a utilitarian object much as it is in the rest of our lives. I think there's the constant illusion that the kind of reportage that I was mentioning earlier becomes representative of some "integrity," this courageous witnessing of any kind, personal or political. We've been allowed as poets to be persuaded that the Puritan plain style is the most appropriate language for our poetry. This seems to me an absolute perversion of William Carlos Williams' ideal about American speech, a poetry that reflects an American vernacular. I think the isolationist tendency that leads us to honor a poetry of utter banality and "accessibility" has become very, very dangerous. I want to see poetry treating language with more respect and pleasure. I want to feel as if mystery and ambiguity have a place in American poetry again. At present, American poetry lives in terror of ambiguity as we do in our politics as well. We'd much rather be lied to than not know. There's such a tremendous range, stylistically, of wonderful poetry being written; I don't mean to suggest that I want a poetry only of one kind. But, at the same time, we've abandoned our love of sensual language. We've abandoned the idea that poetry can be powerful and pleasurable. We've begun to be so reductive in our idea of the language that is proper to poetry that we've excluded a whole realm of verbal experience. This seems to me saddening in that we can't afford this impoverishment in our poetry. The other thing that disturbs me is that poets want to align themselves with particular poetic trends and poetic schools. I think we should always be suspicious of poets who run in packs. Poets who run in packs are hungry for fame; the ambition for oneself is different, obviously, than the ambition for one's work.

JULIUS SOKENU: What can't you write about? What would you not consider writing about?

DAVID ST. JOHN: In other words, what would I consider out of bounds in terms of content or subject matter? I would never rule anything out. I think poems can address anything. But there are certain subjects, there are certain arenas of subject matter that seem to me inherently melodramatic and sentimental. In the hands of other poets perhaps they would not be so. This is a decision, I think, that each poet has to make. I'm constantly reading the poems of poets who I feel have chosen sentimental and melodramatic subject matter and yet two days later I'll see a great poem on the same subject matter by a different poet. So, it was the style not the subject matter that was sentimental. I think the point is that subject matter is not the issue; it's the imagination, perceptions, talent, and craft of the poet who chooses that particular subject matter.

JULIUS SOKENU: You'll be forty-three soon. You are most definitely considered one of the best poets of your generation. If you were to take an inventory of the world and your writing, what questions would you ask?

DAVID ST. JOHN: I would ask myself why I haven't written more than I've written and my answer would be that I have written more, but so much of it is so bad that no one has ever seen it. I would ask myself did I truly believe in the power of poetry with the kind of passion that I seem to hold. I would say no, even more so. I believe poetry has an absolutely central place in the life of the culture and one need only look at South American, European, East European cultures to find the centrality of poetry there. I think it's misleading if we look only to the place of poetry in America. Those who say that poetry is in bad shape, or "What's wrong with poetry," are completely misguided. I think it's tremendously strong. I think the number of terrific poets writing and the variety of the poems that they're writing has never been greater. In spite of the fact that trade publishers have backed away from publishing poetry, an impressively large number of books of poetry are being published. The audience for poetry has never been larger. I think the accusation that the audience for poetry is entirely academic is completely wrong. It shows that the person who says it has spent no time in any mildly metropolitan community in America. I think in world communities as well you'd find the same broad appetite outside of the academy for poetry. What impresses me is precisely how broad-based and widespread the audience for poetry is today. I not only don't believe any of the doomsayers about contemporary poetry, all the evidence I see is absolutely to the contrary.

JULIUS SOKENU: In your interview with *The Seneca Review* you commented on being "pissed" about the assumption that most young poets know nothing of traditional prosody. *Terraces of Rain* has been praised for its formal devices. Are you still pissed and what do you think of the new formalism?

DAVID ST. JOHN: Formal concerns take various shapes. Whether they involve traditional metrics and rhymes or not, poets are always dealing with formal concerns. In *Terraces of Rain* some of the poems use traditional schemes, obviously the villanelle, and the Pasolini poem, which uses terza rima, and which is meant to be a specific echo of Pasolini's own use of terza rima. Of the new formalists, whom I prefer calling the new traditionalists, in their defense I think most of them are made nervous by being lumped together since stylistically and temperamentally they seem to me varied. What's most disturbing about many of those poets is that they incorporate the mechanics of traditional metrics without being musical. It's very, very disturbing to see a poem that is technically quite proficient and yet painfully unmusical and unpoetic. This is my main complaint. There are fabulous poets writing in traditional forms and metrics, poets like Gjertrud Schnackenberg, Tom Sleigh, Molly Peacock, to name just a few. And yet the idea that poets like, say, Larry Levis don't know anything about prosody couldn't be farther from the truth. If Levis wished tomorrow, he could sit down and write a dazzling cycle of sonnets.

JULIUS SOKENU: Guillaume Apollinaire once referred to poetry as existing between chaos and adventure. Do you think of your work as Dionysian or Apollonian in its structure or origin?

DAVID ST. JOHN: I think in its origin it's completely Dionysian. The Apollonian gets invited to participate in the shaping of what's Dionysian about it.

Any poetry that I admire seems to me to invite both gods into the arena. I think one of the difficulties in making the choice is that one is never simply one or the other. There is always the sense of the yin and the yang. There's always the process of reciprocity in the making of the poem. But I think I'm looking toward something more mysterious, even primitive and ecstatic in the poems. I do want to stand in that lineage of mystical poets from St. John of the Cross to Blake to Dino Campana. I don't know about you, but to me it seems like a great place to stand.

# DAVID ST. JOHN

This interview was conducted by Karen Fish for the *American Poetry Review.*

*The following conversation occurred over a few days in January, 1994 at the home of David St. John in Venice, California. The interview was completed by mail during the last weeks of February, 1994.*

KAREN FISH: How would you like this interview to begin, if you were given your choice?

DAVID ST. JOHN: Well, I love those descriptions of writers' houses that open all the *Paris Review* interviews; I also used to love that old feature from *Esquire,* I think it was, called "Why I Live Where I Live," that was done by various writers.

KAREN FISH: O.K. Describe yourself for us in those terms.

DAVID ST. JOHN: I'd say, "David St. John lives with his wife, poet Molly Bendall, and their daughter Vivienne in a 1910 Craftsman bungalow on a historic, palm-lined street in Venice, California. Like other poor poets living in expensive cities, he rents. A fascinating feature of this house is that it has, as the mantle to its fireplace, a piece of the original Venice pier, salvaged when the pier first burned down. It is important that poets live in houses and apartments with character. His previous place of residence was a large, beautiful apartment just half a block from Muscle Beach on the Venice Boardwalk; this was an apartment that had been frequented over the years by members of the bands The Eagles and, more recently, Suicidal Tendencies. At the end of this block, Jim Morrison, singer and near-poet, lived in a building fronting the Venice Boardwalk; there is now a three-story mural of Morrison on the building to memorialize this fact. In the midst of this charged cultural atmosphere, David St. John has lived for the past seven years."

KAREN FISH: *(Laughs)* Do you often refer to yourself in the third person?

DAVID ST. JOHN: As often as socially acceptable. You know, in spite of the irony in that description, I do love living in California, even though there's so much academic and literary condescension about the work—both scholarly and literary—that's done by people west of the Hudson; but it doesn't really bother me. After all, I lived outside of California, mainly on the East Coast, for seventeen years, so I saw all of that truly moronic prejudice first-hand. I think I'm pretty immune to it by now. But I confess that sometimes I miss living in the East, where, at least in a few places, the cultural icons still tend to be a bit more literary. I also miss living on the Amtrak corridor and having access to museums in New York and Washington, D.C. Even so, there's only one other place in America like Venice, and that's Key West. It's not an accident that both of these places are at the literal ends of the road—take one more step and you hit the waves. As a result, all kinds of fascinating human jetsam collects. Venice, of course, has a long history as an artistic and poetic community, though now it's mostly known through TV and movies as a place where colorful weirdos collect and beautiful women roller skate nearly nude. This is all true of course, and the degree of physical display is often quite astonishing, but the mix of the place is really the most amazing thing: lawyers, painters, junkies, movie producers, Sixties refugees of every stripe. Down the alley is a guy with two Rollses and another with a DeLorean. Then there's me with my fifteen-year old Mazda. Often, here in Los Angeles, we like to rank success by the simple measure of your wheels, so you can see where I come along the status food chain. When I was trying to decide whether to come and teach at USC, I promised myself that if I did move to LA I'd definitely live by the beach, where the air is great and the sound of the waves is endlessly consoling. Besides, I saw all those Route 66 episodes as a kid.

KAREN FISH: When you write a poem, do you have a particular audience in mind? Also, if you had to be critical of contemporary poetry, what aspect of the current climate would you describe negatively?

DAVID ST. JOHN: My sense of audience has changed over the years. At times it's been very specific, a group of four or five people—friends and other poets—I knew would see and read the poems. Then for a while I had a sense of a wider audience, but I think that only lasted for about ten minutes, fortunately. I think poets often write for themselves, that is, for their sense of the language. We all know poets who suddenly begin writing for posterity or for particular critics who have praised them in past reviews; their work turns to shit as a result, of course. I'm not saying that one's ambitions shouldn't be enormous, but there's a difference between one's ambitions for the work and one's ambitions for oneself. As to the second part of your question, I'd have to say that I'm most upset by the extraordinary and pervasive terror that has emerged in American poetry—a terror of ambiguity, the utter terror of any mystery in our poetry. Or our lives, for that matter. We've become so dogmatically literal-minded in our poetry that most of the work I read is a mildly glorified domestic journalism with a little *frisson* of revelation (always a minor revelation) or a tiny twinge of conscience thrown in, in order to convince you it's poetry and not an article for your local neighborhood newspaper.

KAREN FISH: Could you be a bit more specific?

DAVID ST. JOHN: You know the kind of poem I mean: A male poet is driving in his car; he's listening to the radio and an especially meaningful song from his past comes on, interrupting his train of thought about the stripper that he secretly wants to see in the club he's just passed. But he's an intelligent man, of course, and very sensitive (otherwise he wouldn't be a poet), so he grows ashamed of himself, and admits this in the poem, to show us how enlightened he is and yet still really just an ordinary Joe. Then, inevitably, he thinks of his wife and the way she holds her white coffee cup in the pure light of the morning and, well, he's moved to tears, right there on the highway on his way home to his pathetic life and patronized wife. We're supposed to be moved at this poor posturing jerk and his confession of human fraility. It's all so calculated and precious. More chardonnay angst.

KAREN FISH: But don't you think poems concerning domestic situations can sometimes be moving?

DAVID ST. JOHN: O.K., I'd be moved if there was one ounce of interesting language there, but it's always just tedious reportage, either self-pitying or self-congratulatory. There's a version of this poem for female poets too, of course. As well as a whole new cadre of poets, male and female, who all owe Anne Sexton royalties on their books. We all know who they are. And I certainly hope Sexton is keeping accounts somewhere.

My point is that these poems are simply catalogs of bald reportage; the imagination—especially any verbal imagination—has been brutally banished to the hinterlands of that dreaded realm that has come to be called "obscurity." These days, anything in poetry that deals with the least shading of verbal imagination, anything that is not banally plain-spoken is now said to be obscure, decorative, and elitist. What extraordinary and incredibly destructive bullshit.

Look, American poetry is entirely too full of statement—that is, highly overt statement of purpose, or judgment, or emotion. It's really everything we tell young writers NOT to do, then they bring in a prize-winning book or poem by Boring Poet X or Boring Poet Y and they say, well, she does it, he does it. The works of mystery or suggestion, by which we used to mean poetry, seem to be in short supply.

As our poetry has grown increasingly discursive and didactic, we are offered less and less to *discover* even when reading the poems of those poets we once liked and admired; I feel a great many poets have opted for a plainer style in the hopes of finding a wider audience. Good luck to them; but this doesn't seem to me worth the sacrifice of art. Being told everything, from beginning to end, gets really boring, doesn't it? Really, isn't everything I've just said embarassingly obvious? I would hope so.

KAREN FISH: Is there an antidote?

DAVID ST. JOHN: Think of the last poet you read from whom you felt a sense of real poetic "vision." I believe that poetry is all about the nature of perception in experience. And, a good poem always lets us share the *experience* of the process of that perception or sequence of perceptions, that poetic vision.

The best poets allow us to experience aspects of perception and vision that are new, yet which remain harmonic with our poetic expectations. That is, visionary poems reach out towards the future and the unknown while echoing the very fabric and origins of what we call poetry—hymn, chant, prayer, song. They echo both in and out of the tradition, and allow us entry into those realms of both langauge and experience that help to console and to instruct us. Every poem carries with it its own vision, of course, its own poetic perspective. It just so happens that some are painfully ordinary and some are truly visionary.

KAREN FISH: You seem to have a pretty bleak view of American poetry.

DAVID ST. JOHN: On the contrary; I believe American poetry is the healthiest it's been in years. I just have become annoyed with and frustrated by this prejudice *against* the very nuances and complexities of language that I feel poetry does best. In spite of this user-friendly, back-porch, look-at-the-owl, aw-shucks-I'm-just-one-of-the-real-folks poetry, I think there are a number of terrific poets writing; these are poets who are breaking new ground for us, and some of them have been doing it for years, of course.

No, I'm not one of those who says what dire straits we're in; I actually believe there are more readers of poetry than there ever have been, and I don't believe it's because most readers like this dull and banal poetry I've been describing. I believe it's because people are desperate for anything that might possibly connect with their lives, with their neglected inner, intellectual, and spiritual lives.

KAREN FISH: Then, could you make your complaints clearer for me?

DAVID ST. JOHN: Part of it is that Americans distrust eloquence; we're an intensely Puritan country, still. The idea of "pleasure" is scary, whether it's sexual, spiritual, *or* poetic. We're terribly suspicious of pleasure and eloquence; we believe that the plain-spoken should be equated with "truth." Our tradition is one that honors silence and straight-talk—you know, the reticent farmer and the blank laconic cowboy—which implies that everything *else* is snake-oil, the words of some lying foreigner. We prize instead the illusion of sincerity; eloquence is seen as a kind of fopism.

KAREN FISH: Ibsen says, "The task of the poet is to make clear to himself, and thereby to others, the temporal and eternal questions...." Do you think a work of art can be temporal and eternal at the same time?

DAVID ST. JOHN: I think it *must* be. To some degree, every question of temporality and passage is by its very nature also a question of the eternal—or the lack of it. But you'd certainly get a very different answer from many contemporary poets, as most have chosen to deflect any questions of the "eternal" entirely to more basic and quotidian terms and concerns. As I've begun to move towards a more arcane and mystery-oriented poetry, well, I keep looking for answers to these questions in the very act of language itself, that is, in the simple enactment of language as "poetry." It's the mysterious and perhaps mystic resonance of this act that intrigues me; I've gone back to Mallarmé to find a poet whose poetics seem appropriate to what I'm after now.

The most interesting contemporary poet writing critically on these issues is Allen Grossman, who has some brilliant pieces that explore these concerns in far more complex ways than I ever could. He's steeped in Yeats and Crane, of course, but his activity is an amazing melding of the vatic and a true social responsibility. Grossman's recent work on poetry and what he calls "the human interest" is really dazzling; it strikes me as some of the most important critical prose of many years. But let me go back to your original question.

It seems to me that all of the greatest art finds its most lasting and universal appeal in what we call, in fact, its temporal aspects. Perhaps that's its most glorious paradox. Yet those temporal aspects need to reflect the resonance of something *other*, whether you want to call it the "eternal" or to give it yet another name. Otherwise, we're left with a kind of grocery list of the daily. I mean, I've happily read the grocery lists of many poets because they're so well written, and so entertaining, but those poems aren't the ones that truly move me.

Besides, one of the traditional purposes of art is to defeat time, to create something that is so truly and profoundly expressive of the *moment* that is, it is eternal; we create out of what passes through and beyond our lives, seeking to embody in language that transitory moment. When we can enact that in language, in a poem, then we have something that can defy passage and stand against time.

In other words, the temporal and transitory in our experience are given a lasting—or, if you wish, eternal—form in art, a form which expresses (by which I mean, in poetry, enacts in language) that moment in and across time. Yet, poems don't "hold" or "freeze" that moment, that experience; the best poems provide the kinetics of an experience in time. The poems we remember most clearly and powerfully are those that enact the *experience* of the moment. Poetry is never static; it's kinetic. It's enactment. If we go back and read Stevens's "Of Modern Poetry," it's all there. Then, if we substitute the idea of cinema for the idea of dramatic staging in that poem, we pretty much have a sense of the arc of twentieth-century poetry.

KAREN FISH: I wonder if I could ask you about your writing habits?

DAVID ST. JOHN: My writing habits have always been a little odd; also, they've changed over the years just as the circumstances of my life have changed. Twenty-five years ago, at nineteen, I had an infant son, so I wrote very late at night, often well into the early morning, as it was the only truly quiet time of the day. Later, at Iowa, I kept that habit of writing after midnight. Once I began teaching, I necessarily had to adjust. I began to work in the mornings, or at odd moments when there was any time at all. At Johns Hopkins and at USC I've held to that schedule, as my classes usually meet in the afternoons. Still, it's never that neat. I write when I can; I'm not that regular about it all. In fact, I go long periods without really writing, just taking notes while reading bits and pieces of things. Then, I'll work very intensely and in a very consuming way for a few weeks on end, while the rest of my life completely falls apart.

When I was a Fellow at The American Academy in Rome, I had the luxury of working in either the morning or the afternoon and then spending the rest of the day out in the city. It was fabulous. Now, I have an infant daughter, so who knows what my writing habits will become in the days ahead. I don't worry about it; I just try to write when I feel like writing, if I have the time.

KAREN FISH: How does a poem start for you?

DAVID ST. JOHN: Almost always a poem will begin for me with a piece of verbal music, some musical phrase I hear in my ear, or some collision of language and resonance that appeals to me. I'll often have a very visceral sense of what I want the poem to be, especially its rhythmic architecture, before I know what images or language will embody that music. But it's important to me that the writing of a poem be an act of discovery. I suppose it's important to remember that I always think of a poem as an *experience*, not an object, not a literary artifact; so, the poem often announces itself to me as a series of tensions or vague apprehensions. I just know *something* is about to happen, though often I don't know what. Certainly, I think most writers must feel this way as they move into the real writing of a poem or story. To me, I write to discover what I'm about to write; that's the excitement and thrill.

Look, once you've written for a number of years, it's not that hard to write a poem that looks like a poem and walks like a poem, even one that people will praise. But so what? If I go into a poem already knowing exactly what I'm going to do or how I'm going to work it out, well, it'll be a disaster. It'll be a decent poem, because I have enough facility to pull it off, but it won't have a shred of interest for me and I'll have learned nothing in the process of the writing. Besides, why tell a reader something he or she already knows? Unless a poem involves some discovery for me—and for the reader as well— then what's the point? Besides, I want my poems to be speculative and investigative, and I want them to be verbally sensual.

KAREN FISH: But don't you think that you run the risk of sometimes leaving the reader behind in the process?

DAVID ST. JOHN: I don't think so; I trust my readers more than that. I think they're willing to cut me some slack, if only to see where and how far I'll go. It doesn't bother me, though, if somebody doesn't understand one of my poems on a first reading. I hope they'll want to live with the poem a bit. I want the poems to become experiences for the reader, experiences they may actually want to return to. The poems have to have music and beauty, first of all; all of their concerns have to emerge from that enacted language. The poems that I feel closest to are those in which I've discovered what they were "about" in the course of the writing; again, this is common among all poets, right? First of all, we all know poems should never be "about" something the way that essays are "about" something; they are, as I keep saying so tediously, meant to be experiences for the reader. What they're "about" is the experience they offer.

KAREN FISH: Would you mind commenting more on this idea of the poem as an "experience"?

DAVID ST. JOHN: Just as we become engaged with the experience of a painting as we view it, so too we become engaged with the experience of a poem as we read it. A poem happens to us just as a film happens to us, or a piece of music. We encounter it, we experience it. The best poems engage us as an experience engages us, with the same visceral immediacy. Poems are not simply objects for contemplation, though some great poems are both.

For me, the finest poems are those that continue trying to locate and echo the mystery or mysteries that resonate most profoundly throughout our lives; you know, sex and death, love and faith. And poets have to do that with the most awkward of artistic tools—language.

Allowing mystery to be present in language is one of the most trying and difficult endeavors in the arts; yet, it's a summoning that is as ancient as time. It's an activity that is at the heart of poetry; it's an elementary facet of all religions, and the source of the dramatic as well. In any case, the poems of my own that I continue to care most about are those in which I feel I have embodied for the reader some experience of those mysteries—spiritual, sexual, corporeal—that constantly inform and trouble our lives.

KAREN FISH: This leads me to ask about your own influences.

DAVID ST. JOHN: Well, I suppose they're pretty much like everybody else's of my generation. This kind of literary name dropping makes me nervous, but here goes. At the immediate level, I was quite lucky in that I had marvelous poets for my teachers, poets who also became my friends. Philip Levine, Peter Everwine, C.G. Hanzlicek, Donald Justice, Marvin Bell, and Norman Dubie were all important figures for me. As an undergraduate in the late 1960s, I was also able to meet Galway Kinnell, Mark Strand, Charles Wright, Adrienne Rich, and W.S. Merwin, all of whom I admired tremendously and all of whom became friends. They are poets who stand as examples of literary integrity, of what it costs in one's life to be a poet. And, throughout the years, Larry Levis has helped me to continue to care about poetry during periods when I questioned whether it was really worth it or not. Larry's love of and total dedication to poetry have been a model for me. He's been a truly exceptional friend as well as being one of the most amazing poets now writing. Of course, Norman Dubie is a dear friend whose poetry is a source of perpetual envy and astonishment to me. *No Heaven* is dedicated to Larry and Norman for serious reasons.

Ashbery and Bishop were both enormously powerful presences for me in the early seventies, a bit before the great vogue for their work hit. Then their work seemed to all of us young poets like a personal gift, not an institutional entity. To me, it's been really delightful to watch Ashbery side-step all the truly awful, crushing nonsense that accompanies such tremendous acclaim; he just seems to laugh it off and write even better poems, thus defying the latest pigeonhole some academic has tried to put him in. It has been sad, at least to me, to see such an industry spring up around the work and life of Elizabeth Bishop. It's inevitable, of course, and with terrific exceptions like the books by David Kalstone, Bonnie Costello, and Lorrie Goldensohn, at least all doesn't seem completely lost.

Let me say too that Adrienne Rich has always been a vital and important poet for me; I can't say enough about how much I admire and respect her as both a poet and an individual. I think she's still writing some of the most powerful and beautiful poems around. For that matter, W.S. Mervin's *Travels* and Mark Strand's *Dark Harbor* are gorgeous books. It's become very fashionable to dismiss and ignore some of the poets of that generation, but my own feeling is that many of these poets are writing some of the very finest poems of their careers. Also, look at the luminous and brilliant poems that John Ashbery and Charles Wright have been writing. That said, we need too to recognize more gratefully the extraordinarily ambitious work of so many of our younger poets. Jesus, how the hell can anyone complain about contemporary poetry? It just astonishes me to read this crap about "the fate of poetry" or "the death of poetry" or all of these endless boring discussions about whether poetry can "matter" or not. I'm sorry, but I'd rather be reading a book of poems than reading one of these endless, deadly discussions; they're what's killing poetry.

All of these self-serving complaints about contemporary poetry drive me nuts; they're so dully self-righteous and ill-read. Besides, the amazing poetry that's being written simply by the young women in this country and by so many minority writers should knock the socks off these idiots. Here's a whole dimension of writing that has been absent from our poetry suddenly making itself felt with tremendous power and force; to me, it's very exciting. I don't want to start naming names, as there are so, so many terrific poets out there and I'll feel stupid later leaving somebody out. But if you haven't read Adrian C. Louis, who is a Native American poet, go out and buy all of his books.

I think this is also the place to say how much I despise the whole notion of poetic schools and camps. I resent anybody who tries to tell me that I can like Robert Creeley but I can't like James Merrill, or vice-versa; that I can like

Trude Schnackenberg but not a poet like Eleanor Lerman. *All* of these poets are important to me; they make my life richer and my own idea of poetry much more complicated. Poets who run in packs are to be distrusted, as they're out for fame, not poetry. I've said this in the past, but I believe it profoundly. Anybody who has a program or agenda for poetry is dangerous and stupid. I believe that the real aesthetics appear in the poetry and not the polemics, even if the polemics themselves are entertaining to read, as they often are. Trust the poem and not the self-glorifying poet who tells you *why* his or her poem is great. And when critics or reviewers start throwing around the terminology coined by one so-called school or another, run for cover. Truly, we need *all* of our poets.

KAREN FISH: I've heard you talk a lot recently about the Symbolist poets.

DAVID ST. JOHN: I've just written an essay for *The Ohio Review* about the tremendous influence of Yeats upon my work; in fact, he may be the greatest single influence, though Eliot and Stevens are right there close behind. With Yeats, the importance of music and the idea of song in poetry were galvanizing to me; I also loved his melding of the vatic and demotic. I suppose it's terribly unfashionable to say this, but Eliot was a very important early influence. While I was still in high school, I heard a record of Eliot reading, and even with his dry manner it was the music and image making that astonished me. I also came upon the poems of Dylan Thomas about this time, and the glorious clamor of those poems seemed to me sensually overwhelming in a way I didn't know poetry could be. Rimbaud and Baudelaire were favorites too, but not so much for the usual romantic flair as for their extraordinary sense of a special vision of modern consciousness. For me, this was also the case with Rilke, whose spiritual resonances have always infected my poems perhaps more than they should. It was Eliot who first sent me back to the French Symbolists, who remain for me even today a central and nourishing influence, especially the astonishing and timeless work of Mallarmé.

I didn't feel the influence of Stevens until my early twenties, but then it hit me like a freight train. The music of the mind and the imagination finding verbal enactment in Stevens' poetry still seems to me one of the most consoling and satisfying experiences in all of art. I was also always very attracted to D.H. Lawrence's poems, especially the books *Look! We Have Come Through* and *Birds, Beasts, and Flowers,* with their Whitmanic flair. At the same time I came upon the work of Trakl, Dino Campana, and Gérard de Nerval, and even at that relatively early point—still my early twenties—I'd begun to see myself in this more arcane and mystic tradition of poetry, though I'm not sure how much it was showing up in the work itself. But, perhaps more than anyone, Celan turned my head around. As he still does. It's odd to see how he's become such a talismanic figure in a variety of the conversations that swirl around poetry today. I'm not sure what he'd have thought of it. As both a figure and a poet, he's now being appropriated almost everywhere, by almost everyone. But, more and more, that seems to be the fate of great poets, doesn't it?

KAREN FISH: Louise Gluck has said that each book she wrote, "Culminated in a conscious diagnostic act, a swearing off." Your four books are stylistically different and, because of that, I was wondering if her statement might be true for you?

DAVID ST. JOHN: I've tried to do something distinct with each book stylistically, but I hope that certain of the stylistic concerns have remained constant throughout. Some poets have made careers by simply repeating themselves until critics and reviewers *got* it, you know? Then they've been condemned to having to repeat themselves, or risk the ire and disappointment of their critical patrons. It's easy to sympathize with the impulse to do that, but what a fate. The book I like best of my own, stylistically, is *No Heaven*. Though I should say that, with *Study for the World's Body*, I'm very happy with how the book has fallen together as a whole, the way poems from all of the books talk back to one another and stand as a body, so to speak, of work.

KAREN FISH: If I understand the poem, "No Heaven" (and the notion of the book) correctly, it ends with an amazing climax—a huge twist. This twist is a question, or a revelation, that hits the speaker as he stands with his lover on the horizon of the modern, apocalyptic, crumbling European landscape: "That we're to be given no heaven/No heaven    but this." The book seems dramatically organized to that end; was that deliberate? Would you say something about how these poems were written?

DAVID ST. JOHN: *No Heaven* was to some extent written to be my own version of *The Book of Nightmares*; it's no accident that the opening of the title poem echoes Galway's final poem of that book. The poems of *No Heaven* were written almost entirely in the sequence in which they appear in the book, the only one of my books where this is true. I wanted *No Heaven* to feel like a book-length poem; I wanted a real sense of progression through the poems, from the fairly desperate state marked by the linguistic wreckage of the book's opening two poems to a more spiritually hopeful (if still ambivalent) sense of closure with the book's final two poems. Yet the ending you refer to is certainly a double-edged revelation, at best.

While writing *No Heaven*, I should say, I was writing against what I saw as a highly conservative turn in American poetry. I don't mean the return to traditional meters and forms; I mean the extraordinary pursuit of plain-spoken banalities that I saw erupting in poems everywhere. I suppose I was trying to write something that was unique against that landscape of 1983, when the poems of *No Heaven* were actually written. I wanted the aggressive line breaks and the lack of punctuation, for example, to be at first a little disconcerting; likewise, the dark tone of the poems. I wanted readers to have to pay much closer attention to what was happening before their eyes.

KAREN FISH: How would you respond to somebody calling you a "philosophical" poet, in the spirit in which we call, for example, Walker Percy a philosophical novelist?

DAVID ST. JOHN: I'd probably fall to my knees and kiss their sandals.

KAREN FISH: In an interview a few years ago, James Green asked Norman Dubie what his response was to the charge that some of his work was "obscure, willfully obscure." Dubie's response was, "If current readers of poetry were as imaginative with the arts, let's say poems in particular, as they are with eavesdropping on the bus, there would be much less discussion of meaning, of obscurity." Then Dubie gave this wonderful descriptive example of imaginative energy while eavesdropping and concluded with, "We're getting good poems, and I think very often we're getting reactionary or lazy readers." You've had similar charges of obscurity leveled against your work; what do you think?

DAVID ST. JOHN: Well, those charges began with the poems in *Hush*, if you can believe it. It's a bit comic to look back and remember that, given how immediate and available they seem to most readers today. But remember that in 1976, when *Hush* was published, the work of Ashbery was just beginning to have broader recognition and wider acceptance; the first rush of prizes for

Ashbery came in 1975, and this really changed the way many readers began to approach "difficult" poetry. Of course, Ashbery also engendered a reaction; and so we still have readers who need to have it all spelled out for them.

*No Heaven* was also accused of "obscurity" because the poems are concerned with mystery and, I imagine, because they are often stylistically somewhat elliptical. I honestly don't feel any of my work is obscure, just filled with different kinds of mystery. I also don't mean "mysteriousness," which I feel is altogether different. "Mysteriousness" is just a tease; mystery is sacred. Certainly, my poems are no more "obscure" than a Francis Bacon painting, or a Bertolucci movie. They're also not in the same league as the work of either of those artists, of course, but you see what I'm getting at.

KAREN FISH: I'd like to follow that question with this: what have been some of the most interesting misreadings of your poetry?

DAVID ST. JOHN: Well, many readers took *The Shore* to be straight autobiography. Even friends I'd been somewhat out of touch with made the assumption that it was a kind of poetic diary. In fact, the poems are all fictions that enact, or re-enact, situations or dilemmas that did truly belong to me, that were part of my experience, but the names, places, and contexts had all been altered significantly. But I was pleased that the poems had enough immediacy to be convincing.

I think the poems of *No Heaven* weren't misread so much as just lazily read. Once, over a meal in Boston, my friends Rosanna Warren and Howard Norman were talking about the way the poems of *No Heaven* were influenced so markedly by Bertolucci and Yannis Ritsos. Don't forget that these are two friends talking, but it struck me then as it does still as being an unusually perceptive comment about the stylistic ambitions of those poems. But I *was* surprised by how many people seemed scared off from discussing the decadent elements of the poems in *No Heaven*. They couldn't decide whether the poems were a critique of decadence or an embrace. I think too that the whiff of that deep, bone-numbing nihilism rising off the poems was, to some, unsettling.

KAREN FISH: In an interview with David Wojahn that you did in 1986, you said, "If we indulge in memory, in poetry, and engage ourselves in that process, we have to be artisans equal to it. We can't be slack about naming memory, because that naming is, in fact, renaming that allows memory to exist with both its names, its first names and its later names as well." That seems to me to be very political.

DAVID ST. JOHN: I believe it is very political. I believe the renaming that poets are engaged in when writing is an inherently political act. I believe the true political force of poetry is not contentual, it is stylistic; that is, the movement of consciousness within a poem—the reconstitution of and the enactment of consciousness in language, by which we mean "poetry"—carries with it a revisionary and political force. Some of these movements of consciousness are radical in our poetry and some are reactionary; both reflect a particular view of the world, a specific orientation and manner of perception that, I feel, has to be considered "political." This means, I suppose, expanding our definition of what is political, but isn't it about time?

At the moment, we have an extremely narrow view of what we consider "political" in our poetry, and it is a view that is usually based upon content and narrative and anecdotal "witnessing." This perversion of the idea of "witness," about which so many poets, primarily Eastern European, have written so movingly, disturbs me deeply. Again, Allen Grossman is one of the very, very few American poets who has clearly approached the subject of "witness" with the profound responsibility it entails, and he has done so in both his poetry and his prose. To my mind, many of the poets who make political claims for their poetry promulgate ideas of the "political" that are both archaic and quite dangerously sentimental; I believe that their view of the political simply encourages us to remain inactive, judgmental, and self-involved voyeurs.

So that I'm not misunderstood, however, let me just say I do feel poems are capable of enacting consciousness in ways that are inherently revisionary and therefore political.

KAREN FISH: But wouldn't you call your poem "To Pasolini" a political poem?

DAVID ST. JOHN: Yes and no. There, in places, I allowed a clearly overt political subject matter to enter the poem, and "To Pasolini" seemed to me the perfect occasion to do this. The fact that I was writing the poem in *terza rima* no doubt helped create the tension I needed to feel the freedom to do that. It was the form Pasolini had used in his own political elegy, "The Ashes of Gramsci," so even the formal choice, for me, had political overtones in this instance. And, in using the epigraph from "The Ashes of Gramsci," that extraordinary passage of Pasolini's about living in history, I tried to signal to readers the clear political intentions that might arise. But the project of the poem as a whole strikes me as being far more insidious and much less overt than it might seem from that statement. That is, I hope that its "political" resonances can be seen simply as one of several patterns formed by the threads that run through the whole fabric of the poem.

KAREN FISH: Wojahn said, "One of the things that seems clear about the way recollection is viewed in your poems is that your speakers never seem to come to terms with the process of memory beyond ackowledging its obsessive hold on them." Do you think that is accurate and if so would you talk about that a bit?

DAVID ST. JOHN: Poetry is about the reclaiming of time, lost time, as the man said. We invoke memory in order to engage in that recovery, that recuperation, of time. I mean "recovery" and "recuperation" in their healing sense as well. But how do any of us "come to terms" with memory? With those pasts that we so carefully reconstruct with our highly selective memories? Well, poetry is one way. Yet our pasts and our invocations of memory are realms that can both haunt and heal us, aren't they? It's this tension that interests me, obviously, more than any "answer" to this clearly unanswerable question we all carry around with us.

KAREN FISH: Could you talk for a moment about the poem "The Man in the Yellow Gloves"? Where did the idea for that poem come from?

DAVID ST. JOHN: From a single image in a movie. Dirk Bogarde pulls on yellow leather gloves before he goes to murder somebody. Suddenly, with that image, the whole sense of the conflict/paradox of beauty and artifice on the exterior and the corrupted or damaged on the interior presented itself to me pretty much full blown. It seemed a great presiding metaphor for a dramatic monologue that would be, for me, a kind of *ars poetica*. Also, I was asked at that time, the early 1980s, to do a lecture on poetics. As a response to that request, I wrote a four-part poem that included, as two of its parts, "The Man in the Yellow Gloves" and "The Swan at Sheffield Park."

To return briefly to the question of memory and its vicissitudes, let me tell you a fascinating story. You know, at the time that I wrote "The Man in the Yellow Gloves," I believed that the poem was entirely invention. Then, several years later, I read the poem in Fresno, where I grew up, at a reading where my mother and two of my aunts were. They were intrigued, they told me afterward, by the way I had used the story of their father—my grandfather, who was a baker part of his life—burning his hands in an oven accident. I was stunned. I had no memory of that story at all, though I had memories of other stories about my grandfather as a baker. Yet I had clearly drawn upon that incident, pulled it from my subconscious, from memory, and rearranged it for the purposes of the poem without truly "remembering" its source.

KAREN FISH: A great many artists and writers trace their original desire for a profession in the arts to pecularities of family life. Can you talk about your childhood?

DAVID ST. JOHN: Well, my father's father was an English professor and a dean of humanities at the local college, but my father was a coach (of basketball and track) and an ace tennis player. I was raised to be a tennis player, which isn't bad training for somebody who wants to be a writer. It's solitary and demands tremendous discipline. But my father was, because of his father, terribly literate, so there were tons of books all around. I know this sounds like self-mythologizing, but my father sat me on his lap as he read to me from the *Illiad*, the *Odyssey*, the *Aeneid*, and *The Jungle Books*. I suppose these were the books *his* father had raised him on. In any case, this was how I learned to read. He also had collected as a boy all of the Scribner's edition books in black covers, with illustrations by N.C. Wyeth and others, books like *Treasure Island*, *A Boy's King Arthur*, and *The Deerslayer*. These were the books I grew up on. But I think more than anything in the world, he always loved best the opening of the *Aeneid*. My mother had a degree to teach drama, and was an actor herself; so, I come by my dramatic impulses honestly.

KAREN FISH: Was there anything else that was untypical about your childhood?

DAVID ST. JOHN: Maybe the most unusual aspect of this childhood, as it relates to the poetry, was my interest in music. I had piano lessons, beginning at eight, for a couple of years, but I really wasn't any good. Still, at eleven I started subscribing to *Down Beat*, the jazz magazine. I became very involved with folk music in the early sixties, by which I mean I read about it, listened to it, and started trying to play guitar. Then, I played in rock bands in junior high and high school.

But the most interesting part of this to me now, looking back, is seeing the tremendous influence of the folk music and especially the early English ballads. It was fun, when I went to college, to open the Norton and discover I knew all of the ballads already. This internalizing of the actual and verbal music of these ballads was important to me. I loved Robert Johnson and I loved The Carter Family; I loved Howlin' Wolf and I loved John Handy; I had the John Jacob Niles ballad book and the Chess albums of Muddy Waters. That great stew of styles, both musical and narrative, really educated me.

Last October, when my daughter was born, I had this incredible urge to go back to those folk songs, those ballads, because I wanted to learn them again to play for her. They seem to me a fine first stepping stone for both music and language. So I went out and bought CDs of all the folk albums that had instructed me; it was really fascinating to see how much those songs and anonymous ballads had structured my sense of the music of English. They're all part of the tradition of our poetry, of course, but I had no idea I was absorbing it at the time. By the way, Vivienne seems to prefer sea shanties to all else.

KAREN FISH: John Ashbery has compared the poems in *No Heaven* to the films of Godard and Rohmer. I was wondering if film has influenced your work, your use of images, and how you use the visual.

DAVID ST. JOHN: It has influenced my work enormously. I think the imagistic release and the movement of consciousness in poems have more in common with cinematic grammars than with what we consider conventional narrative progressions. Christian Metz and Stephen Heath are both writers who have been very important to my own sense of a filmic aesthetic. Earlier, I mentioned Bertolucci; I think it was seeing *The Conformist* that first gave me permission to try a certain kind of verbal texture in my poems, to try a kind of lushness undercut by a raw psychological ravagement. I've always loved Antonioni and Fellini, of course, but who doesn't? But I was amazed and pleased when Ashbery saw the Rohmer in my poems, as he's always been one of my very favorite directors.

KAREN FISH: We've spent some time talking about the particular influences of literature and film; it also seems obvious that the visual arts, especially paintings, have left a mark on your work. Would you address that for a moment?

DAVID ST. JOHN: One of my aunts, my father's sister, was a painter, and I was fascinated by the visual arts from a very young age. The only problem was that I was completely untalented as a painter, and my interests, obviously, were mainly literary. Yet in college I spent a lot of my time hanging out with painters and sculptors; after all, every writer knows they're a lot of fun to party with, as they tend to be more extroverted than writers. The materiality and physicality of the visual arts had a profound effect on me; I wanted that kind of density and plasticity for language as well. I think poems have more in common with paintings and film than they do with prose. I can't help but feel fortunate to have seen so many great paintings at this point in my life; it's changed the way I think about the world and about my own poetry. I hope this doesn't sound insufferably pretentious. I just really love paintings. They make me see the world in new ways, and that helps me stay alive as a poet.

KAREN FISH: What's been the most difficult thing for you about being a poet?

DAVID ST. JOHN: The fact that the literary world is fueled by rumor, by endless and often malicious gossip. It's great fun at times, but I've also seen it be devastating to people. I can't fucking believe all the shit that's been tossed around about me. If only a quarter of it were true, Jesus, I'd be such an interesting guy. Larry Levis and Norman Dubie and I used to all check in periodically, just to find out what the latest rumors about ourselves were, then we'd giggle like mad. Lately, I don't care enough even to ask. I've had periods in my life when I've heard totally untrue stories repeated about me as if they were gospel, even by poets I hardly knew. But, as we all know, information is power, so the gossip and rumor mills rage on. Still, I actually don't mind those people who just love to gossip, since we all do, let's face it. It's the people who try to use rumor or gossip to harm other writers, to keep them from getting something they deserve. Believe me, I've been in meetings where this has gone on; I've been at the table when the shit's been thrown. It's ugly. But poets don't like to talk about this, just like they don't like to talk about drugs or alcohol, or sex. Or, when they do, it's with that glow of mixed self-pity and self-congratulation. It all just hits much too close to home, and poets are, like everyone else in the world, terrific at denial. Finally, though, I suppose it all angers me because I want to be known in the world by the things that I've done, not by the things people say or imagine that I've done.

KAREN FISH: The poem "Study for the World's Body" is a poem that makes it obvious you are interested in the visual presentation of work on the page. Can you comment about the structure of this new poem?

DAVID ST. JOHN: I'll try to talk about it without giving too much away. In the most general, even reductive terms, the left hand column is erotic, souled by the sexual, and composed of a highly charged, very dense language; it uses the elements of earth and fire. The right hand column is the spiritual and unearthly column, an elegy for a friend and, to some degree, also an elegy for my father; it uses the elements of air and water. It's of a more conversational nature, addressed to someone specific, and is riddled with meditations on time and art, specifically dance. Obviously, the realm of the body is at stake in both of the columns. But that's as much as I care to say, as I feel that I shouldn't try to give any operating instructions for readers. I'd prefer it if the reader finds his or her own way through the poem, through each of the columns, then he or she can begin to consider why they are congruent, or facing, or mirroring. Or, if one is a gloss for the other. All of these questions need to be addressed by the poem's readers, if they care to; I want the sense of discovery to still be there, so I feel uneasy about sorting out the poem's difficulties, its mysteries. They seem to me also the poem's greatest pleasures.

KAREN FISH: This new poem makes the reader aware of audience, with its dual address. How would you read the poem aloud?

DAVID ST. JOHN: Well, I'm told that John Ashbery and Ann Lauterbach once did a reading of Ashbery's poem "Litany" by reading the two columns simultaneously. I don't think that would work with this poem. My feeling is that I would choose to read one of the poem's columns or the other. I could read them back to back, of course, but that seems like something close to punishment for an unsuspecting audience.

KAREN FISH: Would you mind talking about another new poem, "My Friend"?

DAVID ST. JOHN: "My Friend" was the first in a series of recent poems in which I tried to push extremely long passages of breath, to keep the meditation running on the rails for a while before the energy just collapsed. The poem "Los Angeles, 1954" is another of these, as is the poem "Lucifer in Starlight," which takes its title from the George Meredith sonnnet, and is set in Rome. I'm curious to see how readers respond. Some of these new poems are dramatic monologues and some are not, but they all share a kind of breathlessness.

KAREN FISH: It seems that year at The American Academy in Rome had a profound effect on your work. Do you think this is true?

DAVID ST. JOHN: Certainly. It gave me permission to live in an unusual way, a writerly way, and to give poetry a kind of attention that is often difficult to sustain in one's workaday world. I'd found the same to be true living in both Paris and London, but every city alters one's own sense of oneself as a writer, even Baltimore, and now Venice.

KAREN FISH: Do you think writers have a responsibility to be lookouts, or critics for a generation, a society? Often, in hindsight, we discover writers have been the conscience of their times.

DAVID ST. JOHN: One's duty as a writer is to one's own driving interior demands concerning the nature and resonance of one's work. To be truly faithful to that is to be faithful in serving one's culture. Likewise, to be also responsible to the fierce ethics of poetry itself is inevitably to be responsible to one's, and perhaps for one's, generation or society.

KAREN FISH: You make your living as a teacher and you also work as an editor. Is there anything negative for a writer in these activities?

DAVID ST. JOHN: They are both done at one's own peril. First, let me say that as a teacher I am both a teacher of poetry writing and also a regular academic, responsible for doctoral students and graduate literature seminars the way anyone in an English Department is. This combination in and of itself would be mind-warping, but I've also been editing the poetry for *The Antioch Review* for more than twelve years now, and certainly that takes its toll as well.

Yet I feel a kind of duty as both a teacher and as an editor. I love teaching young writers; there seems to me nothing quite as exciting. I love teaching hard-core literature seminars to rabid theory-crazed doctoral students. And I feel an obligation to help young writers find their way into print in *The Antioch Review*. It's also my good fortune, I should add, that I have a real poet, Judith Hall, who acts as my Assistant Poetry Editor. Also, I get to see a lot of poems I'll never have to write, since somebody else has already written them.

KAREN FISH: You are married to a poet; how has her work influenced yours?

DAVID ST. JOHN: Molly's work has encouraged me to take some chances that I'm not sure I would have taken otherwise. As you know, her poetry is an enormously textured and richly layered poetry, filled with a lot of surprising tonal shifts and dislocations, as well as with gorgeous and highly inventive language play. Her poems also have some of the most savagely ironic moments I know, coupled with real humor. I do neither of those things— irony or humor—very well, I feel, so it's been good for me to see how she pulls it off. Maybe I'll learn something for once.

As we all know, living with another artist, especially another poet, is fraught with difficulties. Molly has been astonishing in making those difficulties seem quite invisible and insignificant. In life as well as in poetry, occasionally one just gets lucky.

KAREN FISH: With the appearance of *Study for the World's Body*, what do you imagine for yourself, that is, for your work, in the future? Is there anything you are trying to do now that wasn't an interest, say, twenty years ago?

DAVID ST. JOHN: I think one doesn't have to be enormously perceptive to see that my work has always had these two impulses: on the one hand, to write a deeply hermetic, dense, and nearly mystic poetry, and on the other to write a more available and transparent poetry. The title poem of *Study for the World's Body* tries, in its own small way, to show that both of these impulses reflect aspects of the same sensibility. As to the future, I imagine myself still struggling with this odd war of impulses. Yet I still see my concerns as being very much those that interested me twenty years ago: the slow dance of men and women, the mystery of the sacred, and how those two sometimes weave together. If I knew what was truly in store, that is, for the future of my work, then it wouldn't interest me to pursue it. The excitement will be in the discovery. I have a sense of the map, of the way, but not of those backroads I'll need to follow nor of those dead-ends where I'm sure I'll find myself. But, as always, I think the poems we can't yet imagine are those we're the most desperate to write.

# David St. John: A Bibliography of Uncollected Prose

"An Introduction," *Screen Gems: The Poems of John Bowie 1950-1977*, edited by Robert Herz. W.D. Hoffstadt & Sons, 1978 (book).

"On the poem 'Elegy,'" from *45 Contemporary Poets: The Creative Process*, edited by Alberta Turner. Longman, 1980.

"The Syntax of Disquiet: The Poetry of Michael Burkard," *The Sonora Review*, No. 3, 1982.

"On Workshops," *Poet and Critic*, Vol. XIII, No. 3, 1982.

"Our Masters' (And Other) Voices: Poetry On Cassette," *The Antioch Review*, Vol. 41, No. 1, 1983.

"Poetry (A Review of New Books by Stanley Plumly, Gary Snyder, Norman Dubie, and David Wagoner)," *The Washington Post Book World*, December 25, 1983.

"Poetry (A Review of New Books by John Ashbery, Richard Kenney, Seamus Heaney, and Charles Wright)," *The Washington Post Book World*, May 20, 1984.

"The Crucifixion Series: 1984-1985, Marsh Pels' cast bronze sculptures," catalogue essay for the Oscarson Hood Gallery, New York, 1985.

"Roman Pleasures," *The Baltimore Sun Sunday Magazine*, October 26, 1986.

"Ultramarine," a review of Raymond Carver, *The Los Angeles Times Book World*, February, 1987.

"On Keith Douglas," *Poetry Pilot*, March, 1987.

"Ars Poetica/Editorial," *The Antioch Review*, Vol. 45, No.1, 1987.

"Home: The Poetry of Donald Hall and Robert Francis," *Western Humanties*

*Review*, Vol. XVI, No. 4, 1988. Robert Francis review uncollected.

"Some Notes On Style," *The Denver Quarterly*, Vol. 23, No.3/4, 1989.

"Neruda's Wings," *Quarry West*, No. 25, 1989.

"Revealing Mirrors: A Review of David Mura's *After We Lost Our Way*," *Hungry Mind Reader: A Midwestern Book Review*, No. 11, September, 1989.

"Hush: A Coming of Age," *Hayden's Ferry Review* No. 6, Summer, 1990 .

"Poetic Justice: Robert Mezey at Pomona College," with Tom Wood, *Pomona College Today* (Alumni Review), Autumn, 1990.

"Poetry, Hope, and the Language of Possibility," *The Antioch Review*, Vol. 48, No. 3, Summer 1990.

"On Editing," from *Spreading the Word: Editors on Poetry*, edited by Warren Slesinger. The Bench Press, 1990.

"Teaching Poetry Writing Workshops for Undergraduates," from *Creative Writing in America*, edited by Joseph Moxley. NCTE Press, 1990.

"On Grief," *Giving Sorrow Words*, by Candy Lightner and Nancy Hathaway. Time-Warner Books, 1990.

"Angels and Other Poets," an editorial, *The Antioch Review*, Vol. 48. No. 3, Summer 1990.

"Dramatic Monologue: Carving the Voice, Carving the Mask," *The Practice of Poetry* (text), edited by Robin Behn and Chase Twitchell. HarperCollins, 1992.

"The Long Poem as Meditation and Event," *Pequod*, # 32, 1991.

"Foreword" to *Again the Gemini are in the Orchard* (poems), by Gail Wronsky. The New Poets Series, 1991.

"Good Hope Road," a review of Stuart Dischell's book of the same title. *The Boston Review*, Vol XVIII, No. 2, March/April, 1993.

"The Old Irish Choirmaster and Me," (an essay on W.B. Yeats), *The Ohio Review*, No. 51, Fall, 1993.

"A Watershed: Contemporary Poetry on Cassette," *Denver Quarterly*, Vol. 28, No. 2, Fall, 1993.

"The Sensual World," an editorial, *The Antioch Review*, Vol. 52, No. 1; Winter, 1993/4.

"Delmore Schwartz," *Oxford Companion to Twentieth Century Poetry in English*, edited by Ian Hamilton. Oxford University Press, 1994.

*Acknowledgements, continued:*

*The Los Angeles Times Sunday Book Review:* Ancient Eyes (Hall); Home At Last (Merwin); Dark Harbor (Strand); Immaterial Girl (Graham)

*Open Places:* Roman Noon.

*Parnassus:* Oxygen and Small Frictions.

*Poetry Miscellaney:* Renaming the Present.

*The Seneca Review:* Or Yours To Keep: The Poetry of Pamela Stewart; (an early version of) Charles Wright's *Country Music*; An Interview With David St. John.

*Telescope:* I vs. You: The Romantic Ambivalence of Self.

*Western Humanities Review:* The Happy Man, under the title "Home ."

"Charles Wright's *Country Music*" appeared as the forward to the book of that title published by Wesleyan University Press. In addition to *The Seneca Review*, an early version also appeared in *Charles Wright: A Profile*, published by Grilled Flowers Press, 1979.

"The Happy Man" also appeared in *The Day I Was Older: Essays on Donald Hall*, edited by Liam Rector, published by Story Line Press, 1989.

"Where the Angels Come Toward Us: The Poetry of Philip Levine," also appeared in *Under Discussion: Philip Levine*, edited by Christopher Buckley, published by The University of Michigan Press.

"A Generous Salvation: The Poetry of Norman Dubie" also appeared in *Conversant Essays: Contemporary Poets on Poetry,,* edited by James McCorkle, published by Wayne State University Press, 1990. An edited version also appeared in *Contemporary Literary Criticism*, edited by Dale Marowski, published by Gale Press, 1985.

"Renaming the Present" also appeared in *Acts of Mind: Conversations with Contemporary Poets*, edited by Richard Jackson, published by The University of Alabama Press, 1983.